THE BLOODY
TRIANGLE

THE BLOODY TRIANGLE

THE DEFEAT OF SOVIET ARMOR IN THE UKRAINE, JUNE 1941

VICTOR J. KAMENIR

ZENITH PRESS

First published in 2008 by Zenith Press, an imprint of MBI Publishing Company, 400 1st Avenue North, Suite 300, Minneapolis, MN 55401 USA.

Zenith Press titles are also available at discounts in bulk quantity for industrial or sales-promotional use. For details write to Special Sales Manager at MBI Publishing Company, 400 1st Avenue North, Suite 300, Minneapolis, MN 55401 USA.

Designer: Diana Boger

Front cover, top: *National Archives*; **bottom:** *The Tank Museum, Bovington, England*

Photo insert: All photos: *Author's collection*

ISBN-13: 978-0-7603-3434-8

Printed in the United States of America

I think that those who never experienced
all the bitterness of the summer of 1941 will never be
completely able to appreciate the joy of our victory.

—*Vassiliy Grossman, Soviet writer*

Contents

APPENDICES

MAPS

NOTES

BIBLIOGRAPHY

INDEX

Preface

AS THE YEARS GO BY, the white areas on a historical map of World War II continue shrinking. However, to most Western military history enthusiasts, the four bloody years of struggle on the Eastern Front continue to be *terra incognita*. Most people have only heard about the Siege of Leningrad, the slaughter of Stalingrad, and, of course, the Battle of Kursk.

The weeklong armored clash near the Russian city of Kursk in 1943 has been widely known as the largest tank battle in history, involving over six thousand armored combat vehicles on both sides. During this bloody battle, the backbone of the German Panzer Corps was broken forever, leaving it unable to mount significant operations for the rest of the war. However, this was not the first large-scale armored struggle on the Eastern Front. Another weeklong conflict featuring massive tank formations took place immediately following the German invasion of the Soviet Union on June 22, 1941.

Just two days after launching Operation Barbarossa, from June 24 to July 1, roughly 650 German tanks and 180 assault gun and tank destroyers fought over 1,500 Soviet tanks in a roughly triangular area of approximately 1,800 square miles between the northwestern Ukrainian towns of Lutsk, Dubno, and Brody.

The fighting in Ukraine did not parallel fighting in Byelorussia, where the armored warfare on the Eastern Front became associated with exploits of the most famous German panzer leader—Heinz Guderian. Instead of heady dashes by "Hurrying Heinz's" armored spearheads, the difficult terrain of northwestern Ukraine limited German advances to a grinding series of battles along a miserable road network.

Events that took place there, when covered by Western historians, are usually glossed over by an encompassing title of "border battles." Yet, here, in the swampy and marshy terrain, the German blitzkrieg was for the first time slowed down to a crawl and even halted for several crucial days. The Soviet side lost the battle. However, even in defeat, the Red Army demonstrated that the vaunted German *Wehrmacht* could be stopped and bloodied, even if only for a time.

This experience was costly for the Soviet Union. Numerically superior mechanized forces of the Red Army were savaged by the smaller, more proficient and professional German opponents. In this, and similar border battles, the Soviet armored force, larger than all other armored forces in the world combined, melted away under the relentless assault of the German combined-arms style of warfare.

Describing the events above, this work relied heavily on numerous memoirs of Soviet and, to a lesser extent, German participants in the conflict. These first-hand accounts provide genuine insights into the unfolding events. While some of them cover the same events, no two of them are exactly alike, each man's own personality coming through in his interpretation of the events. I intentionally weighted my research towards the Soviet/Russian sources because I wanted to present this conflict from the Soviet point of view.

Starting shortly before the war, the Soviet officers, their reports and memoirs describe, often in minute detail, the condition, preparedness, and morale of the Red Army at the outbreak of the conflict. I was not the first writer to rely on these works, and, like others, I drew my own conclusions.

Russian writer and former military intelligence officer Vladimir Rezun (pen name Viktor Suvorov) helped fuel the debate whether Soviet Union was planning to attack Germany first. Very persuasively, albeit not very convincingly, Rezun argued that presence of certain types of weapons or personnel in large quantities was the indicator of immediate Soviet aggressive intentions. I found his claim that the Soviet Union had one million paratroopers by the start of the war preposterous. While parachute jumping was immensely popular among Soviet youth before the war, a teenager who has several jumps off a tower under his belt does not a trained airborne soldier make.

While I do not dispute Stalin's aggressive intentions overall (it is hard to argue with this, knowing of his swallowing up the three tiny Baltic states and chunks of Finland, Poland, and Rumania), I do not believe that the Red Army was in any shape to conduct major offensive operations in July 1941, as advocated by Rezun/Suvorov. On a much more personal note, I find him usurping the venerated surname of Suvorov as an insult to Russian and Soviet history.

Rezun alleged that the sheer number of over twenty-four thousand Soviet tanks as clear demonstration of aggressive intent. However, a significant number of them were so obsolete as to be not much more than targets for German gunners. This could be unscientifically explained by Russian propensity not to discard anything. Large numbers of inoperable tanks rusting in their motor pools were still carried on the rosters as viable combat vehicles.

Along with inflated quality and quantity of materiel, unrelenting propaganda of the Communist Party lulled the Soviet citizens into a false sense of security. In early 1939 a movie called *Tractorists* was released in the Soviet Union. Two new songs written by songwriter Boris Laskin and featured in its soundtrack became instant classics, "The Tree Tankers" and "March of the Soviet Tankers." The latter song featured words which symbolized the naïve pride which the Soviet people had in their armed forces: "The armor is strong and our tanks are fast."

The unrelenting stream of propaganda convinced a majority of the citizens of the Soviet Union that their country possessed the strongest armed forces in the world. The whole country took pride in its armed forces. Millions of young men and women had membership in paramilitary clubs teaching a variety of military skills—flying, parachute jumping, shooting, and radio operating. Military pilots, dubbed "Stalin's Falcons," strutted with their chests puffed out with pride. Tens of thousands of young people proudly wore their "Voroshilov's Marksman" pin, named after Stalin's crony Marshal Kliment Voroshilov and earned for outstanding rifle shooting.

After the German invasion on June 22, 1941, shaken out of their sense of security, the Soviet people with great disbelief listened to radio broadcasts naming long strings of cities and towns captured by Germans with insulting ease. Common questions were, if not on everybody's lips, certainly on everybody's mind: "What happened to our armed forces? Where are our planes, the fastest in the world? Where are our tanks, the strongest in the world?"

This work will, hopefully, shed light how the Soviet tank park melted away under merciless German hammer blows in 1941.

Part I:

OPPOSING FORCES

CHAPTER 1

German Plans, Dispositions, and Organization

ON THE HUMID EVENING OF JUNE 21, 1941, all the camps of the 11th Panzer Division around the small Polish town of Stalowa Wola were a beehive of nervous and excited activity. While the drivers revved up their engines and ran through the last-minute maintenance checks, the troops were busily loading up their vehicles. Every available inch of space was crammed to overflowing with extra ammunition, jerry cans, and metal drums of fuel, indicating a long and busy drive. Anxious weeks of training and waiting were replaced by relieved anticipation.

For the past month their bivouacs were buzzing with rumors. Oh, there was no doubt that they were going to war again. The veteran tankers had been through this already and knew the signs. Their panzers had trampled the wheat fields of Poland, rolled down the tree-shaded roads of France, and rumbled through the twisting mountain valleys of Yugoslavia.

Well armed, superbly led, and experienced, the young troopers of the 11th Panzer Division were cockily spoiling for another fight. Knowing only victories brought about by Hitler's ambitious daring, theirs was a generation unencumbered by memories of humiliating defeat of World War I. Did they not thrash the French, their fathers' tormentors? Did they not make the British wade through the cold waters of the English Channel, scrambling up the boats whisking them to the safety of their island home? How about the Polish, their ancient enemy? The Poles lasted but four weeks, crushed under panzer onslaught and screaming dive bombers.

Only some of them believed the official version claiming that they were training for the invasion of the British Isles. There were better and closer places to train than this backward corner of Eastern Europe. Born out of half-truths and wild guesses, the rumors ran unchecked through the bivouacs. Some said that the Russians were going to let them pass through their territory and attack India, the crown jewel of British Empire, from the north. Others claimed that they were to head south through Romania and Turkey to link up with Rommel's Africa Corps in Palestine. Only a few thought that they would fight the Soviet Union. After all, didn't the Führer sign a nonaggression treaty with the commissars? Whichever way they would turn, the men and machines of the 11th Panzer Division, bearing the white stencil of a sword-wielding ghost, the symbol of their unit, were ready.

All the rumors were dispelled later on this muggy evening. Hitler gave the nod, and like wildfire, the code words "The heroes say: Wotan! Neckar fifteen!" spread through the German cantonments in Poland. The greatest invasion in history would begin tomorrow morning! It was now Russia's turn to submit to the will of the master race!

In his second-story office in a commandeered tavern-turned-headquarters, commander of the 11th Panzer Division Maj. Gen. Ludwig Crüwell was poring through the almost-memorized operational plans. He already prepared the address which would be read to his troops tomorrow morning, shortly after the artillery of all calibers would make its own poignant announcement. The brief statement read:

> Soldiers of 11th Panzer Division!
> The Führer calls to war against the Bolshevism, the supreme enemy of our National-Socialist realm. The fight will be tough, calling for sacrifices everywhere. The Ghost Division will fall upon the enemy as it did in Serbia, wherever meeting it, attacking it and destroying it.
> I know that I can rely on you absolutely, as in the southeast, from the oldest officer to the youngest man.
> Our slogan remains—Attack! Our goal—the Dnieper [River]. We want to be the first again, as before in Belgrade.
> Heil Führer![1]

The stocky, bespectacled major general was immensely proud of his tankers, recruited mainly among the sturdy Silesians with their long military traditions. Like the overwhelming majority of German officers, Major General Crüwell had no doubts about the necessity of destroying the communist Russian state. Belonging to an older generation than his men,

Ludwig Crüwell remembered well the cancerous influence of Bolshevism on post–World War I Germany. Now it was time to wield the scalpel.

Down in the street below, Crüwell could see his driver, paint brush in hand, refreshing a large "K" on the side of his armored command vehicle. The three-foot letter indicated that Crüwell's division belonged to the Panzer Group 1, commanded by Col. Gen. Ewald von Kleist. In just a few short hours, the 11th Panzer Division would begin moving to its pre-attack staging areas near the tiny Polish town of Laszczow, just twenty-five short miles west of the Soviet border.

GERMAN PLANS AND DISPOSITIONS

Crüwell's division belonged to *Wehrmacht*'s Army Group South, commanded by a stiff-backed, old-school Prussian field marshal, Gerd von Rundstedt. This powerful group of forces was aimed at the strategically important Soviet Ukraine, with its vast natural resources desperately needed by resource-poor Germany. The original plans of Army Group South called for a two-pronged pincer movement, penetrating the Soviet border defenses and advancing with all haste on to the great Dnieper River, almost four hundred miles east beyond the border. Once there, the northern and southern pincers were to link up on the eastern bank of the river, trapping the bulk of the Red Army in Ukraine on the western side.

The stronger of the two, the northern wing of Army Group South, was composed of Sixth and Seventeenth Field armies, plus its strike force of Panzer Group 1. This force was designated to contend with its primary Soviet counterpart, the Kiev Special Military District. While the Seventeenth Army was to operate against the northern flank of Lvov pocket, the forces striking directly for the Ukrainian capital were the infamous Sixth Army, marching towards its doom at Stalingrad. The Sixth Army, commanded by Field Marshal Walther von Reichenau, was given the task of breaching the Soviet border, paving the way for Panzer Group 1 under von Kleist, an army in all but name, to break into operational maneuver space.

The Eleventh Army deployed in Rumania was the southern pincer of Army Group South, originally tasked to attack against Odessa Military District. However, Hitler's last-minute modification ordered the Eleventh Army to stay put and to guard against a possible Soviet counteroffensive into Rumania, protecting Ploesti oil fields, vital for the German war effort. The Rumanian Third and Fourth armies, supported by over five hundred aircraft, were also part of Army Group South. The gap between the two parts of Army Group South, running along the craggy Carpathian Mountains, was thinly held by a Hungarian mobile corps.

Stretching from a small Polish town of Wlodawa in the north, to the Danube Delta in the south, along almost five hundred miles of border, the Army Group South numbered 41 German divisions, supported by 772 aircraft of Luftflotte 4. The above number reflects strictly the number of German divisions. Even though there were additional Rumanian and Hungarian divisions included in the overall strength of Army Group South, the German planners did not trust their abilities or motivations. This attitude is clearly illustrated in a diary entry by Generaloberst Franz Halder, chief of Army General Staff: "It would be pointless to base our operational plans on forces which cannot be counted on with certainty. As far as actual fighting troops are concerned, we can depend only on German forces. . . . On Romania we cannot rely at all. Their divisions have no offensive power. . . . Hungary is unreliable. Has no reasons for turning on Russia."[2]

Breaking down German mission objectives, from the long-range strategic goal of reaching Kiev, individual German corps and armies were to strike for intermediate operational objectives. On the extreme left, north, flank of Army Group South, the XVII Corps was to attack in direction of Kovel, safeguarding the left flank of German Sixth Army, whose intermediate objective was the city of Lutsk. Aimed against it was the XXIX Corps of the Sixth Army, tasked with breaching Soviet defenses along the Western Bug River and allowing the III Mechanized Corps of Panzer Group 1 to race onto Lutsk. The ancient town of Lutsk, founded in the eleventh century, was the first important stop on the road to Kiev. Termed *Panzerstrasse* by Gen. Eberhard von Mackensen, commander of III Mechanized Corps, this major artery ran from German-occupied Poland to Lutsk, then Rovno, Zhitomir, and, finally, to Kiev.[3]

South of them, aimed at Sokal, the LV Corps of Sixth Army was echeloned in front of XLVIII Mechanized Corps of Panzer Group 1, with the XLIV Corps farther south. Finally, in reserve of Army Group South, located in the area of Lyublin, was the XIV Motorized Corps.

The German units were deployed in very compact, concentrated formations, achieving density of one division per three miles of front. Compared to up to thirty miles of frontage occupied by some Soviet divisions along the border, the Germans were well-positioned to penetrate porous Soviet defenses by bringing the maximum amount of forces at the place and time of their choosing. Still, von Rundstedt and his senior commanders clearly understood the complexity of launching a major invasion with the northern wing alone, as underscored by command staff exercises in Saint Germain, France, in early February 1941:

> It shows the difficulty of accomplishing an enveloping operation west of the Dnepr [Dneiper], with the northern wing alone, particularly in view of the possibility that this wing might be threatened or at least slowed in its advance by enemy attacking from Pripet area. . . .[4] By any attack against the Russian army, one must avoid the danger of simply pushing the Russians back. We must use attack methods which cut up the Russian army and allow its destruction in pockets. A starting position must be created which allows the use of major envelopment operations.[5]

It is common nowadays to lambaste German military planners for underestimating Soviet military capabilities. The often-quoted Heinz Guderian, godfather of German panzer operations, estimated the Soviet tank park at over ten thousand in 1937, knowing that these numbers would only grow yearly at an ever-increasing pace. In 1933 he visited one tank factory in the Soviet Union, producing twenty-two tanks a day.[6] Extrapolating from this figure and allowing for a modest five-day week, fifty-two weeks per year, these numbers amount to an output of 5,720 tanks per year. And these numbers are just for one factory in 1933. Doubtless, the German planners made projections of what the Soviet tank strength would be in 1941. In a similar vein, a Luftwaffe officer, Maj. Rudolf Loytved-Hardegg, tasked with preparing intelligence estimates about the Red Air Force, placed the number of Soviet combat-ready aircraft at fourteen thousand.[7] The two men were echoed by Halder:

> Comments on Russian tanks: Redoubtable; 4.7cm gun (AT) a good medium weapon; bulk of tanks obsolete. Numerically Russia's tank strength is superior to that of any other nation, but they have only a small number of new giant types with long 10cm guns (mammoth models, 42 to 45 tons). Air force very large in number, but mostly outdated; only small number of modern models."[8]

This mention about the "new giant types" of tanks dispels the notion that Germans were unaware of the new generation of large Soviet tanks. However, this particular entry was not clear to which model Halder was referring; KV-1 armed with a long gun but 76mm in caliber, or KV-2, which was armed with a heavier but shorter 152mm howitzer.

Despite being contemptuous of Soviet combat capabilities and leadership, the German planners were wary of the sheer numerical enormity of their future opponent. Underscoring that it would be a giant undertaking to topple the Soviet colossus, a terse entry in Halder's famous war diary on January 28, 1941, read: "Commit all available units."[9] It appears that Hitler himself placed his support behind the best possible chances of success: "AAA (Anti-Air Artillery). Führer wants no serviceable piece to remain inactive. Personnel for thirty batteries. AAA Corps, of six battalions, for Sixth Army (Panzer Group 1) and Panzer Group 2."[10]

Nor were logistics underestimated; another entry on the same day: "Satisfaction is possible only when the point of main effort is prepared through the collaboration of all forces in order to solve the most significant supply issues concerning transportation, tires, fuel, and storage. The air force and army must use the available transportation through careful, coordinated effort."

Halder comments on the sheer size of the Soviet state:

> Problems of Russia's vastness: Enormous expanse requires concentration of critical points. Massed planes and tanks must be brought to bear on strategic points. Our air force cannot cover this entire huge area at one time; at the start of the campaign, it will be able to dominate only parts of the enormous front.[11]

Immensely hampering German planning efforts was the closed nature of the Soviet society. Tourism by private western citizens into the Soviet Union was practically at zero, virtually negating German efforts to explore the Soviet defensive and industrial capabilities lying in the hinterland of the vast country. Even the most basic building block of any planning, maps, was in short supply: "Difficulty with Russian maps. Especially the tactical maps (1:100,000) are very poor. Lower echelons must be warned on how staff work will be affected by such bad maps."[12] However, the new territories which Soviet Union acquired after the 1939 partition of Poland contained large numbers of locals either sympathetic to Germans or hostile to the Soviets, providing German intelligence with accurate tactical information about the border areas.

Overall, German planners were well aware of the effects Stalin's purges had on condition, capabilities, and morale of Soviet military in general and its officer corps in particular. German intelligence rightly determined the Soviet command and support structures to be slow to respond, bulky, cumbersome, and not ready to adapt to rapidly changing tactical situations.

GERMAN ORGANIZATIONS

The striking power of Army Group South rested with its five panzer divisions, all veteran formations. Impressed with the performance of armored units in 1939 and 1940, Hitler ordered the number of panzer divisions doubled from twelve to twenty-four for the 1941 campaign. However, this increase in numbers of divisions was not matched by a proportionate increase of total number of tanks. In 1940, the maneuver portion of a panzer division was composed of two panzer regiments and one motorized infantry regiment. The doubling of panzer divisions was achieved by shuffling the balance of regiments within a division. The 1941 panzer division had one panzer regiment with two motorized infantry regiments.

Suffering from chronic shortages of raw materials, production capacity, and availability of specialist workers, the German armament industry was not able to deliver the number of tanks required for twenty-four panzer divisions. While a panzer division of 1940 numbered close to 300 tanks, the start of the campaign against the Soviet Union in 1941 saw German panzer divisions numbering less than 160 tanks each.[13] The table below is based on A. V. Isayev's book, in turn quoting Thomas Jents:[14]

Table 1.

Tank Strength of Panzer Group 1

	Unit total	Pz I	Pz II	Pz III	Command Pz IV	Division tanks
9th Panzer	8	32	71	20	12	143
11th Panzer		45	71	20	10	146
13th Panzer		45	71	20	13	149
14th Panzer		45	71	20	11	147
16th Panzer		44	71	20	8	143
Total	8	211	355	100	54	728

In addition, there were two battalions of assault guns and two more of tank destroyers assigned to Panzer Group 1, numbering approximately 180 more armored vehicles.

A typical German panzer entering Soviet Union in 1941 numbered just short of fourteen thousand men, roughly 150 tanks, 50 cannons, and howitzers ranging from 75mm to 150mm, and 30 81mm mortars. These heavy weapons were supplemented by 42 37mm and 9 47mm or 50mm antitank guns, virtually noneffective against the new and heavy Soviet tanks, but plenty deadly to older and lighter models. In addition to field artillery, each German tank division possessed 12 20mm flak guns and 8 to 12 88mm guns. Adding to the deadly cocktail were the heavy artillery and self-propelled assault gun battalions, belonging at the corps level and distributed to individual divisions in mission-oriented battery packages.

While panzers received the lion's share of glory, the mainstay of the German army remained infantry, some motorized, but overwhelmingly regular, of a foot-slogging, gravel-agitating variety. Motorized infantry divisions, although lacking tanks, had the same number of combat battalions, six, as a panzer division, also with roughly fourteen thousand men, while regular infantry division numbered over sixteen thousand men with nine infantry battalions. However, both motorized and regular infantry divisions possessed stronger artillery than their panzer brethren. While the motorized divisions had roughly the same numbers of guns as panzer ones, they were of heavier calibers. The regular infantry divisions, on the other hand, had an additional twelve-gun 105mm battery.

Despite being regularly portrayed as a mechanized force *par excellance*, the German army brought 625,000 horses with it into the Soviet Union in 1941, more than Napoleon did in 1812. Equally difficult was the situation with wheeled transport. While a shortage of wheeled vehicles before the opening of the campaign was partially made good by captured or commandeered French trucks, their suspensions, developed for well-maintained European highways, did not last long on the rutted roads of the western Soviet Union. While the bulk of the German army marched on foot, almost all of its artillery was horse-drawn, and the typical Landser of 1941 did not look much different from his father in 1914. Still, a significant advantage that German troops enjoyed over their Soviet counterparts was the fact that they were at almost full manning levels, were well-provisioned and superbly trained, and experienced and enjoyed inspiring and confident leadership.

CHAPTER 2

Soviet Military on the Eve of War

STARTING IN THE LATE 1930s, the Soviet military experienced dramatic growth. Its numbers rose from over 1.5 million men in 1937 to 5.2 million by June 22, 1941, a more than three-fold increase. However, this drastic increase in quantity was not paralleled by an increase in quality. This dilution of fighting capability can be underscored by taking a closer look at the prewar Soviet officer corps.

By 1936 Stalin's bloody hand had already raked through the Communist Party and the country's administrative apparatus. Concerned with "Bonapartism," the fear of a charismatic military leader arising to lead a successful challenge to his authority, Stalin turned his jaundiced eye towards the military.

Marshal Mikhail N. Tukhachevskiy was one of the earliest and the most prominent victims of military purges. Implicated along with Tukhachevskiy, many other officers connected to him socially or professionally were swept away. Unfortunately for the Soviet armored forces, many of its proponents were found among Tukhachevskiy's circle of friends and colleagues and perished along with him. Not only the theoreticians of tank warfare were affected. In a wave of paranoia seeing saboteurs and enemies everywhere, access of enlisted Soviet tankers to their machines was severely restricted to minimize or prevent them from damaging their equipment and stealing parts and supplies.[1]

The men swept up by the purges were normally dubbed "enemies of the people." Their arrests were regularly followed by arrests of their wives, siblings, friends, and adult children. Minor children were generally placed into state orphanages. Elderly parents were often turned out of their homes without means to support themselves. An arrest of one man created expanding ripples of arrests among people associated with him, in turn creating more waves of arrests.

Marshal of the Soviet Union Georgiy K. Zhukov was later to describe the atmosphere of fear in the country:

> The Soviet people and [Communist] Party had to pay a heavy price for the unprincipled suspicion of the political leadership of the country, headed by J. V. Stalin. Horrible situation existed in the country. Nobody trusted anybody, people became afraid of each other, avoided meetings and any conversation, and if such were necessary—attempted to talk with a third party present as witnesses. An epidemic of false denouncements unfolded. Often crystal-clear honest people were falsely denounced, sometimes among close friends. All this was done out of fear to be suspected of disloyalty. This horrible situation continued getting worse.
>
> The Soviet people, from young to old, could not comprehend what was happening, why the arrests among our people were so wide-spread. Not only [Communist] Party members, but even non-party affiliated people, with incomprehension and internal doubt, watched the rising tide of arrests and, of course, nobody could openly voice their incomprehension, their doubt that those arrested were indeed involved in any anti-Soviet activity or membership in counter-revolutionary organizations. Every honest man, going to bed, could not be sure that he would not be taken that same night under some false denouncement."[2]

Unfortunately, human nature being weak, false accusations were often used to settle scores or to clear an avenue for advancement. General Grigorenko made a somewhat generalized observation: "Those who were crude and of limited intelligence seemed to avoid being purged. Those destroyed were mainly cultured, tactful, thoughtful people."[3]

In his memoirs, Zhukov described his own close brush with the deadly menace of the purges in 1937. Danilo Serdich, commander of III Cavalry Corps, in which Zhukov commanded a cavalry division, was arrested. Upon Zhukov's arrival at corps' headquarters in Minsk, he was met by F. I. Golikov, commissar of the Belarusian Military District. This district just had its commander and Golikov's predecessor arrested. Golikov presented Zhukov with a report by commissar of III Cavalry Corps Nikolai Yung, full of false accusations, including a charge that Zhukov's wife baptized their daughter

Ella in church. He also grilled Zhukov about his associations with officers already arrested. The hot-blooded Zhukov was ready to explode, with quite possibly deadly consequences for himself. This scene was interrupted by acting commander of Belarusian Military District V. M. Mulin. He calmed Zhukov down and sent him back to his division. Zhukov spent two very uncomfortable months waiting for the outcome of his confrontation with Commissar Golikov. When he was finally appointed to command the III Cavalry Corps, he found out that his accuser, Yung himself, was arrested.

By then, Zhukov's new command was in shambles:

> Two weeks later I managed to familiarize myself in detail with situation in all the subunits of the [III Cavalry] Corps and, unfortunately, had to admit that majority of units, due to arrests, suffered severe drop in combat and political readiness of command and political personnel, accountability lowered and, as follows, discipline and service of all personnel weakened.[4]

Besides sheer numerical losses of experienced and capable men, the pool of knowledge that was lost was staggering. A prime example of this was the General Staff Academy. The disgraced Marshal Tukhachevskiy was a great proponent of this institution and personally selected many talented military educators and theoreticians to staff the faculty at the academy. After the fall of Tukhachevskiy, a wave of arrests swept through the General Staff Academy in late 1936 and 1937, decimating the faculty.

Arrests were not limited to faculty but included students as well. Future marshal of the Soviet Union Ivan Khristoforovich Bagramyan, whose memoirs will be extensively quoted in this work, was a student at the General Staff Academy during the purges. Normally, the first step before arrest was denouncement at a Communist Party meeting, followed by expulsion from the Communist Party. At one such meeting, Bagramyan was accused of being a former member of Dashnaks, an anti-revolutionary Armenian military formation during the Civil War. Despite documented proof that Bagramyan, in fact, fought against this organization, he was expelled from the Communist Party and was expecting an arrest to come at any minute. Following a friend's advice, Bagramyan appealed the expulsion and, astonishingly, was fully cleared and reinstated.[5] However, a black mark stuck to him, and this episode slowed down his rise through the ranks before the war.

During the late 1920s, Bagramyan attended an advanced course for cavalry officers in which two of his classmates were the future Marshals Georgiy Zhukov and Konstantin K. Rokossovskiy. Rokossovskiy was later arrested for his association with Marshal Tukhachevskiy. He underwent severe beatings and tortures at the hands of the People's Commissariat of Internal Affairs (NKVD) interrogators and, during multiple brutal beatings, all of his teeth were knocked out. Miraculously, Rokossovskiy was released shortly before the war and appointed to command a mechanized corps. Some men, like still-pugnacious Rokossovskiy, with his mouth full of gold teeth to replace the ones knocked out by NKVD men, survived the purges with their characters intact. Others, like the former Chief of General Staff General Kiril A. Meretskov, emerged from the NKVD basements broken men. During his two months of imprisonment, Meretskov's tortures were so particularly brutal that even the sinister NKVD chief Lavrentiy Beria described them as a "meat grinder." Even though released and reinstated like Rokossovskiy, Meretskov was nonetheless a changed man, meek and indecisive.

Men, who unflinchingly faced death on multiple battlefields during World War I and the Russian Civil War, were tortured into signing false confessions, implicating themselves and other innocent men for nonexistent crimes. The most common charge was "agent of foreign power."

The havoc created in the Soviet military by the purges was terrifying. Men who replaced those shot or dismissed the previous year would find themselves similarly dealt with, and their successor would often share the same fate. The extraordinary upheaval moved men several steps up the command chain in a space of a year or two, resulting in young and inexperienced officers promoted far beyond their competency and ability.

The effect of the loss of so many senior officers had a tremendous effect on Soviet enlisted personnel. The generally poorly educated Soviet enlisted men were more susceptible to trust Communist Party propaganda. Many of them believed that their former superior officers were traitors and "enemies of the people," which undermined their trust in their commanding officers and drastically lowered discipline and combat readiness in the armed forces.

In the Soviet Far East, another charismatic Soviet commander, Marshal Vasiliy Blyukher, was in a position of great power, far from Moscow's reach. This popular and capable commander shared Tukhachevskiy's fate and was executed. The officer ranks under his command suffered particularly heavy cleansing. Then-Colonel Grigorenko, upon assignment to the Far East in 1940, found the situation to be dismal:

> Almost two years had passed since the mass arrests had come to an end, but the command pyramid had not yet been restored. Many positions remained unfilled because there were no men qualified to occupy them. Battalions were commanded by officers who had completed military schools less than a year before. Some battalion commanders had completed only courses for second lieutenants, and their experience had been limited to several months of command of platoon or company. . . . In the 40th Infantry Division, not only had the officers of divisional and regimental administrations been arrested, but also the commanders of battalions, companies, and platoons.[6]

Stalin's purges cost the Soviet military close to fifty thousand officers, mostly in field-grade and general ranks, who were executed, imprisoned, or cashiered. While some of them were nothing more than Communist Party hacks in uniform, an overwhelming greater part of them were men with military experience. A majority of them saw service with the old Russian Imperial Army and fought during World War I and the Russian Civil War. In the aftermath of World War I and immediately following the communist takeover of Russia, virtually all the former czarist officers were driven out of the military. Listed among "class enemies," allegedly hostile to the nascent Communist regime, the officers of the old army were slaughtered in large numbers during the Red Terror. Numerous others immigrated, joined the burgeoning counter-revolutionary "White" royalist formations, or melted into civilian society.

In 1918, as the young Communist government was faced with the life-or-death struggle against armed insurrections of various anti-Bolshevik military formations, foreign interventionists, and home-grown peasant rebellions, the need for qualified officers to lead the brand-new Red Army became dire.

Recognizing the severity of the situation presented by a lack of trained cadres, first commander of the Red Army Leon Trotskiy instituted a wide-scale program of bringing the former czarist officers back into uniform under unobtrusively sounding title of "military specialists." The purist communists howled at such pollution of proletarian ranks, but Trotsky dug in his heels, and eventually over two hundred thousand former officers were re-integrated into the military. Some went willingly, some not, and more rejoined out of a need to make a living. In many cases, these officers' participation was obtained only by the Reds holding their families as hostages to ensure men's cooperation.

However, a majority of officers who rejoined the ranks were not the same men who led the Russian army at the start of World War I. The old, mostly aristocratic, officer corps of 1914 was largely wiped out during the first bloody years of the conflict. They were replaced overwhelmingly by men from the middle class and often from the working class. Many among this new generation of officers were more sympathetic, or simply nonhostile, to the Communist regime. Yet more men served out of sense of patriotic duty to Russia, regardless of political views of those at the helm. A prime example of such men was the Russian General Staff, almost to a man joining the Red Army out of sense of serving their country. Such "military specialists" provided the needed backbone, and some of them went on to distinguished careers in the Red Army. Some, like Zhukov, a former noncommissioned officer (NCO), and Tukhachevskiy and Boris M. Shaposhnikov, former aristocratic officers, went on to gain the highest ranks and top positions in the Soviet military.

Attempting to alleviate shortfall of officer cadres before the war, the Red Army leadership increased the number of officer schools, shortened the course of study at the existing ones, and called up numbers of reservist officers. According to Colonel Bagramyan:

> From 1939 to 1940, 174,000 reserve officers were called to active duty. Numbers of students at military academies doubled. In 1940 alone, 42 new military schools were created. . . . Numbers of students at military schools rose from 36,000 to 168,000 men.[7] All military schools switched from three-year curriculum to two years. At the same time, numerous courses for junior lieutenants were organized. . . .
>
> I recall that in our district alone by May 1941 there was a shortage of over thirty thousand command and technical personnel. We were placing great hopes in 1941 upon the May graduating class of military schools. However, the young lieutenants arrived at their units several days before the start of war and, of course, did not have an opportunity to get their bearings and become familiar with their subordinates.[8]

A dearth of staff officers was felt at all command echelons. For example, the headquarters of a field army on peacetime footing was set at 268 personnel, 225 of them being officers. Switching to wartime footing, the numbers were to increase to 1,530 and 550, respectively.[9] However, the wartime staffing could be achieved only with declaring full mobilization, which the Soviet government tried to avoid or delay at all costs. Calling up a number of reserve officers for short refresher training was not sufficient to alleviate staff officer shortages.

The influx of called-up reservist officers somewhat improved the situation mainly at the junior officer level. Rapid expansion of the army, combined with purges of senior and experienced cadres, resulted in inexperienced officers promoted and assigned beyond their competence level. From company level to district command, the shortfall in experience and military education drastically reduced the Red Army's war fighting capabilities.

A prime example of this Peter Principle was Col. Gen. Mikhail P. Kirponos, who ascended to command the Kiev Special Military District in January of 1941. He had large shoes to fill, and he did not fill them well. This district, besides being the most powerful among Soviet border districts, was the most prestigious as well. Command of Kiev Special Military District was often a direct stepping stone to the highest strata of Soviet military establishment. Among the former commanders of this district were such distinguished Red Army personalities as I. E. Yakir, M. V. Frunze, A. I. Yegorov, S. K. Timoshenko and G. K. Zhukov. The first three did not live through Stalin's purges; the last two went on to pinnacles of the Soviet military.

Kirponos' direct predecessor was none other than the irascible Georgiy K. Zhukov, promoted to become the chief of general staff. A veteran of World War I and the Russian Civil War, the war with Finland in November 1939 found Kirponos in command of the 70th Rifle Division. Competent division commander, Kirponos was one of the few Soviet senior commanders who achieved any distinction in the Winter War. He was awarded the medal of Hero of the Soviet Union, the highest Soviet military award, for successfully leading his division through a dismal campaign.

When the deadly wave of purges decimated the Soviet military command establishment in 1937, General Kirponos rose up on the follow-up wave of promotions needed to fill the gaping vacancies. April of 1940 found him in command of a rifle corps; three months later, in a jump of two ranks, he headed the Leningrad Military District. In June 1941 came the fateful appointment to command the Kiev Special Military District, with rapid subsequent promotion to the rank of colonel general.

Similar to the officer corps, the Red Army forces were short of everything: men, combat and utility vehicles, armaments, and equipment. Despite many changes in military science and technology since World War I, one commodity remained an almost constant—the Russian, now Soviet, soldier. Other than a general increase in basic literacy levels, the typical Red Army soldier closely resembled his predecessor that marched off to war in August 1914. The proletarian makeup of enlisted personnel was paralleled by the officer corps. "By 1937 workers and peasants made up over 70 percent of command cadre; more than half of commanders were communists and Komsomol members," wrote Zhukov in his memoirs.[10]

Removing millions of men from the civilian sector of the economy to sweepingly increase the military negatively reflected on productivity of the Soviet economy. Further call-up of men had to be balanced against the needs of the military without straining the economy. This resulted in a majority of Soviet military units operating even below their peacetime personnel requirements.

In April of 1941, the People's Commissariat for Defense established a new organization for a rifle division to include three rifle regiments, two artillery regiments, plus a number of separate specialist battalions, including a battalion of sixteen light tanks. On paper, the new organization of a Soviet rifle division amounted to 14,438 men. However, the vast majority of Soviet rifle divisions did not have time to upgrade to the new organization before the war started and were in transition. Even with the increased manpower of called-up reservists, a Soviet rifle division in June 1941 had over 2,300 fewer men than its counterpart German infantry division. What's more significant, a German infantry division was much stronger in antitank weapon systems and was infinitely better equipped with wheeled vehicles.

Simultaneous with reorganization, ninety-nine rifle divisions were ordered brought up to full wartime strength of 14,483 men from peacetime establishment of 8,000 to 10,000 men. However, when the Germans crossed the border on June 22, only twenty-two of these divisions were so beefed up.

Two to three Soviet rifle divisions, plus supporting units, were organized into a rifle corps with paper strength of 51,061 men. The next higher formation in the Soviet ground forces was an army, composed of one to three rifle corps, one or two mechanized corps, and supporting units. The Fifth Army, for example, on June 1, 1941, was composed of two rifle and two mechanized corps and, including garrisons of its fortified regions, numbered 142,570 men. More were assigned in May, when reservists were called up for training.[11]

Out of all the ground forces of the Red Army, its armored corps went through possibly the most severe upheaval during the prewar years. Initially, there was major opposition to the mechanized forces from the generation of senior Red Army officers, steeped in the long-standing tradition of the cavalry. Gradually, however, the cavalry fell into decline, as dominance of armored forces became apparent.

Unlike the meat-grinding trench warfare on the Western Front during World War I, operations conducted by the Russian Army during that conflict were of a more fluid nature. In the Civil War that came close on the heels of the world war, far-ranging cavalry played a major part in combat operations over the vastness of far-flung Russia. From the very start, there were sufficient numbers of influential and eloquent theoreticians that moved the Soviet armored forces forward in the face of traditionalist cavalry opposition.

Like England and Germany, the new Soviet proponents of tank warfare had diverging ideas on the best use of tanks on the battlefield. Some, still clinging to World War I warfare concepts, believed that tanks should operate exclusively in support of, and be subordinate to, the infantry. Others boldly advocated sweeping, far-ranging independent operations by massed tank formations. The difficulty lay in the fact that virtually no Russian officer had any combat experience in tank warfare. The few World War I vintage tanks captured from the loyalist forces during the Civil War did not see much field service and, by the mid-1920s, were largely nonoperational.

While efforts were made to begin developing Soviet tank designs and production, the Red Army cast about for a source of knowledge of tank operations. The opportunity, presented by Germans, came knocking in 1926. Germany's top political and military leadership were actively taking steps in circumventing the Treaty of Versailles and rebuilding the German military machine. Article 171 of the Treaty of Versailles prohibited Germany from developing and producing an armored force. The Soviet Union eagerly provided a clandestine place where new ideas and secretly designed tanks could be tested and knowledge shared.

By the end of 1926, Hermann von der Lieth-Thomsen, the German representative and strangely enough an air force officer, and Jan Berzin, chief of Soviet military intelligence, signed an agreement to establish a tank school in Kazan, Russia, in 1927. Germany was to pay for building and running the school and provide training and command cadre, while the Russians would see after the upkeep of the facilities. Due to various delays, political and logistical, the school actually commenced operations in mid-1929 with the arrival of the first three tank prototypes secretly built in Germany. A class of twenty officers, ten German and ten Russian, began their theoretical studies at approximately the same time.[12]

Close cooperation continued until 1933, when the divergent military and political goals resulted in closing down of Kazan tank school, along with its sister school for aircraft at Lipetsk. All German personnel, along with now ten tanks, returned to Germany. Still, they left behind a significant amount of equipment worth over 1.2 million rubles,[13] plus the physical facilities, used to great extent by the future generations of Russian tankers. Both sides benefited greatly from their joint venture, acquiring a great deal of theoretical and practical knowledge. Experience gained at Kazan allowed both countries to become world leaders in armored warfare.

While Germany was tied hand and foot by the vengeful restrictions of Treaty of Versailles, the Soviet Union, unencumbered by any outside limitations, began serious design and development of armored vehicles, even though it did not yet have a cohesive doctrine on their use. Handicapped by the devastating Civil War, the Soviet Union initially lagged behind the western countries in tank design. However, the late start was partially made up by purchasing a limited number of armored vehicles in the West and producing them under license at home. The British Vickers six-ton tank became the cornerstone of the Soviet T-26 tank series, which underwent numerous modifications and upgrades. In a similar vein, American inventor Walter J. Christie's M1931 tank and suspension system became the basis for Soviet BT series and the T-34 tank, arguably the most successful tank of World War II. Conversely, the Soviet Union copied, both legally and illegally, a number of other mechanical equipment, notably American Ford trucks and cars and Caterpillar tractors.

At approximately the same time as the experimental tank school opened in Kazan in 1929, the Red Army formed its first experimental mechanized unit. By the end of the next year, the regiment was expanded to a brigade numbering sixty MS-1 tanks plus numerous other vehicles including tankettes and armored cars.[14] Training and progress of the new experimental unit was closely monitored by such high-level observers as K. E. Voroshilov, B. M. Shaposhnikov, and V. K. Triandafilov. The armored force continued to expand steadily, and in 1932 a first mechanized corps was born, followed soon by several more. By 1936 the Soviet armored force already numbered four mechanized corps, each with over five hundred tanks, plus six tank regiments and six separate tank battalions.

In 1936, as the Spanish Civil War flared up a scant three years after the productive cooperation at Kazan ended, Germany and the Soviet Union found themselves looking at each other over gun barrels. Both countries, backing opposing sides in a politically second-rate country, thought Spain useful as testing grounds for their armored doctrines in a live-fire environment.

The disparity between German and Soviet armored formations in Spain favored the Soviets. Thin-skinned, machine-gun armed, German light Panzer I tanks were no match for Soviet T-26 machines armed with a 45mm cannon. Unfortunately for the Spanish Nationalist forces and their Soviet patrons, they usually employed their tanks in roles where their advantage was decreased or nullified. In many instances, the Soviet tanks were doled out in penny-packets among Nationalist infantry, who hadn't had the slightest inkling of how to cooperate with the armored vehicles. On several occasions tanks were used in street fighting, where their advantage of mobility and armor was thrown away on narrow cobblestone streets of Spain. Fortunately for the Soviet Union and its Nationalist allies, the Germans with their allies employed their armored vehicles in a similarly ineffective manner.

Germany and the Soviet Union reached different conclusions based on armored operations in Spain. German high command understood that no concrete decision could be made about the course of tank warfare based on circumstances in Spain. Germans realized that their armor was incorrectly used, subordinated to infantry, and the number of tanks was too small to have had significant effect on operations. In addition, the Spanish terrain was largely unsuitable for tank operations. One major offshoot of tank warfare in Spain was the emergence of antitank artillery as a primary factor in halting armor attacks. Germans took this lesson to heart, and the start of World War II found them significantly ahead of the Soviet Union in antitank weapon tactics and implementation.

On the other hand, the Soviets regarded their experiences in Spain as a valid litmus test of armor warfare. Based on their experiences, the image of tanks as an infantry-support weapon began taking precedence over the "deep battle" independent operations.

In 1938 and 1939, two conflicts were fought against the Japanese in the Soviet Far East at Lake Khasan and Khalkhin-Gol River. Even though emerging victorious in both instances, the Soviet military managed success only after bringing overwhelmingly superior manpower and firepower to bear on the Japanese. While the tank units that participated in both conflicts, especially at

Khalkhin-Gol, played a significant role in the Soviet victories, armor was used unimaginatively and suffered far greater casualties than necessary.

In September 1939, while Hitler was crushing Poland from the west, the Soviet Union delivered a crippling stab into the Polish back from the east. As a result of partitioning Poland between Hitler and Stalin, the Soviet Union came away with large portions of western Ukraine and western Byelorussia. The Soviet tank units that participated in this "liberation" presented a particularly poor showing, being slow, unwieldy, hard to maneuver, and prone to mechanical breakdowns. Lieutenant General Dmitriy Ryabyshev, later talking with his friend Commissar Nikolai Popel, a big tank enthusiast, teased him: "In 1939 your tanks fell behind my horsies."

Many German officers who had the opportunity to observe Soviet armor units in operation during this conflict came away with decidedly unflattering opinions about Soviet capabilities. Poor performance of the Red Army in western Ukraine had a significant influence on German planning when preparing for invasion of the Soviet Union, misleading German planners into underestimating Soviet capabilities.

In late fall of 1939, a blue-ribbon Soviet commission, evaluating the poor Soviet showing and the outstanding German one, recommended the disbandment of Soviet mechanized corps in favor of forming tank divisions on the German model. Combined with the devastating purges of mid- and late-1930s, the Soviet armored forces slid into a period of decline and stagnation. However, almost immediately after the original Soviet mechanized corps were disbanded, the senior Soviet leaders decided to re-form these corps, albeit on a more flexible basis. They studied very carefully the German experiences during the French and Polish campaigns and became more open to opportunities presented by armored and mechanized forces.

Each reconstructed mechanized corps was composed on paper of two tank divisions and one motorized rifle division, a motorcycle regiment, one or two artillery regiments, plus supporting units. Tank divisions were largely formed around the existing tank brigades. In the wholesale expansion of the armed forces, smaller units were expanded on paper into larger ones, without full complement of equipment and personnel. For example, a signal company would be expanded into a signal battalion, receiving a majority of additional lower enlisted personnel, but without appropriate numbers of officers and NCOs, radio and telephone equipment, and transportation.

In a similar vein, tank divisions of the mechanized corps resembled a skeleton to be fleshed out by muscle over time. The Russian Civil War, less than twenty years in the past, left the Soviet Union a devastated country. Only the draconian measures during the industrialization instituted by Josef Stalin and the Communist Party allowed the country to begin playing catch-up with the western nations. Starting with no tank industry in 1929, the Soviet Union produced almost four thousand of these vehicles during its first economic Five-Year Plan of 1929-1933. Still, by the start of war with Germany, Soviet industrial capacity in producing the required number of tanks fell far short of the desired goal. Combined with a Russian propensity to hoard their old equipment, the seemingly impressive number of almost twenty-four thousand at the start of the war was a mismatched collection of modern new tanks, decrepit older ones, and some in between.

The Soviet tanks fell into three distinct categories: light, medium, and heavy. Depicted in multiple books and film, the T-34 medium tank carved out a niche as a quintessential Soviet tank. However, at the start of Operation Barbarossa:

> The mainstay of the tank park of the RKKA consisted of light T-26 and BT tanks of various models, making up nearly 75 percent of total number of vehicles.[15] The new medium T-34s and heavy KVs composed only almost 8 percent. Majority of old tanks, such as early versions of T-26 and BTs, plus the T-28, T-35, T-37, and T-38 were seriously worn out: 9 percent of these machines required major overhaul, and 44 percent, intermediate-level overhaul.[16]

By far, the most numerous armored fighting vehicles of the Red Army at the start of Operation Barbarossa were the T-26 light tanks, developed on the basis of the British Vickers light tank. In the scope of the "Deep Battle" concept, this tank was designated as an "infantry escort tank"—supporting the infantry on the offensive and carrying out limited follow-through attacks in the enemy rear. Starting from late 1931 and up to the start of the war, over 11,200 different variations of this tank were produced, and some 10,268 were still carried on the rosters of the Red Army armored units, representing close to 40 percent of the total Soviet tank park.[17] Many of the very early models, like the two-turreted machine gun–armed versions, while officially designated as "training park," padded the total numbers, adding practically no value to the overall strength of their units.

Eventually upgraded to mount a 45mm cannon, the T-26 could successfully outshoot all German light tanks. However, a significant weakness in the design of the T-26 rendered this most-numerous Soviet tank an easy prey to German antitank defenses. Endemic to all T-26 versions, it suffered from inadequate armor protection, being able to mainly withstand machine-gun fire, and in some cases, not even that. The frontal armor of T-26, the thickest part of the tank, was only 15mm thick, making it vulnerable even to the most outdated 37mm antitank cannons. This was illustrated time and time again in Spain, Finland, and Mongolia. Attempts to up-armor the T-26 came to naught due to the vehicle engine's inability to accommodate heavier armor. Still, the basic design of the T-26 proved to be a very versatile basis for many mission-specific purposes. T-26 chassis were used as a platform for such specialist vehicles as flame-throwing tanks, bridge layers, self-propelled artillery, tank recovery tractors, prime movers, and others.

The Bystrokhodniy Tank (fast tank, or BT) series consisted mainly of the BT-2, BT-5, and BT-7 versions. As mentioned previously in this chapter, both the BT series and the T-34 were based on the work of American tank designer J. Walter Christie. The light and fast BT series of tanks were developed to operate as a mobile branch of the "deep battle" concept—striking far into the rear of the enemy. Characteristic to all BT models, these tanks could operate in tracked mode for traversing cross-country and wheeled mode on the road. Successive designs of BT tanks, mainly the BT-7, featured upgraded armor, engine, and armament, plus a series of other vital improvements.

While the BT-2 and BT-5 versions could not successfully contend with medium German panzers, the BT-7 could trump the German Panzer II and Panzer 38(t) tanks and was generally on par with the Panzer III, especially the BT-7s produced after 1937. However, in the upcoming contests, the Germans would almost always come out victorious due to their superior training, command and control, and communications.[18]

Rounding out Soviet light tanks were T-37, T-38, and T-40 swimming reconnaissance tanks, which could be grouped together, being essentially similar in design and purpose. Tanks in this category were developed based on the prototype models of Vickers tanks, created by two British designers Sir John Valentine Carden and Vivian Lloyd, appropriately called the Vickers-Carden-Lloyd Amphibian Tanks. While several other countries successfully experimented with amphibious tanks, the Soviet Union was the only country to ramp up serial production of these vehicles. By the time the war started, over four thousand of these machines were produced, with significant numbers of them still found among Soviet mechanized formations.

The T-37/38/40 family of tanks was, in reality, one short step up the armored ladder above the tankette. The tankette was a small armored vehicle, usually lacking a rotating turret and crewed by two men, sometimes one, armed almost exclusively with one or two machine guns. Its thin armor and light armament proved totally inadequate for survival in the struggle with German panzer formations and their formidable antitanks defenses. Virtually all of the Soviet T-27 tankettes and superlight T-37/38/40 perished within the first several months of the German invasion.

The next weight category, the medium tanks, was represented by the older T-28 and the famous T-34. This category of armored combat vehicle was envisioned to operate in support of infantry breaking through heavily fortified areas and for limited follow-up exploitation. Once again borrowing from the British, the T-28 was based on the Vickers A6E1. Like many contemporary designs of its class, the T-28 sported three turrets and was manned by a crew of six. As the already familiar malady, the early versions of the T-28 suffered from insufficient armor, which had to be upgraded later. Overall, this was not a successful model, and its serial production was discontinued in 1939. Slightly over six hundred tanks of this type were produced between 1932–1939, with a significant portion of them still in service at the start of war.

Sharing its weight category, the vaunted T-34 was the most mass-produced tank of World War II. The basic design by the American Walter Christie laid the groundwork for this versatile combat vehicle. Its thick-sloping armor was virtually impervious to most of the German antitank artillery and tank-based guns except at extremely close ranges. The wide-stable platform and wide tracks gave the T-34 an exceptional mobility on poor Russian roads and in difficult cross-country terrain. Starting in 1940, by the beginning of conflict with Germany, roughly 1,225 T-34s were produced. By the time the war ended, over 35,000 of them took the field. Undiscovered by German intelligence before the war, these combat vehicles came as a rude surprise to advancing Germans.

While the numbers of heavy tanks were relatively low in the Soviet Army, the German *Wehrmacht* did not have any heavy panzers in serial production, other than several experimental prototypes. The heavy tanks were envisioned by the Red Army commanders as close support for infantry in breaching enemy defensive works. The early Soviet heavy T-35 was a veritable land behemoth, weighing in at forty-four to fifty-five tons, depending on the year of modification, and mounting five turrets. Manned by a crew of ten or eleven, the five turrets, mounted in two levels, were armed with one 76mm cannon, two 45mm cannons, and six 7.62mm machine guns.

Being large and heavy, the T-35 was a surprisingly fragile vehicle, extremely prone to mechanical breakdowns. Its sheer size and mass made this heavy tank exceedingly difficult to operate in any terrain but the most favorable. In the era of no power steering, it was physically exhausting for its drivers to maneuver the heavy tank. Before the war, almost all the operational T-35s were concentrated in the VIII Mechanized Corps of the Kiev Special Military District. Less than a handful actually came to grips with the enemy on the battlefield, the majority of them being lost to breakdowns and air attacks on the march. In all, between 1935 and 1939, only sixty-one of these monstrous tanks were produced.[19]

Another heavy Soviet tank, the KV-1 (named after Kliment Voroshilov, a leading Soviet marshal and Stalin's crony) was a much more successful version. Designed to replace the T-35, the KV-1 initially resembled a heavier version of the T-34, even being armed with the same caliber cannon, the 76mm. Slightly over six hundred KV-1s were produced from mid-1940 to mid-1941.

The KV-2 was the poor relation of the KV-1. Designed specifically for suppressing and destroying enemy fortifications, the KV-2 mounted a 152mm howitzer in a tall, square naval gun turret mounted on KV-1 chassis. Even though slightly over 330 of these tanks were produced in 1940 and the first half of 1941, less than 100 of them were operational when the red balloon went up. Like the T-35, very few of them engaged the enemy on the battlefield. When they did, the results were almost invariably pathetic. Designed to engage stationary fortifications, the KV-2 did not have armor-piercing ammunition and, being armed with a howitzer, could not effectively engage enemy in a tank-versus-tank combat. Virtually all of the KV-2s perished in 1941.

Well into the first year of the brutal campaign against the Soviet Union, Hitler has been said to have stated: "Had I known that the Soviet Union had so many tanks, I would not have attacked." Indeed, the number of tanks in the Soviet arsenal has been almost unanimously placed by historians between twenty-three thousand and twenty-four thousand machines. This number, even though including older versions of these combat vehicles, was larger than almost all other tanks in the world put together.

On paper, the Red Army tank park was indeed impressive. Regulations of 1940 created eight mechanized corps numbering 1,031 tanks each, with twenty-two more corps added the next year. At full strength, this would have amounted to a staggering 30,930 tanks in just the mechanized corps alone, plus a large fleet of armored cars, many of which had mounted cannons capable of defeating light tanks. In addition to the above numbers, additional thousands of light tanks and armored cars were to be assigned to rifle and cavalry divisions and training institutions.

A significant portion of 1,031 tanks comprising a new mechanized corps was to be composed of the medium T-34 and heavy KV-1 machines (420 and 126 respectively), amounting to 53 percent of the total number. These new machines were superior to any tank in the world. While the senior German military command had an inkling about the existence of new Soviet heavy tanks, this information was not disseminated down to the lower echelon, and the presence of these new combat vehicles came as a rude shock to German troops within the very first days of the war.

The T-34 medium tanks went into serial production in July of 1940, and by June 22, 1941, only 1,225 of these machines had been produced. Their distribution was uneven. Almost all of the T-34s were delivered to the mechanized corps created in 1940 and were located in the first echelons of the western border districts. The mechanized corps created in spring of 1941 and garrisoned deeper in the Soviet territory either did not receive any new tanks by the start of the war or received them in single-digit numbers. Diluting their strength further, the new tanks were often not concentrated in units but were distributed in penny packets among many formations within a mechanized corps.

To further exacerbate the problem, the tanks that were available to the mechanized corps were an ill-matched collection of vehicles. By 1939 the existing mechanized corps were disbanded and the armored vehicles were organized into tank brigades and separate battalions. There were two types of tank brigades, the light and heavy ones. The heavy tank brigades were assigned the mission of cooperating and supporting the infantry in breaching enemy defenses. The light tank brigades were to operate independently or in close cooperation with cavalry in exploiting breakthroughs and carrying out attacks in depth.

The heavy tank brigades of 1939 to early 1940 were equipped with T-28 medium tanks and a small number of heavy T-35s. The light brigades were allocated fast BT tanks and light T-26s. Reconnaissance detachments of both also had a sprinkling of light T-37 and T-40 reconnaissance tanks capable of swimming. No other country in the world at the time had amphibious tanks.

When the first nine mechanized corps were reconstituted in late 1940, the new T-34 and KV-1 began arriving in small numbers. Demand for these new vehicles totally exceeded production capacity. Despite being produced in numbers unheard of in western Europe, the Red Army needed another two to three years to acquire the proposed number of tanks.

However, before the first wave of the nine mechanized corps was fully organized, the Soviet government high-handedly ordered creation of twenty-one more corps. Bottoms of barrels were scraped to come up with the needed combat vehicles. Almost any tank was used to make up the desired numbers. This resulted in many nonoperational tanks being delivered to units so that their inventory would show numbers on hand. This created a bewildering array of vehicular hodge-podge. Zhukov described the situation:

> We did not objectively consider capabilities of our tank industry. To completely equip the new mechanized corps [we] needed 16,600 tanks of just the new types, with 32,000 tanks being the total number. It was practically impossible to obtain these numbers in one year; there were shortages of technical and command personnel as well.[20]

As mentioned previously, there were multiple models of BT tanks, with the BT-5 and BT-7 being most common. However, small numbers of earlier versions, like the BT-2, were still around. Even within the BT-5 and BT-7 series there were multiple models. As one type or model was taken out of serial production, manufacturing of spare parts for them ceased as well. However, the existing tanks of discontinued models were not taken out of circulation, instead being retained for training purposes. When the new mechanized corps were formed, the "training park" vehicles were again listed as operational. This resulted in units still being equipped with obsolete models without means to replace the worn-out parts to keep them operational. A small number of them were kept running by salvaging parts from vehicles beyond repair or manufacturing replacement parts in local machine-shops on an individual basis. The German invasion found large numbers of these older versions still sitting immobile in their motor pools. A similar situation existed for earlier versions of still T-26 and for still T-28 and T-35, the last two already being taken out of production.

When the red balloon finally went up, the Soviet mechanized corps differed drastically in strength and composition. The corps re-created in the first wave in 1940 were the most combat capable. Some of them, like the IV and VIII Mechanized Corps, deployed in the first echelon of the Kiev Special Military District, numbered over nine hundred tanks each and contained hundreds of new T-34s and KV-1s. On the other hand, their poor brethren of the second wave of spring in the 1941 were mere shadows of their envisioned selves. The IX and XIX Mechanized Corps, also located in the Kiev Special Military District, but further east, numbered less than three hundred tanks each, mainly T-26s and BTs. Neither corps had the modern models, and around 15 percent of the tanks that they did have were nonfunctional. The July 1940 directive that reconstituted the mechanized corps envisioned each comprised of two tank divisions, one mechanized infantry division, a motorcycle regiment, and supporting units, including an air force squadron. None of these aviation squadrons were actually created and remained on paper only. Otherwise, the mechanized corps were allotted formidable 38,000-plus personnel, 1,031 tanks, 358 artillery pieces and mortars, and 384 armored cars.[21]

By the time the war started, none of the corps were fully formed. While most of them had required numbers of lower enlisted personnel, a great portion of them were either new recruits or recently called-up reservists. None of the mechanized corps had the assigned strength of 1,031 tanks, with the actual strength being between 300 to 900 machines.

The round-out of the Soviet armored fighting vehicles would not be complete without mentioning the armored cars. These numerous vehicles were generally represented by wheeled light BA-20 and medium BA-10 armored reconnaissance cars. While the BA-20 was armed with one 7.62mm machine gun, the BA-10, in addition to the same machine gun, also mounted a turret with a 45mm cannon. These were the same turrets as the two secondary ones mounted on the heavy T-35 tanks. Overall, over 5,300 of these two types of vehicles were made, with most of them perishing in combat by the spring of 1942. The cannon-armed BA-10, if used properly, would have presented a significant challenge to German vehicles of the same type. As it was, Soviet commanders proved completely incapable of effectively employing these weapons platforms in the type of missions for which armored cars were designed.

The Red Army's artillery was technically on par with the German Army. Regimental artillery batteries were mainly equipped with 76mm and older 107mm guns. Divisional and corps artillery regiments were equipped largely with 120mm guns and 152mm howitzers. There were additional separate battalions and regiments of large-caliber 210mm guns, 203mm and 305mm howitzers, and 280mm mortars that belonged to the Reserve of Supreme Command and were doled out to support the field armies.

At the start of the war, the vaunted BM-13 rocket launcher artillery systems, later nicknamed Katyushas, existed only in seven experimental models. Ironically, their serial production was ordered on June 21, 1941, one day before the war started.[22]

The mortars were largely represented by 50mm mortars of limited effectiveness. The more-effective 82mm and 120mm mortars existed in smaller numbers.

However, the greatest weakness of Soviet artillery was in its lack of mobility. The majority of artillery was still horse-drawn, and there were insufficient numbers of draft horses, the shortage of which was supposed to be made up from the civilian economy upon the announcement of mobilization. The heavier-caliber artillery was supposed to be towed by slow-moving tractors, of which there was also a dearth.

The drive to increase the antitank capability to counter possible (German-led) armored threat started late. Only in May 1941 the Soviet high command began forming ten antitank artillery brigades in the western border districts. Five of such brigades were being formed in the Kiev Special Military District. However, due to the common tone of shortage of everything, only one such brigade was more or less completed by the beginning of war. These brigades were to be assigned one per field army and designated to cooperate with the mechanized corps of these armies. To keep up with the mechanized formations, these antitank brigades were also to be completely mechanized. However, with the exception of the 1st Antitank Artillery Brigade, due to overwhelming shortages, most brigades were at 40 to 80 percent of assigned guns, and many brigades were without a single tractor to tow them. There were also severe shortages of wheeled vehicles to transport supplies, personnel, and ammunition.

► CHAPTER 3

Dispositions of Kiev
Special Military District

FROM THE SOGGY VASTNESS OF PRIPYAT MARSHES, then south along the meandering Western Bug River and to the craggy Carpathian Mountains, the Kiev Special Military District was responsible for defending slightly over six hundred miles of Soviet Union's western frontier. In the center of district's border, a salient of land, centered on ancient Ukrainian city of Lvov, protruded into German-occupied southern Poland. The importance which the Soviet leadership allocated this area was underscored by the amount of troops deployed in and around Lvov salient. This area could have been easily used as a beachhead for a thrust southwest, threatening Rumanian oil fields, crucial for German war effort. In a similar manner, a Soviet attack could have been launched northwest, into the southern flank of German-controlled Poland.

There has been much discussion whether Soviet deployment was indicative of their offensive or defensive intentions. The official version presented by the Soviet Union was that its peace-loving country was treacherously attacked by predatory Nazi Germany. This version has many adherents, especially in the former Soviet Union. Others advocate the dense concentration of Soviet troops in the Lvov salient as indication of offensive intentions. However, documentation and memoirs of participants on both sides of the conflict could be interpreted in favor of either viewpoint, massing for a powerful offensive or concentrating for a determined defense in depth.

The truth, as it often tends to, most likely lies somewhere in the middle. In this writer's opinion, Soviet Union did have aggressive intentions, but not in July 1941, as presented by sensationalist writer and ex–Chief Intelligence Directorate (GRU) defector Victor Suvorov (pen name of Vladimir Rezun), but in spring of 1942. Declassified documents and numerous memoirs consistently paint the picture of the Soviet military on the eve of World War II as a cumbersome organization in a state of flux. Based on my own research for this work, I do not believe that the Soviet Union was in shape to conduct invasion-scale offensive operations in 1941.

The nonaggressive rhetoric decried by the Soviet propaganda does not bear scrutiny when compared against the actual course of action carried out under Stalin's stewardship. Just as Hitler browbeat the aging Czech president Emil Hacha into permitting the unopposed entrance of German troops into Czechoslovakia in March 1939, Stalin similarly bullied the three small Baltic states of Latvia, Estonia, and Lithuania in September/October of that same year into accepting Red Army garrisons on their soil, effectively subjugating them by the Soviet Union. In the similar manner, Rumania was forced to cede the province of Northern Bukovina to Stalin in 1940.

Once threats failed, the communist state had no qualms about using force. When, in November 1939, unlike the Baltic states, Finland defiantly refused establishment of Red Army bases on its territory, the Soviet Union invaded its small northern neighbor. And, almost simultaneous with swallowing of the three small Baltic democracies, the Soviet Union lopped off for itself a large chunk of eastern Polish territory in September 1939.

However, these territorial acquisitions reached the limits of Soviet offensive capabilities. Performance of Red Army troops during the easy campaign against Poland was dismal and was duly noted by the German observers. The Winter War against Finland was downright disastrous, exposing for the whole world the weaknesses of the Soviet military machine. Faced with cumulative effects of purges, humiliating Finnish campaign, and need for rearmament and reorganization, Stalin required at least two years of peace to rebuild his offensive potential.

The backbone of the Soviet defensive network was a series of "fortified regions," a system of field and semi-permanent defensive fortifications based on strategically important localities and usually named after them. Prior to late 1939, the Soviet Union possessed a very strong line of these fortified regions, called "The Stalin Line," situated along its western border. Constructed at great expenditure of time, money, and resources, these fortified regions protected vital areas along possible avenues of invasion into the Soviet Union. The fortified regions, comprising a formidable array of defensive fortifications manned by independent machine-gun and artillery battalions, formed the framework in which the Soviet field forces were expected to first halt and then expel the enemy from Soviet territory.

However, after a period of extensive land acquisitions in 1939, the Soviet borders were moved roughly two hundred miles due west, and the old system of well-developed fortified regions soon became redundant. The following year, Soviet government began construction of a new line of fortified regions called "The Molotov Line" along the new border. The old fortified regions, being superfluous and expensive to maintain, were largely mothballed, their equipment and armaments either partially stored or partially moved to the new border.

On May 21, 1941, the People's Commissariat for Defense (NKO, or Narodniy Kommissariat Oborony) ordered the fortified regions along the western border to be brought up to full readiness and manning. This measure was to start on June 4, but by June 22, not a single fortified district was at full readiness, due to shortage of manpower and equipment, endemic to the rest of the Red Army. At the start of the war, battalions manning the fortified regions were at below 50 percent strength, and less than 50 percent of actual fortifications were constructed.

According to Zhukov, an admonishment from Timoshenko and the General Staff on June 14, 1941, stated: "Despite series of directives from the General Staff of the Red Army, emplacement of [appropriate] bunker armaments into long-term field fortifications and bringing these bunkers to combat readiness is being conducted inexcusably slow[ly]."[1]

Had the Soviet Union had time to completely build the system of fortified regions along the new border, similar to the one along the 1939 border, it would have presented a formidable barrier to German invaders. As it was, construction of new fortified regions was progressing slowly, hampered by huge financial expenditures needed for these works.

A major weakness of the new defensive lines lay in the fact that many bunkers were evenly distributed along the the border, rather than being concentrated along the most-likely routes of enemy advance. In addition, many of these field fortifications were constructed in full view from the German side and weren't even camouflaged. Being in the early stages of construction, a majority of already-built fortifications were still isolated islands of resistance, not tied in together by trenches and concealed lanes of approach. Means of telephone communications among them were also lacking, with only 32 percent of land lines completed and 12 percent of buried telephone cable in place. A majority of bunkers in these strong points, if armed at all, were equipped with machine guns, leaving them at only 25 percent of the required norm for antitank defenses.[2]

In accordance with the Soviet defensive plans, upon declaration of mobilization, the first echelons of Soviet field armies were to move directly to the border and take up defensive positions in the field between the strong points of the fortified regions, augmenting their garrisons and linking together the whole system. The second echelons of these armies were to concentrate roughly twenty miles east of the border in order to contain enemy breakthroughs and eliminate enemy forces that did penetrate Soviet territory. Behind the screen of these covering armies, the reserve armies of the South-Western Front were to organize and deliver follow-through strikes into enemy territory.

On paper, reserves of the South-Western Front, backing up the four covering armies, were formidable. They were five separate rifle corps (XXXI, XXXVI, XXXVII, XLIX, and LV), one airborne corps, and two field armies (Sixteenth and Nineteenth). These last two armies began arriving in Ukraine in mid-June from military districts deeper within the Soviet Union, and parts of them were still in transit when the war started. Had the Red Army been given time to sufficiently equip, organize, and man these formations, the outcome of German invasion in northwestern Ukraine would have unfolded drastically differently.

> CHAPTER 4

Organization and Strength of Kiev Special Military District

As mentioned previously, the Kiev Special Military District was the strongest of other similar groups of forces. Its major combat components numbered sixty-one ground divisions: sixteen tank, thirty-three rifle, eight motorized rifle, two mountain rifle, two cavalry, plus eight air force divisions. Additionally, there were five antitank brigades and six artillery regiments belonging to the Reserves of Supreme Command. These formations, formidable on paper, in reality were a mixed bag of bad and mediocre combat units, sparsely sprinkled with some good ones.

The mechanized corps of Kiev Special Military district were a representative sample of the Red Army's armored forces as a whole. In this work I will concentrate only on five mechanized corps which directly participated in the border armored battle: the VIII, IX, XV, XIX, and XXII Mechanized Corps.

In his summary report on July 17, 1941, Maj. Gen. Rodion N. Morgunov, chief of the armored forces of the South-Western front, described condition of the front's mechanized formations on the eve of the war:

> Mechanized corps were not yet cohesive formations and were not fully provided with equipment. The strongest mechanized corps were the IV, VIII, and XV corps, but even in these corps the tank regiments of their mechanized rifle divisions had only the armored vehicles designated as training park. There were no vehicles designated for combat in the

motorized divisions.

The rest of mechanized corps appeared in the following manner as far as combat capability was concerned:

- XVI Mechanized Corps: the only combat-capable division was the 15th Tank Division, but it was equipped with older tank models; the other two divisions had limited numbers of armored vehicles designated for training.
- XIX Mechanized Corps: only the 43rd Tank Division was combat-capable, but even it had old equipment.
- XXII Mechanized Corps: only the 41st Tank division was combat-capable, which was equipped with T-26 tanks and thirty-one KV tanks; the other divisions had "training park."
- XXIV Mechanized Corps: all divisions had only the "training park."
- IX Mechanized Corps: only the 35th Tank Division was combat-capable, mainly equipped with T-26s, some of them two-turreted machine-gun versions; the rest had "training park."
- The armored train detachment had two light armored trains and one heavy.

By the start of combat operation the South-Western Front had 4,536 tanks and 1,014 armored cars distributed in the following manner:

KV x265	T-34 x496	BT x1,486	T-26 x1,962
T-35 x44	T-28 x195	T-40 x88	BA-10 x 749
BA-20 x 365			

Such equipping of the mechanized corps led to such events that on the first day of war the tank regiments of IX, XVI, XIX, XXII, and XXIV Mechanized Corps, not having specific armaments, were equipped with 45mm and 76mm cannons and were, in effect, antitank regiments.[1]

XXII MECHANIZED CORPS

As mentioned in the previous chapter, the XXII Mechanized Corps was the closest unit to the border in the Fifth Army's area of operations. A new formation, numbering 712 tanks and 82 armored cars and formed in March 1941, the XXII Mechanized Corps was commanded by Maj. Gen. Semyon M. Kondrusev. Major combat units of the XXII Mechanized Corps were the 19th and 41st Tank and 215th Motorized Rifle divisions.

Corps headquarters, along with 19th Tank and 215th Motorized Rifle

Divisions and corps support units, were located in Rovno, over sixty miles from the border. The 41st Tank Division was situated in Vladimir-Volynskiy, with its motorized rifle regiment in direct vicinity of the border at Lyuboml.

In the previously mentioned report, Major General Morgunov described the XXII Mechanized Corps at the start of war: "Only the 41st Tank division was combat capable, equipped with T-26 tanks and thirty-one KV-2 tanks; the other divisions had 'training park.' " Taking a closer look at the 41st Tank Division would demonstrate the bleak shape the other two divisions were in, if the 41st Tank was the best one.

Even though KV-2s were not exactly new tanks, they were new to the 41st Tank Division. Various sources place them between eighteen to thirty-one machines. These vehicles were received by the 41st Tank Division in the evening of June 17. Needless to say, by the time the war started six days later, not a single crew was trained to effectively operate these new tanks. Division's Chief of Staff Colonel Konstantin A. Malygin remembered:

> In the evening of June 17th, a train with KV-2 tanks for the heavy tank battalion arrived at the Vladimir-Volynskiy railroad station. There were eighteen machines, five each per company and three for the command platoon. These tanks were classified [secret]; we were permitted to unload them and move them to [our] division only at night, covered by tarps. . . . With the exceptions of drivers who were sent to the factory to receive and escort the KV-2s, no one in the division has seen them yet.
>
> In the morning of June 20th, division's commanding officer [Colonel Petr P. Pavlov] delegated his deputy for technical affairs, Lt. Col. D. A. Vasilyev, to conduct a briefing for command personnel about these new machines. Reading from the manual, Vasilyev pointed out that due to the extreme weight of these tanks, close to fifty tons, they could be towed only by a specially made heavy "Voroshilovets" tractor, of which the division had none. If one of the new KV-2s would become immobilized, it could only be moved by one or two other KV-2s.
>
> It soon became clear that KV-2, even though being a mighty combat vehicle, had major shortcomings: heavy, with poor maneuverability, could not fight against tanks because its 152mm cannon had a steep . . . trajectory. . . . Examining the tank, everybody voiced their opinions, but common opinion was sketchy: the tank, of course, is powerful, but . . . we

counted many of these "buts."[2]

In his summary report of July 25, 1941, Col. Petr P. Pavlov described condition of his division on the eve of the war:

> The artillery regiment, equipped with sixteen 122mm and 152mm howitzers, did not have a single tractor. Thirty-one KV tanks with naval turrets [KV-2], armed with 152mm cannons, did not have a single round of ammunition. The air defense battalion had four cannons and no ammunition either. Shortage of wheeled vehicles was seven hundred trucks, which were not received from the civilian sector. Drivers of KV tanks were not trained, since these tanks were received seven to eight days before the war. 15 KV tanks, arriving before the start of the war, turned out to have major defects. . . . At the start of combat operations, the following tanks were made ready for action, albeit without spare parts: 312 T-26s and 31 KV-2s.[3]

Colonel Malygin seconded his commanding officer:

> While the tank regiments were formed on basis of two good existing tank brigades, the 41st Motorized Rifle Regiment was formed from scratch. Personnel, armaments, and equipment for it began arriving at the beginning of May. Overwhelming majority of soldiers were brand new recruits, never having held a rifle in their hands. The 41st Howitzer Regiment by that time received men and cannon, but did not have a single tractor. The 41st Air Defense Battalion had three batteries–worth of personnel, but only one of [the batteries] had four 37mm air defense cannons.[4]

Table 2.

Tanks, XXII Mechanized Corps, June 22, 1941

	Totals	KV-2	BTs	T-26	OT-26	T-37
XXII MC	707					
19th TD	163		34	142	7	
41st TD	415	31		342	41	1
215th MRD	129		?	?		

Table 3.

Artillery, XXII Mechanized Corps, June 22, 1941

	Totals	37mm	76mm	122mm	152mm
XXII MC	102	12	16	48	26
19th TD	32	4	4	12	12
41st TD	24	4	4	12	4
215th MRD	36	4	8	24	-

Table 4.

Transport, XXII Mechanized Corps, 1941[5]

	Trucks	Tractors	Motorcycles
19th TD	295	52	10
41st TD	682	15	-
215th MRD	405	62	-

The 19th Tank Division was not a combat-ready unit. Formed from scratch, by the start of the war the division had 163 tanks, all of them light BT and T-26 models, many of which were nonoperational, plus 58 armored cars. Lower ranks of the 19th Tank Division, being mainly recent draftees, were not fully trained. In addition, almost 60 percent of lower enlisted personnel came from various non-Slavic ethnic groups. Of this number, approximately 30 percent, or almost two thousand men, did not speak Russian language.[6]

The 215th Motorized Rifle Division was formed around a previously existing rifle brigade and had a relatively well-trained core of enlisted personnel, supplemented by a large number of recent draftees. Like many other motorized rifle divisions, the 215th suffered from dearth of wheeled transport and, in effect, was a regular foot-slogging formation. The tank regiment of this motorized division, however, had almost as many tanks as the whole of the 19th Tank Division, albeit most of them being old and in poor condition.

XV MECHANIZED CORPS

XV Mechanized Corps, commanded by Maj. Gen. Ignatiy I. Karpezo, was another corps located close to the border. Its major components were 10th and 37th Tank and 212th Motorized Rifle divisions. Even though the 15th Mechanized was formed in the second wave, in March 1941, it was a relatively strong formation, numbering sixty-four KV-1s and seventy-two T-34s among its 740 tanks, plus 160 armored cars.

The new T-34 tanks were split roughly equally between the two tank divisions of the XV Mechanized Corps. All but one KV-1 were concentrated in the one battalion of 10th Tank Division. This division was transferred from the IV Mechanized Corps in the summer of 1940 and was a veteran formation with well-trained personnel. They were augmented by an influx of new recruits, called-up reservists, and transferred personnel. The 37th Tank Division was created in the spring of 1941 around the 18th Light Tank Brigade relocated from the Baltic region.[7] Like its brethren corps, the XV was almost fully staffed with lower enlisted personnel, but suffering from shortage of commissioned and noncommissioned officers.

Colonel Yermolayev, who in late June replaced wounded Major General Karpezo, shed light on the condition of the XV Mechanized Corps immediately before the war. The following two charts were made from his report.[8]

Table 5.

**Strength of XV Mechanized Corps,
Expressed in Percentage of Assigned Personnel**

	Corps HQ	Motorcycle Regiment	10th TD	37th TD	212th MRD
Officers	50%	30%	87%	50%	56%
NCOs	44.5%	53%	75%	45%	60%
Privates	78%	105%	91%	101.5%	94%

Table 6.

Armored Fighting Vehicles

	KV-1	T-34	T-28	BT-7	T-26	OT-269
10th TD	63	38	51	181	22	8
37th TD	1	34		258	22	1
212th MRD				32	5	
Totals	64	72	51	471	49	9

An additional seventeen T-40s were in the 131st Tank Regiment of the 212th Motorized Rifle Division. Also, there were additional tanks assigned to command elements of the divisions that were not reflected among the above totals. Five more armored cars were in the motorcycle regiment.

According to Yermolayev:

> The 212th Motorized Rifle Division was not fully organized, staffed, or trained . . . and did not have transportation means. This division, while being almost fully manned by lower enlisted personnel, did not have any vehicles to transport them and could not even provide itself with enough trucks to deliver ammunition, food, and POL (petroleum-oil-lubricants). . . . The artillery regiment had eight 76mm cannon, 16 122mm howitzers (12 of them without sights) and four 152mm [cannon], but only five tractors. The lower enlisted personnel of the motorcycle regiment, while at full strength, were not trained and have not conducted even one rifle practice. . . . Communications and combat engineer battalions were staffed by brand new recruits, still conducting Phase I of their basic training, and were experiencing severe shortage of command personnel, with companies being commanded by junior officers. [Both battalions] just started receiving equipment, were not fully organized, and could not carry out combat missions.[10]

Yermolayev is seconded by Lieutenant Colonel Sukhoruchkin, who in similar manner to Yermolayev ascended to command the 10th Tank Division: "At the start of the war, division was short 583 junior leaders, 37 medical personnel, 813 privates, and 25 technical personnel. Out of 1,092 men which division was supposed to receive at mobilization, only 333 privates arrived."[11]

Sukhoruchkin, however, was more optimistic about the overall condition of his division's materiel, reporting that out of assigned fighting vehicles the following numbers actually left the garrisons and deployed forward: sixty-three KV-1s, forty-four T-28s, 147 BT-7s, eight OT-26s, nineteen T-26, fifty-three BA-10, nineteen BA-20, and eight hundred wheeled vehicles. He summarized their overall status:

> BT-7 tanks were a mixture of machines with various engine usages of 40 to 100 hours, and only 30 of them had brand new engines. However, there were practically no spare parts. T-26s were in overall good shape, averaging 75 hours of usage. Armored cars were in good shape overall, with ten BA-20s being brand new machines. Therefore, KV, T-34, and

T-26 were in good overall shape and were mission-capable. T-28s and BT-7s needed engine replacements and could not be used in prolonged operations.[12]

The following table illustrates the actual numbers of armored combat vehicles of the XV Mechanized Corps that were able to leave their garrisons and lumber towards the border:

Table 7.

Combat-Capable Vehicles, XV Mechanized Corps

	KV-1	T-34	T-28	BT-7	T-26	OT-26
10th TD	63	37	44	147	27	8
37th TD	1	32		239	13	1
212th MRD				32	5	
Totals	64	69	44	418	45	9

Additionally, 152 out of 160 armored cars were combat capable.

The 37th Tank Division under Colonel Anikushkin wasn't in as good shape as the 10th:

> In accordance with [Timoshenko's] directive #ORG/1/521114, the 37th Tank Division of the 15th Mechanized Corps was supposed to be completely formed by July 1st, 1941. As of June 22nd, 1941, division had 41.2 percent of senior command personnel, 48.3 percent of junior command personnel, and 111 percent of lower enlisted.
>
> As far as tanks were concerned, there was 1 KV-1 (1.6 percent of TO&E [table of organization and equipment]), 34 T-34 (11.4 percent), 258 BT-7s (on hand, but not on TO&E), 22 T-26 and one flame-throwing OT-26. Artillery: 37mm air-defense artillery guns 33 percent, 122mm howitzers—56 percent, 152mm howitzers—33.3 percent. While, counting extra-allotted 258 BT-7, the division was at almost 90 percent strength, having 315 tanks, it was lacking in sticking power. . . . Sixty percent of privates were recruits called up in May 1941, who have not yet completed their basic training. Six hundred of them in the motorcycle regiment did not even have personal weapons issued to them.[13]

He continued:

The motorized rifle regiment, far from being completely equipped with wheeled vehicles, and initially located ninety-five miles away from the [rest of] division, at first could not operate in concert with the division.

The artillery regiment was also not completely equipped with materiel and left its deployment area (Kremenets) having only one 122mm and one 152mm howitzer [battery]. Separate air defense battalion out of [allocated] twelve guns (three batteries) only numbered four guns (one battery).[14]

As part of the conclusion section of his report, Anikushkin wrote:

1. Division left its [peacetime] deployment area of Kremenets with approximately 70 percent of its assigned personnel. The rest [of personnel] were left in Kremenets, where it later conducted, along with units of 14th Cavalry Division, defensive battles in Kremenets vicinity.
2. There were 315 tanks (approximately 90 percent of assigned numbers), and out of them, 258 BT-7 tanks were not part of TO&E, which negatively reflected on division's striking power and firepower.
3. The maneuverability of the motorized rifle regiment, which set off on foot due to lack of wheeled vehicles, was extremely low, which did not allow [this] motorized rifle regiment to operate as part of the division until June 25th, 1941. This situation forced the tank regiments to allocate large number of tanks for support missions instead of utilizing them as striking power.
4. Lack of fully equipped artillery regiment . . . negatively reflected on division's combat operations.

Ironically, contradicting himself and obviously putting on a brave face to present it to higher echelon commanders, Anikushkin stated: "Despite everything mentioned above, the 37th Tank Division represented a solid combat formation and . . . successfully carried out all assigned missions."[15]

VIII MECHANIZED CORPS

The VIII Mechanized Corps, belonging to the Twenty-Sixth Army and headed by Lt. Gen. Dmitriy I. Ryabyshev, was one of the strongest Soviet mechanized formations. Various sources place the number of tanks in this corps between 850 and 932 machines of at least six different models, plus 172 armored cars. The main punch was provided by one hundred T-34 tanks and approximately eighty KV-1 heavies. However, this corps included a staggering variety of older models as well, including obsolete BT-2 tanks. Corps' 34th Tank Division also included a battalion of flame-thrower OT-26 tanks and forty-eight giant T-35 tanks.

The VIII Mechanized Corps began its conversion in July of 1940 from the IV Cavalry Corps. Its 12th and 34th Tank Divisions were formed around cores of two light tank brigades, plus smaller tank units withdrawn from other formations.

The 7th Motorized Rifle Division was a distinguished unit, tracing its history from the Russian Civil War. This well-trained unit with high esprit de corps was handicapped by a lack of wheeled transport.

Sources on the breakdown of armored vehicles in this corps are too varied to present a cohesive table. However, the majority of new T-34s and KV-1s were concentrated in the 12th Tank Division, while the 34th Tank had all forty-eight of slow T-35s.

The chart below illustrates the difference between the number of tanks on rosters of VIII Mechanized Corps and the number of tanks that were actually able to leave their garrisons and move towards the border.[16]

Table 8.
Tanks Available, VIII Mechanized Corps

	KV-1	T-34	T-35	T-26	BT	T-37/40	Total
On Hand	71	100	49	344	277	17	858
Inoperable	11	5	11	33	92	0	152
Deployed, June 22	60	95	38	311	185	17	706

There was an additional small number of tanks that was not reflected in the above totals that were assigned to command elements of the VIII Mechanized Corps.

IX MECHANIZED CORPS

Even though the IX Mechanized Corps was formed in the first wave in November 1940, at the start of German invasion it was one of the weakest mechanized corps in the Red Army. Its commander was pugnacious Maj. Gen. Konstantin K. Rokossovskiy, recently released from NKVD jail. Major combat formations of IX Mechanized Corps were the 20th Tank, 35th Tank, and 131st Motorized Rifle divisions. Part of the reserves of the South-Western Front, this corps was located ninety miles from the border, having its regular garrisons in and around Novograd-Volynskiy and Shepetovka, along the pre-1939 border.

At the start of war, the corps had 298 tanks, all of them light and older models, most of which were gathered from training facilities, consisting of 269 BT and T-26 tanks and 29 very light reconnaissance T-37, T-38, and T-40 tanks. There were 11 light and 62 medium armored cars, 1,069 wheeled vehicles of all types, 133 tractors, and 181 motorcycles. The dearth of armored combat vehicles caused Rokossovskiy to bitterly call his tank divisions the "so-called tank divisions" in his memoirs.

Rokossovskiy was bitter for good reason. Among the tanks in his corps, there was not a single modern one. His 20th Tank Division numbered only 36 light tanks. The 35th Tank Division numbered 142 light tanks, 40 of which were armed only with a machine gun. Ironically, the 131st Motorized Rifle Division was stronger in tanks than the 20th Tank Division, having 122 tanks, including 18 T-37 swimming reconnaissance tanks and 21 outdated BT-2s.

Table 9.
Tank Distribution, IX Mechanized Corps [17]

	Total	T-37	T-26	OT-26	BT
IX MC	296				
20th TD	36		3	3	30 (BT-5)
35th TD	142		141	1	
131st MRD	122	18			104*

*including 21 BT-2s; the remainder were BT-5s and BT-7s

In the 35th Tank Division, seventy-nine T-26s were armed with 45mm cannons, and an additional forty mounted only machine guns. Four T-26s had 37mm cannon, and ten T-26s did not have any armament at all, being used only for towing.

Table 10.

Status of Artillery on June 22, 1941

	76mm cannon	37mm ADA	152mm howitzer	122mm howitzer	82mm mortar	50mm mortar
20th TD	4	4	12	12	18	28
35th TD	-	4	4	6	18	27
131st MRD	16	4	8	16	12	59

Table 11.

Status of Transportation

	Wheeled Vehicles	Tractors	Motorcycles
20th TD	244	38	10
35th TD	188	7	-
131st MRD	595	69	17

In his memoirs, Marshal Rokossovskiy wrote:

By the beginning of war our corps had an almost complete complement of personnel, but was not fully equipped by primary materiel: tanks and wheeled transportation. We had no more than 30 percent of quantities allocated under the TO&E. Combat vehicles were worn out and not ready for prolonged operations. Basically, the [9th Mechanized] Corps was not combat ready under these circumstances. Neither the headquarters of Kiev Special Military District nor General Staff could have been ignorant of this situation.

XIX MECHANIZED CORPS

The XIX Mechanized Corps under Maj. Gen. Nikolay V. Feklenko was a virtual twin to Rokossovskiy's IX Mechanized. Feklenko's corps was also part of reserves of South-Western Front and was also located along the old border, centered on towns of Zhitomir and Berdichev. Major combat units of this corps were the 40th Tank, 43rd Tank, and 213th Motorized Rifle divisions. The chart on the next page illustrates the approximate strength of XIX Mechanized Corps at the start of the war.

Table 12.

Tank Strength, XIX Mechanized Corps[18]

	Total	T-37	T-26	T-34	KV-1
XIX MC	450				
40th TD	158	139	19		
43rd TD	237		230	2	5
213th MRD	55	13	42		

Colonel Tsibin, commander of 43rd Tank Division, described the condition of his unit on the eve of war in the following manner:

> Division had 711 out of 1,253 senior commanders; 1,054 out of 2,172 junior commanders; 6,669 out of 6,451 lower enlisted; for a total of 8,434 out of 9,876 allotted, i.e. 50–60% of commanders, over 100% in privates. Core of division was formed from the veteran 35th Tank Brigade and was well trained. Command personnel were also well trained, many being veterans of the Finnish War. Motorized rifle regiment was approximately 70% short of command personnel. Lower enlisted personnel of 1st battalions of both tank regiments were mainly new inductees who just finished their basic training.
>
> Combat vehicles were fully ready for combat operations, with complete crews, but were technically seriously worn. Out of wheeled vehicles on hand, almost 150 were in Berdichev, inoperable; partially under repair at the depots and partially without drivers. . . . There were approximately 40%–50% of required spare parts at division's supply depot.[19]

Tsibin describes the vehicles available to 43rd Tank Division (see Table 13).

Table 13.

Vehicles, 43rd Tank Division

	TO&E	On hand	On hand %		TO&E	On hand	On hand %
KV	63	5	7.94%	Wheeled	1,500	571	38.07%
T-34	210	2	0.95%	vehicles			
T-26 and	74	230	310.81%	Fuel tankers	137	69	50.36%
XT-26				Tractors	83	15	18.07%
BT	26	0	0.00%				

Table 14.

Situation of 43rd Tank Division's Artillery

	TO&E	On hand	On hand %
152mm howitzers	12	4	33.33%
122mm howitzers	12	12	100.00%
76mm cannon	4	4	100.00%
37mm ADA cannon	12	2	16.67%

The 37mm ADA cannon did not have any ammunition.

Table 15.

Status of Artillery in the XIX Mechanized Corps

	76mm cannon	37mm ADA	152mm howitzers	122mm howitzers	82mm mortars	50mm mortars
40th TD	-	4	4	8	12	27
43rd TD	4	4	12	12	12	22
213th MRD	8	4	-	4	8	60

Table 16.

Status of Mechanized Transport, XIX Mechanized Corps

	Wheeled vehicles	Tractors	Motorcycles
40th TD	157	5	-
43rd TD	630	15	18
213th MRD	140	47	-

The overall condition of the XIX Mechanized Corps resembled that of the IX. The motorized rifle divisions of both corps were similarly short of wheeled transport and prime movers for artillery:

> [W]heeled vehicles on hand did not by any means provide division with means to begin campaign and upload all the supplies. Because of this, majority of personnel from the motorized rifle regiment . . . did not have transportation. In the similar manner, the soldiers of first battalions of tank regiments could not depart, not having equipment.[20]

Diluting the offensive power of the XIX Mechanized Corps were the numerous very light T-37 amphibious reconnaissance tanks, comprising roughly 60 percent of corps' total tank strength. These tanks, being hardly more than tankettes, were armed with machine guns only and had very light armor.

1ST ANTITANK ARTILLERY BRIGADE

The 1st Antitank Artillery Brigade under Maj. Gen. K. S. Moskalenko was a brand new unit. After evaluating successes of German panzer formations in Poland and France, leadership of the Red Army created a number of antitank artillery brigades, designed to counteract German panzer threat. Moskalenko's brigade, bearing numeral one, was also the most combat-capable of the five such brigades of the South-Western Front.

In his memoirs, Moskalenko described his unit:

> The 1st Antitank Artillery brigade was comprised of two artillery regiments, combat engineer battalion, transportation battalion, and smaller service support units. Each regiment had two battalions of 76mm cannons (24 pieces), three battalions of 85mm cannons (36 pieces) and one air defense artillery battalion (eight 37mm cannon and 36 DShK machine-guns). Therefore, brigade possessed 48 76mm cannons, 72 85mm ones, 16 37mm cannon and 72 DShK machine-guns. We were completely equipped with ammunition, including armor-piercing.[21]

Likewise, Moskalenko's brigade was fully equipped with wheeled and tracked vehicles.

Similar to other military districts, the majority of units under Kirponos' command experienced manpower shortages. Colonel Alexei V. Vladimir-skiy, chief of Operations Section of Fifth Army's headquarters, described the manpower situation in his army on the eve of war:

> Rifle divisions . . . had on the average 10,000 men, or 70%, of assigned personnel. These divisions were staffed at 68–70% with officers, 70–72% with noncommissioned officers, and 66% of lower enlisted. . . . Shortages of officers were planned to be remedied by calling up reserve officers from the eastern regions of Ukraine; shortage of noncommissioned officers— by promoting privates and, in part, by [calling up] noncommissioned officers of former Polish army born in the western regions of Ukraine,

after re-training them at division-level training course; shortages of lower enlisted personnel was to be fully covered by residents of western Ukraine, with the exception of truck and tractor drivers, who were to be assigned from eastern Ukrainian regions.

Significant portion of senior commanders of the [Fifth] Army, as well as commanders of larger units who survived Stalin's purges, participated in World War I and Civil War, and some of them—in fighting with Japanese aggressors or with Finns in 1939–1940—had combat experience, but those who were elevated to their command positions relatively recently did not yet fully know their missions in accordance with the operational plan. Headquarters of armies and rifle [corps] were headed by experienced commanders and were cohesive; however, headquarters of [lower-echelon] units were composed of officers with little experience, needing additional training. Readiness of cadre noncommissioned officer and lower enlisted personnel could be acknowledged as quite satisfactory, but the lower enlisted men called up in the fall of 1940 only finished their training on squad level.[22]

Shortfall in personnel in the Kiev Special Military District was mirrored by chronic and systemic shortages of equipment, vehicles, and armaments. Lieutenant General Mikhail A. Parsegov, chief of artillery of the South-Western Front/Kiev Special Military District, on July 14, 1941, presented an extensive report to the chief of artillery of the Red Army. The tables below were created from his report.[23]

Table 17.

Infantry Weapons

Weapon	Assigned	On hand, June 22	% Shortage
7.62mm carbines	110,434	66,228	40%
7.62mm machine pistols	61,207	15,780	74%
7.62mm revolvers/pistols	245,931	165,206	33%
7.62mm light machine guns	28,336	21,336	25%
7.62mm complex machine guns	2,330	955	59%
12.7mm machine guns	1,087	186	83%
82mm mortars	2,283	1,829	20%
120mm mortars	432	264	39%

In addition, Separate Railroad Corps (arriving from another district in May–June of 1941) was short fifteen thousand rifles and other infantry weapons; at least fifteen construction battalions (formed locally and arriving from different districts) each needed one thousand rifles.

Table 18.

Field Artillery

Weapon System	TO&E	On Hand	Shortage	% of Total
45mm cannon	2,134	1,912	222	89.60%
76mm cannon	1,943	1,722	221	88.63%
122mm howitzer	1,752	1,464	288	83.56%
152mm howitzer	1,483	1,140	343	76.87%
203mm howitzer	193	193	0	100.00%
280mm howitzer	24	24	0	100.00%
Totals	7,529	6,455		85.74%

Note: The Kiev Special Military District also had 213 old 107mm cannons that were not on any table of organization. Including these field pieces, Kiev Special Military District was 88.56 percent equipped with artillery. According to the same report, 487 artillery pieces, or almost 14 percent of on-hand totals, were in need of depot-level overhaul.

Table 19.

Air Defense Artillery

Weapon System	TO&E	On Hand	Shortage	% of Total
37mm air defense cannon	984	210	774	21.34%
76mm air defense cannon	796	599	197	75.25%
85mm air defense cannon	600	542	58	90.33%
Totals	2,380	1,351	1,029	62.31%

A problem plaguing air defense artillery in particular was a shortage of ammunition, especially the armor-piercing type.

The above-mentioned report noted that quantity and quality of equipment varied based on when the unit was created:

Older units . . . were well-provided with all weapon systems, with the exception of 37mm air defense cannons. . . . The corps-level artillery regiments and those belonging to first tier of Reserve of High Command were fully equipped, the shortages in the [Kiev] District were experienced by units formed in the second wave. The new formations, created during April–May, had the following shortages:

- Rifle divisions had their 76mm cannons of model year 1927 replaced up to 80 percent by cannons of 1902/30 year-model.
- Seven rifle divisions were short of 122mm howitzers of 1910/30 year-model.
- Six new divisions were short of 152mm howitzers of 1909/30 year-model.[24]

Parsegov also presented examples of shortages of specialist equipment.

- Binoculars: Old rifle divisions had 65% of allotted amounts; new rifle, tank and motorized rifle divisions and artillery brigades—between 45–50%; corps artillery regiments—100%; Reserve of High Command artillery regiments—75%; all other units—20–40%
- Theodolites: All old artillery regiments—100%; new regiments (formed in 1941)—50–75%; artillery brigades—30–35%.
- Periscopes: Old artillery regiments, corps artillery regiments, and artillery regiments of Reserve of High Command—85–100%; units formed in 1941—40–45%; [antitank] artillery brigades—up to 35%.
- Topographical surveying equipment—15–50%.
- Search Lights—20–50%.[25]

Specialist units like reconnaissance, combat engineers, and signal units were short of equipment necessary for accomplishing their specific tasks. In particular, the reconnaissance units of the Fifth Army had only 25 percent of allocated motorcycles, 48 percent of armored cars, and 54 percent of T-37 and T-40 tanks.[26] Likewise, a majority of units of the Kiev Special Military District, corps and below, had 50–60 percent of radio equipment and 60–70 percent of telephone equipment. The situation was slightly better in army- and front-level formations—roughly 75–80 percent of assigned norm.[27]

CHAPTER 5

Creeping up to War

How was it that the Soviet Union, a country with an acknowledged most-extensive intelligence network, was caught unaware of the impeding danger that came close to bringing the communist state to its knees within the first six months of war?

Winston Churchill's critique was harsh:

> War is mainly a catalogue of blunders, but it may be doubted whether any mistake in history has equaled that of which Stalin and the Communist chiefs were guilty when they . . . supinely awaited, or were incapable of realizing, the fearful onslaught which impended upon Russia. . . . As far as strategy, policy, foresight, competence are arbiters, Stalin and his commissars showed themselves at this moment the most completely outwitted bunglers of the Second World War.[1]

For decades after the war, the government of the Soviet Union steadfastly maintained its position that Germany's attack came as a complete and total surprise. Generations of Soviet children born after the war grew up to believe that myth. The Western governments, knowing the truth, politely kept the silence. After all, the Cold War enemy was yesterday's ally in the fight against Hitler.

These claims of ignorance do not hold up under even the most perfunctory scrutiny. Even without having a widespread and well-placed spy network, how could a country miss over three million potentially hostile soldiers along its borders or completely misinterpret intentions of their leadership?

When Adolf Hitler signed into being Directive No. 21, the "Case Barbarossa," these plans for attack against the Soviet Union contained a caveat:

> In certain circumstances I shall issue orders for the deployment against the Soviet Russia eight weeks before the operation is timed to begin. Preparations . . . will be concluded by 15th May, 1941. It is of decisive importance that our intention to attack should not be known.[2]

German leadership understood very well that massing a large army on the enemy's doorstep would not go unnoticed for very long. Presence of widespread troop concentrations and railroad movements bringing them forward would be impossible to conceal. Therefore, what needed to be concealed was not the troops' presence, but their purpose.

The official explanation for having large-scale German troop concentration in Eastern Poland was given as rest and recreation and training for continuing operations against England, out of reach of the Royal Air Force. As Anthony Reed described it: "Every possible means was used to create a huge double-bluff, by presenting Barbarossa itself as 'the greatest deception operation in military history,' aimed not at the Soviet Union but at Britain, and this remained the principal cover story right up to the end."[3]

Training for Operation Sealion (*Unternehmen Seeloewe* in German), a proposed invasion of the British Isles which was cancelled on October 12, 1940, began again in the spring of 1941. Along with highly visible land forces training, the German Air Force made numerous reconnaissance flights over England, with the sole intent of being noticed.

However, a serious monkey wrench was thrown into Hitler's plans by none other than one of his closest companions, Rudolph Hess. Neanderthalish Hess, Hitler's political deputy and Nazi "old fighter," held a privileged, albeit diminishing, position at Hitler's side. On May 13, Hess flew a Messerschmitt Bf 110 plane to England and parachuted out of it over Scotland on an ill-conceived solo peace mission. Hess' intentions were to bring England and Germany to the peace table; but, realizing that Hess was not completely mentally stable and acting without authorization from Hitler, British authorities disregarded his overtures.

While creating few minor and temporary ripples in the two affected countries, Hess' escapade had a significant effect on Josef Stalin. The Soviet dictator never believed that Hess' mission was not authorized and maintained an opinion that Germany and England were conspiring behind his back.

As Adolph Hitler raged over his old comrade's indiscretion, Dr. Paul Joseph Goebbels, the evil genius behind Hitler's Propaganda Ministry, threw all of his considerable energy in the deception efforts. Anthony Reed quotes from Goebbels' diary: "I am having an invasion of England theme written, new fanfare composed, English speakers brought in, setting up propaganda companies for England, etc."[4] German invasion of the small Greek island of Crete in the morning of May 20, 1941, served as an example of German continued war against England and provided Goebbels with ample fuel to pull off a deception effort worthy of his talents.

With Hitler's full knowledge and approval, on June 13, 1941, Goebbels published an article in *Voelkischer Beobachter*, the official newspaper of the Nazi party, full of bombastic threats against England. In mid-afternoon on the same day, a great stage-managed show of seizing and withdrawing this edition of the newspaper was conducted across Berlin. According to Reed, "Goebbels then placed himself in public 'disgrace', to complete the illusion that he had committed a grave indiscretion." It was quite obvious that he was quite satisfied with his efforts:

> Everything goes without a hitch. I am very happy about it. The big sensation is under way. English broadcasts are already claiming that our troop movements against Russia are sheer bluff, to conceal our plans for an invasion of England. . . . At home, people regret my apparent faux pas, pity me, or try to show their friendship despite everything, while abroad there is feverish conjecture. We stage-managed it perfectly. Only one cable got through to the USA, but that is enough to bring the affair to the attention of the whole world. We know from tapped telephone conversations between foreign journalists working in Berlin that all of them fell for the decoy.[5]

Another aspect of the German misdirection campaign was Hitler's apparent concern about the Soviet Union building a line of strong fortifications along the border and the rumor that Hitler was about to make a list of demands and concessions from the Soviet Union. This last factor confirmed in Stalin's mind the pattern of Hitler's modus operandi: ask first, then demand, and then, if needed, attack. This pattern was present in Hitler's previous adventures with Austria, Czechoslovakia, and Poland.

Although Hitler cautioned for the utmost secrecy, Operation Barbarossa did not stay hidden for long. Within one month, indications of still-distant, but growing, threat, came trickling into the Soviet state. Despite the post-war Soviet claims, there were plenty of warnings, coming from diverse and independent sources. One of the early bell-ringers was Richard Sorge, Soviet deep-cover agent stationed in Tokyo, Japan. Sorge was born in the old Tsarist Empire, son of a Russian mother and a German engineer father working in Russia. In 1898, shortly after Sorge's second birthday, his family moved to Germany. When World War I broke out, young Sorge fought in the German army, receiving an Iron Cross for his bravery. Like many young men of his generation, cast adrift in the aftermath of the world war, Sorge became disillusioned with the present system and became a willing convert to socialism. While living in Russia and idealistically working for Comintern (Communist International), he was recruited into Soviet military intelligence in 1929 by the chief of Fourth (Intelligence) Directorate of NKVD, General Jan Berzin (real name Peteris Kyuzis, a Latvian). His background as a decorated war veteran won Sorge wide admittance into German military circles. The ticket in was Sorge's left leg, almost one inch shorter as the result of a WWI wound, combined with his outward outspoken Nazi views. In his solid cover as a freelance reporter for several German newspapers, most notably the respected *Frankfurter Zeitung*, Sorge was posted to Japan, where he penetrated the highest level of German diplomatic community and established reliable information sources in Japanese government.

Within two weeks of Case Barbarossa being approved, Richard Sorge got wind of this dangerous development and began a stream of warnings to Moscow. Despite his best efforts, Sorge's warnings were ignored, and the tone of his communiqués became frustrated and desperate. Why were Sorge's reports unheeded?

Richard Sorge's former direct superior, chief of Fourth Directorate Jan Berzin, was caught up in the wave of purges. Implicated as Trotskyite, he was imprisoned in 1935 and executed in 1939. Close personal and professional associates of General Berzin shared his fate. Berzin's former deputy and replacement, Semyon P. Uritskiy, also perished in NKVD basements and, in turn, Uritskiy's replacement, Semyon G. Gendin. In 1937, many Soviet intelligence agents operating abroad were recalled to Moscow where they were arrested and executed. These men who had done so much for their country were not trusted by the country's leadership on the grounds that they were likely to have been suborned while living in capitalist countries and turned into double agents.

Besides the loss of experienced intelligence officers, their carefully nurtured networks were destroyed along with them. This decimation of intelligence-gathering resources immediately and negatively reflected on the quality and quantity of intelligence information coming into the Soviet Union.

Sorge was one of those who received instructions to return to the Soviet Union. However, he had access to multiple western European newspapers highlighting the espionage "show trials" in the Soviet Union and naming those convicted and executed, many of whom were personally known to Sorge. An intelligent man, Sorge developed a strong suspicion that he would share their fate. A severe blow to Sorge came in 1940, when newspapers around the world publicized the death of his friend Ignac Poretsky, an NKVD defector assassinated in Switzerland in September of that year.[6]

When Sorge's recall orders came in November 1940, he demurred on the grounds that he could not leave Japan until April of next year. When further summons arrived from Moscow, Sorge always found an excuse not to obey. His refusal to follow the recall orders resulted in Moscow losing confidence in his reports. Therefore, when Sorge continued forwarding intelligence about the upcoming German invasion, his reports were treated with utmost suspicion in the Moscow center.

Still the dedicated patriot, Sorge continued to carry out his intelligence-collecting duties. On May 6 Sorge sent a report to Moscow, in part stating: "Decision on start of war against USSR will be taken by Hitler alone, either as early as May, or following the war with England."[7] Still, Sorge's superiors in Moscow customarily rejected his reports as: "Suspicious. To be listed with telegrams intended as provocations."[8] Stalin himself reportedly categorized Sorge in the following manner: "A shit that has set himself up with some small factories and brothels in Japan."[9] Thus, a priceless intelligence asset was wasted due to mistrust and suspicion, including Sorge's report in late June that the war was about to start within days.

Another of Berzin's recruits was Leopold Trepper, the head of the Soviet intelligence network in Europe, dubbed by German counterintelligence as *Die Rotte Kapelle* (the Red Orchestra). In similar fashion to Sorge, Trepper's reports about the growing threat went unheeded. Another entity loosely connected to Treppler's organization, a German Schultze-Boysen/Harnack Group, also passed on important information. However, this particular group, named after Lt. Harro Schulze-Boysen, a German Air Force intelligence officer, and Arvid Harnak, an official in the German Ministry of Economics, was anti-Nazi, rather than pro-Soviet, and was only marginally trusted by the Soviets.

Another source of impending invasion came from foreign governments hostile to Nazi Germany. British Prime Minister Winston Churchill, while being a staunch anti-Communist, was an even greater implacable foe of Hitler. He was quoted as saying: "I have only one purpose: the destruction of Hitler. . . . If Hitler invaded Hell I would make at least a favourable reference to the Devil in the House of Commons."[10] Beginning in April of 1941, Churchill passed on to Stalin indications of imminent invasion. However, Stalin believed that any information coming from western intelligence sources was an attempt to provoke a war between the Soviet Union and Germany.

A very significant factor feeding Stalin's mistrust of England and France was the fact that these two countries in the recent past were making plans to wage an armed struggle against Stalin. When on November 30, 1939, the Soviet Union attacked its small northern neighbor Finland, this unprovoked aggression created deep outrage in Western Europe. Outnumbered by more than four-to-one, the gallant Finnish army put up a tenacious resistance, thwarting Soviet plans for a quick victory. In late April to early March of 1940, England and France planned to send fifty-seven thousand ground troops into Finland to fight the Soviets. However, Norway and Sweden refused their passage on March 2. French Premier Edouard Daladier made an offer to Finnish leader Baron Carl Gustav Mannerheim to force their way through the two countries if Mannerheim phrased it as an official request. Mannerheim declined, not trusting the fighting spirit of British and French,[11] and in mid-March of 1940, Finland surrendered. This apparent readiness to commit troops, even though this help, judging from British and French meekly observing Poland's and Czechoslovakia's dismemberment, might not have been actually forthcoming, was not something Stalin would be willing to forgive or forget.

Another ill-conceived Allied plan for armed intervention against the Soviet Union was aimed at Baku oil fields. Located on the shores of Caspian Sea in the southern portion of the Soviet Union, the vast oil fields provided roughly 75 percent of country's petroleum needs. Fearing that cordial relations with the Soviet Union would present Hitler with an unlimited strategic supply of oil, French leadership was serious about launching an air attack into the southern Soviet Union via Iraq or Iran in order to destroy Baku oil fields and deny them to Germany. Charles Richardson wrote:

> On January 19, 1940, Premier Edouard Daladier of France issued an order which read in part: "General Gamelin and Admiral Darlan are to be requested to prepare a memorandum concerning eventual intervention for the destruction of the Russian oil fields."[12]

Even though senior British statesmen like Neville Chamberlain and Winston Churchill were opposed to an attack on Baku oilfield, nonetheless several French and British reconnaissance flights were conducted over the area in question in early April of 1940. These overflights were noticed by the Red Army and duly reported, feeding further fuel to Stalin's mistrust of Western democracies.

However, when Germany launched simultaneous attacks against Denmark and Norway on April 9, 1940, the Allied attention shifted to the matters closer to home than distant Baku. And when France's turn to be invaded by Germany came scarcely a month later on May 10, Stalin was undoubtedly ironically amused by France's humiliatingly rapid defeat and the British mad scrabble to avoid a bloodbath at Dunkirk.

But was Stalin really completely ignoring warnings presented by his intelligence services, or was there something else in play? Like his fellow dictator Adolf Hitler, Josef Stalin considered himself superior to his professional military advisers in all matters geopolitical. It is quite possible that while believing some of the warnings, he considered himself better qualified to make the final judgment of their immediacy. His paranoia and cruelty undoubtedly demonstrate a presence of at least a small degree of mental illness. However, despite all his faults, Josef Stalin was not a stupid man. The Soviet dictator clearly realized that his country was not quite ready for war and was stalling for time. Time, the one resource Stalin needed most desperately, was in short supply: time to continue expanding the heavy industry to meet the increased demand of the Red Army, particularly expressed in large numbers of new tanks; time to increase the output of military schools and academies to provide leadership backbone to the expanding military; time for new commanders, who replaced those eliminated during the purges, to become acquainted with their new assignments.

Zhukov agreed with this:

> Stalin was not a coward, but he clearly understood that country's leadership, led by him, was clearly late with undertaking major measures to prepare the country for a large-scale war with such strong and experienced enemy as Germany. He understood that we were late not only with rearmament of our forces with modern combat equipment and reorganization of armed forces, but also with country's defensive measures, particularly being late with creating needed state reserves and mobilization stores. J. V. Stalin clearly knew as well that after 1939, military units were lead by commanders far from being well-versed in operational-tactical and strategic science. On the eve of war, the Red Army did not retain practically any regimental or divisional commanders with academy education. Moreover, many of them did not even attend military schools, with their majority being prepared only in commanders' courses. It was also impossible to discount the moral traumas which were inflicted upon the Red Army and Navy by the massive purges.[13]

A significant factor influencing Stalin's disbelief of Germany's offensive intensions was understanding that while the Soviet military was not at its peak performance, it was numerically and qualitatively stronger than German, quantity having a quality of its own. Stalin was thinking in absolute terms, matching gun against gun, tank against tank, and battalion against battalion. He was well aware that his armored force of nearly 24,000 tanks dwarfed the German tank force of roughly 4,500. The heaviest German tank was a medium Pz IV, completely outclassed by new Soviet medium T-34 and heavy KV-1 tanks. The Soviet air force and navy similarly outnumbered their German counterparts.

Nor did Stalin believe that Hitler would be blind enough to attack the Soviet Union while still engaged against the British in the West. As demonstrated in World War I, Germany simply did not have economic resources or population to fight a war on two fronts. Another huge discrepancy in correlation of forces was the sheer size of the Soviet Union when compared to Germany. Moreover, Stalin was fully aware of what it meant to fight in the vastness of Russian time and space, while German planners were constricted by their experiences in the tight confines of central Europe.

Striving to buy time, in a move that shocked Western governments, the Soviet Union signed a ten-year nonaggression pact with Nazi Germany on August 24, 1939. "War would pass us by a little longer," Stalin stated to those of his closest circle.[14]

One of the key points of this pact was the agreement by both parties to maintain neutrality if one of the signatories became engaged in war against a third party. In a parallel agreement several days before, on August 19, both countries signed a seven-year trade agreement in which Germany paid the Soviet Union in hard currency for raw materials much needed by Germany— grain, timber, oil, and some minerals essential for war industry.

In a secret protocol of the treaty, Germany and the Soviet Union divided Eastern Europe into two spheres of influence. Consequences of this agreement continued to influence the course of European affairs well after the fall of Germany in 1945 and the breakup of the Soviet Union in 1991.

Opportunity to act upon this secret protocol promptly presented itself. On September 1, 1939, merely a week after signing the treaty, Nazi Germany unleashed World War II by invading Poland. While the main portion of the Polish army was defeated in a two-week campaign, giving rise to the term "blitz-krieg," the Polish government still nursed hopes of holding out until France and England intervened. Its hopes were crushed on September 17, when the Soviet Union crossed the Polish borders in the east, mortally stabbing Poland in the back. The fact that Poland and the Soviet Union signed their own nonaggression treaty in 1932 did not carry much weight with Stalin. Hitler would negate the German-Soviet nonaggression pact in a similar off-hand manner just two short years later. In addition to reaching an agreement with the Germans, the USSR signed a neutrality pact with Japan on April 13, somewhat securing the Siberian back door. In a special article of this pact, like the one between Russia and Germany, it was agreed upon that if a third party would attack one of the two signatories, the other one would remain neutral in the war.

As the result of its participation in the 1939 campaign, the Soviet Union acquired approximately 155,000 square miles of territory with a population of over 13 million. This was more of re-acquisition, rather than acquisition. In March 1918 the nascent Soviet state signed a humiliating Treaty of Brest-Litovsk under which it ceded large portions of now-defunct Russian Empire, namely western portions of Ukraine and Belorussia, the Baltic states, and Finland, plus some other minor territories in the Caucasus. After carving up Poland in concert with Germany in 1939, the Soviet borders were returned farther west, a fact that would play a significant role in the early stages of upcoming Soviet-German struggle in 1941.

Now, as the clock inexorably inched closer to fateful June 22, Soviet forces deployed along these new western borders began sounding alarms in increasing frequency and urgency. The most evident of these were over-flights by German reconnaissance aircraft over Soviet territory. Since late 1930s, a *Luftwaffe* formation called Special Purposes Squadron (or Squadron Rowehl after its founder Colonel Theodor Rowehl) had been flying high-altitude reconnaissance missions over Europe. Soviet Union was one of the countries on which it routinely spied. However, as the plans for Operation Barbarossa proceeded ahead, increasing demands for military intelligence about the Soviet Union caused Colonel Rowehl to give top priority to activating directed against the Soviet Union.

In January of 1941, Rowehl added another, fourth, squadron to his unit, which by now expanded into a full air wing. This fourth squadron was tasked solely with collecting information on Soviet Union. According to David Kahn: "Altogether, [Rowehl's] craft violated Soviet air space several hundred times between October 1939 and the German invasion of Russia."[15]

On two occasions when German aircraft were forced to land in the Soviet territory due to technical difficulties, evidence of German intelligence-gathering was irrefutable. On both of these occasions, a camera in working order was found in the wreckage of a German plane. Developed film clearly showed Soviet military installations and road junctions photographed from the air. Despite clear indications of intelligence-gathering activities by German aircraft, numerous requests by Soviet air defense units to open fire were invariably met with instructions to hold their fire so as not to provoke Germans into escalating the issue into a wider conflict.

Sometimes German attempts to cover up intelligence-gathering activities were so porous as to be insulting to the Soviets. Still, Stalin did everything possible to appease Hitler. In the spring of 1941, Germany requested and received permission to search the area on the Soviet side of the border for graves and remains of German servicemen fallen during World War I and the recent campaign against Poland in 1939. While Soviet commanders along the border gnashed their teeth in frustration, the Germans made the most of their opportunity to conduct ground reconnaissance.

When the Soviet border moved west in 1939, a somewhat chaotic situation existed for a time along the new frontier. The new border was easily crossed by people moving back and forth across the border, especially by local residents. Along with smuggling, information trade on a local level flourished. These porous borders, aided by largely difficult thickly wooded terrain, were favorable to penetration by spies and intelligence agents from both sides. Germany, especially, benefited from services of the underground Ukrainian organization, the Organization of Ukrainian Nationalist (OUN, the Organizatsiya Ukrainskikh Natsionalistov) who viewed the Germans as the lesser evil compared to the Soviets. Multiple local sympathizers passed the information directly to Germans or through the OUN. Lieutenant Fedor Arkhipenko, a fighter pilot stationed near Kovel, voiced his suspicious of the locals: "There were many civilians from the neighboring villages employed in building the landing strip, and there were many spies infiltrated among them, who observed the airfield."[16]

Once the Soviet Union joined the western Ukraine to the rest of the country, it began brutally asserting its rule over this newly acquired territory. Tens of thousands people were arrested and jailed locally or transported to concentration camps and jails deeper within the Soviet Union. At this point, executions, while common enough, did not attain the level they would reach immediately after German invasion.

This brutal treatment at the hands of their new Soviet masters created widespread discontent among the Western Ukrainian population. While a majority were sufficiently cowed into sullen inactivity, a small core of Ukrainian militant patriots rallied around the OUN. These men and women provided the Germans with a valuable network of agents reporting on Red Army's dispositions and strengths. Lieutenant Arkhipenko writes:

> I recall that before the war in those areas, often the officers from other units, who were outside the military garrisons, would disappear.... In the spring of 1941, under commissar's orders I had to make a presentation dedicated to the Red Army Day in one of the villages near Kovel. I arrived at the village, introduced myself to the kolkhoz chairman and went to the community center, where many people gathered. I delivered my presentation. During the presentation, several shots were heard outside. It was

possible that the villagers, unhappy with the Soviet authority (kolhozes) decided to test, represented by me, the moral fortitude of the Red Army. . . . The atmosphere was quite tense, and a thought occurred to me that it would be prudent to get out of there while I was still alive. Even though I was invited to spend the night there, I insisted on leaving and set off for Kovel in a horse cart, holding a pistol inside my coat all the way there, while appearing nonchalant.[17]

Several other Soviet memoirists record instances when wives of Red Army officers shopping or running errands in western Ukrainian towns were verbally accosted by local residents. The common thread of whispered threats was: "Just wait till Germans get here. They'll show you!" It was the atmosphere of not whether the war with Germany will happen, but when will it happen.

The feeling of oncoming war ran prevalent among the Red Army personnel as well. Colonel Ivan K. Bagramyan was transferred in December 1940 from Moscow to the headquarters of Kiev Special Military District to take over Operations Section of Headquarters of Kiev Special Military District. Since this reassignment took place in the middle of a school year, his wife and two daughters remained in Moscow, allowing the girls to finish off their school year before moving to Ukraine in the summer of 1941.

Knowing that Bagramyan was in Kiev alone, his direct supervisor, Maj. Gen. Maxim A. Purkayev invited Bagramyan to his apartment to ring in the new year. Shortly before being assigned to his current position, General Purkayev served as a military attaché in Germany. This posting gave Purkayev an insight into the situation in Germany and its military capabilities, giving him ample cause for concern.

Apparently, Purkayev's wife, Antonia, shared some of her husband's apprehensions, for she raised a toast: "Especially, that there would be no war!" Despite the cheerful occasion for their dinner, table conversation was serious. Purkayev related to Bagramyan that major issues were being looked at during a recent high-level military conference in Moscow:

> Some issues are closely scrutinized. Stalin himself is interested in the progress of the conference. Each meeting is attended by some member of Politburo. . . . It appears that the Central Committee [of Politburo] is taking into account the complexity of the international situation and growing threat from the fascist Germany. This explains increased

attention to the defensive potential of [our] country. And without doubt, there will be major changes in our army life.[18]

In the first week of 1941, commander of Kiev Special Military District, Georgiy Zhukov, returned to Kiev from Moscow's conference. Within days of his return, Zhukov called together a meeting that included senior command personnel of the military district, army commanders along with their members of military councils and chiefs of staffs, the same representative groups from corps and divisions, commanders and chiefs of staff of fortified districts, and commandants of military schools.

Zhukov opened the proceedings with statement: "The threat of war more and more hanging over our Motherland." He was no longer hiding the fact that Germany was to be considered a potential enemy; therefore, the main emphasis of the five-day meeting was dedicated to reviewing and updating the district's plans for defending the border in the near future. Zhukov particularly stressed the fact that these plans must be made counting on only the resources at hand:

> Some comrades forget that any, even the most brave, plans must be based on realistic capabilities. While planning measures in case of war, we could not base them on what our army will have in the future. What if the war starts now? *We must be realistic and make plans based on means and abilities which we possess today* [emphasis added].[19]

At the end of the conference, Zhukov officially announced shuffling of command personnel: General Sovetnikov, who was commanding the Fifth Army, was appointed as District's deputy commander in charge of fortified districts. He was replaced by Maj. Gen. M. Potapov, commander of the IV Mechanized Corps. In his turn, Potapov was replaced by Maj. Gen. A. A. Vlasov, who stepped up from command of the 99th Rifle Division. As for himself, shortly after this conference, Zhukov departed for Moscow to take over the General Staff, with Zhukov's replacement, Col. Gen. M. Kirponos, arriving shortly.

Friction between Purkayev, Bagramyan, and Kirponos began within several days of latter's arrival. After reviewing plans for covering the border, Kirponos disagreed with them. He was convinced that there would be some warning, at least several days, before the hostilities begin. Therefore, he thought that too many troops were placed too close to the border. He wanted to have at least one division per army to be held back as a mobile reserve. Purkayev offered a counter that if Germans attack without warning, they will overcome the weak defending units, and there will be no opportunity to organize the defense. Kirponos' counter was purely rhetoric: "We must not allow the enemy to surprise us. What do we have intelligence for?"[20]

The intelligence services, both NKVD and military GRU, had indeed been sounding warnings. Since the beginning of January 1941, Soviet intelligence began noticing significant movement of German forces towards the western Soviet border. Everything that Gen. F. I. Golikov, chief of intelligence directorate of the General Staff, would report to Timoshenko and Zhukov, they would in turn report to Stalin:

> However, I do not know what intelligence information Gen. F. I. Golikov was reporting to J. V. Stalin, bypassing the [Minister] of Defense and Chief of General Staff, and such reports were frequent.
>
> I can only say: *J. V. Stalin knew significantly more than the military leadership.* But even from what he was reported by the military intelligence sources, he could see undeniable increase of the threat of war, but he did not do this, and he, overestimating his abilities, continued farther on the false trail [emphasis added].[21]

In May, People's Defense Commissar M. Timoshenko sent a directive to military districts, outlining their responsibilities in case of a sudden attack by the Germans. Since the official plans for covering the border were being worked on, Timoshenko sent out a special directive to increase readiness of western border districts. In accordance with the plan, the rifle corps were to form the first echelon, mechanized corps, the second echelon. In the Kiev Special Military District, additional defensive positions were to be built thirty to thirty-five kilometers east of the border. The second echelon, occupied by five rifle and four mechanized corps, awaited movement orders from General Staff. A district's command post was also ordered built in Tarnopol.

After the German invasion of Yugoslavia on March 27, senior commanders of covering armies were called for a working conference to Kiev to work out a new defensive plan that called for more troops directly on the border to repel the German first strike. This work was conducted in such secrecy that only generals and officers directly involved in planning could have access to the materials. They had to write and type everything personally. Bagramyan ruefully remembered that he had to brush up on his half-forgotten skills with a typewriter.

At approximately the same time, Timoshenko and Zhukov submitted a joint request to Stalin to call up round-out personnel to bring rifle divisions to full strength. Initially, Stalin denied this request on the grounds that such call up could be interpreted by Germans, intentionally or not, as mobilization and cause for war. In the end of March, however, Stalin relented and authorized a call up of five hundred thousand men earmarked for border districts in an attempt to bring each rifle division to at least eight thousand men. Several days later, an additional call up of three hundred thousand men was authorized. Training periods for them were to last from May to October. This allowed a majority of first-line rifle divisions to be brought up to eight to nine thousand men.[22]

On April 26 they received orders to form five antitank artillery brigades, but only the 1st Brigade under Maj. Gen. Konstantin Moskalenko was formed by the start of hostilities. Additionally, the I Airborne Corps was being formed from the 204th Airborne Brigade, already assigned to the district, plus the 211th Airborne Brigade, which was being transferred from Far East. Additional manpower for the airborne corps came from the excess enlisted men left over after four rifle divisions of the Twelfth Army were reorganized into mountain-infantry divisions.

In the second half of May, command of Kiev Special Military District received instructions from Moscow informing them of arrival of the XXXIV Rifle Corps from the North-Caucasus Military District, consisting of four rifle and one mountain infantry division. The first trains bearing this unit were expected on May 20. On May 25, further order announced relocation of the XXXI Rifle Corps from the Far East. According to Bagramyan:

> At the end of May, significant portion of officers from district's headquarters were occupied in meeting and housing the arriving units. Trains came in one after another. The Operations Section turned into a dispatcher section, gathering all information about movement and condition of units. Divisions were arriving combat capable, even though their commanders complained about not having enough mid-level officers and lack of combat vehicles, transportation, and communication means.[23]

Taking these factors into consideration, during March and April the General Staff was feverishly working on updating their defense plans to reflect German movements. Based on these updated plans, Timoshenko and Zhukov reported to Stalin that there were not sufficient Soviet forces in the western districts and requested urgent mobilization of several armies from internal districts and begin moving them west. *"After long and quite pointed conversation, J. V. Stalin* [emphasis added] permitted two armies to be moved west under the utmost secrecy and under guise of training."[24] At the same time, NKVD received Stalin's instructions to step up construction of airfield networks; however, the workforce was permitted to be employed on these works only after finishing construction of the fortified districts.

At the end of May, the General Staff issued orders to commanders of western districts to urgently begin preparing command posts, with further instructions in the middle of June to move their command elements to these posts. They were to be moved by June 21–25, depending on a district.

Bagramyan picks up the tale:

> In the very beginning of June we found out that command element of the 19th Army has been formed and situated in Cherkassy. [Author's note: it is interesting that formation and deployment of a new army in district's territory was done from without district command's knowledge.] The new army will include all five divisions from 34th Rifle Corps and three divisions of the 25th Rifle Corps from the North-Caucasus Military District. This army will be headed by commander of the North-Caucasus Military District Lieutenant-General I. S. Konev and held under direct control of [Timoshenko]. A day later the General Staff gave us a heads-up: there will be another army coming, the 16th, under Lieutenant-General M. F. Lukin. It will be transferred from Trans-Baikal region during June 15th to July 10th.[25]

Bagramyan remembered being relieved that two more armies would be available to defend the border. Besides reinforcing the Kiev district, two other armies were being moved to its northern neighbor, the Western Special Military District.

As new troops continued rolling into the district, training of units already there stepped up at increasing pace. On May 26, Kirponos, Bagramyan, and other officers conducted an inspection tour of the Sixth Army. Observing maneuvers of a tank company from IV Mechanized Corps, Kirponos did not like what he saw: "One of T-34s slowly moved through the obstacle course. The tank, directed by an inexperienced hand, was barely navigating it. Two other vehicles fared slightly better." Following movements of the tanks,

Kirponos winced: "Not good!" General Morgunov [commander of Kiev Special Military District tank troops] sighed: "It's not surprising, Comrade Commander. The drivers did not have opportunity to familiarize themselves with the new vehicles. They have not even had three hours of driving time with them."[26]

This same unit, while conducting itself better during shooting practice, did poorly during the night march:

> Along the route of tank regiments, we saw large number of halted vehicles along the roads. The farther we went, the more [broken down vehicles] turned up. . . . When division commander arrived and began making a report about the progress of the night march, [Kirponos] interrupted him: "Why, Colonel, you have such a mess? Your tanks are halting on the march; what would happen in combat?" Division commander attempted to explain that only the most-used T-26 and BT tanks, mainly from the training park, had halted, due to lack of spare parts.[27]

Amid heightened activity,

> The intelligence section of Kiev Special Military District began receiving reports each more concerning than the other. [Chief of Intelligence] Colonel G. I. Bondarev practically became the most frequent [Kirponos] visitor. We noticed that after almost every conversation with him M. P. Kirponos became even grimmer. There were plenty of reasons for worry... [Around June 10th] commander called together the Military Council at which [Bondarev] reported all he knew.[28]

Bondarev talked about construction of numerous airfields on the other side of the border and laying roads directly to the Soviet border. Since April there had been increased movements of German forces and large number of trains were arriving every day. He was seconded by General Ptukhin, commander of the air forces, who reported ever-increasing overflights by German aircraft in violation of Soviet air space.

Kirponos told the officers that while general movement towards the border was forbidden, army commanders received orders to have their units ready. Several divisions could be shuffled around without drawing attention from Moscow. Purkayev brought up an issue that greatly concerned him—the fact that the second-echelon corps were not up to strength, and an especially alarming situation was with lack of wheeled transport and tracked artillery movers. In case of sudden attack, a majority of artillery units would not be able to move forward a significant part of their cannons.

Kirponos replied that such addition of manpower and assets from the civilian sector would only be possible with an announcement of mobilization. He called it "an issue of state policy" and the Soviet government's attempt not to give Hitler any chances at provocation. Even partial mobilization would not be possible to conduct in secrecy. Purkayev, though, managed to convince him and Commissar Nikolay Vashugin to return artillery regiments and engineer battalions from training camps to their parent divisions. Besides these measures, Kirponos gave orders to each covering division to move forward small detachments and take up positions in the fortified districts.

Measures to increase readiness of second-echelon forces were taken as well: each regiment to have ready ammunition kept directly with the subunits, and half of the ammunition allocated to machine guns to be loaded into disks and belts; half of hand grenades, artillery, and mortar ammunition to be directly distributed to the units; all vehicles to be topped off and a quantity of fuel sufficient for one refuel to be kept with them in cans.

Approximately a day after Kirponos instructed small units to occupy the fortified districts, a telegram arrived from the General Staff. In no uncertain terms, Kirponos was chastised for possibly giving Germans the pretext for an armed clash. Kirponos was ordered to immediately cancel these orders and return the units to their garrisons. Kirponos and his staff later found out that his initiative was undermined by someone at the headquarters of the NKVD border guards, who had an additional task of making sure that no actions to provoke the Germans were taken. As it were, this incident completely snubbed out Kirponos' initiative to take prudent precautionary measures. Heavily weighing on Kirponos' mind was the understanding that Stalin personally considered Ukraine as a strategically vital area. According to Zhukov:

> J. V. Stalin was convinced that during the war with the Soviet Union, the Hitlerites will be striving first to capture the Ukraine, the Donetsk basin, in order to deny our country the most important economic regions and capture the Ukrainian grain, Donetsk coal, and then—oil from Caucasus. While considering this operational plan in the spring of 1941, J. V. Stalin said: "Without these vital resources the Fascist Germany could

not wage a prolonged and large-scale war." These considerations were signed off on in February 1941, and these plans became known as MP-41. While updating the operations plans in the spring of 1941 (February to April), we did not completely correct this oversight and did not allocate sufficiently large forces for the western [Belorussian] direction.[29]

Kirponos was torn between wishing to do his best to protect the vital areas as outlined by Stalin and, at the same time, realizing that his measures were not enough, not wanting to be labeled as an alarmist.

However, some of Kirponos' subordinate commanders were secretly making their own preparations. Around this time, commissar of the VIII Mechanized Corps, Nikolai Popel, visited his friend, commander of the Twenty-Sixth Army, Maj. Gen. Ivan N. Muzychenko, at latter's headquarters in Drogobych. During a frank conversation, Muzychenko told his friend: "Between us, I moved infantry from garrisons into fortified districts. I'm not in a hurry to report this to my superiors. Don't want to be labeled panic-monger."[30] Likewise, Popel's own commander, Lt. Gen. D. I. Ryabyshev, under his own authority and also not reporting to higher echelon, moved parts of each regiment in his corps to their staging areas.[31]

Officers from subordinate armies continued bombarding Kirponos with warnings of increased German activity and questions about when they could take up positions in the fortified districts. Kirponos, while agreeing with them, could not give them concrete answers, other than reassuring them that Moscow knows what it's doing.

However, from senior officers down to the lower-ranking ones, few doubted what was coming. Lieutenant Arkhipenko wrote:

> In the spring of 1941, German reconnaissance planes constantly violated our border and conducted reconnaissance flights over the Soviet territory and our airfield, but there were instructions not to shoot them down and not even to scare them, but only escort them to the border. Everything was done as to *postpone* [emphasis added] the war, prevent the development of attempted German provocation.[32]

In an attempt to allay growing concerns and fears, Telegraph Agency of the Soviet Union (TASS) published a statement on June 14, 1941. In this officially sanctioned statement, the Soviet government categorically denied worsening relations between Germany and the Soviet Union and reiterated wishes of both governments in maintaining peaceful coexistence. However, this statement only served to further bewilder those Soviet officers in key positions and those deployed along the border, who were well aware that what they saw daily with their eyes did not match rosy official prognostications.

In Moscow, Timoshenko and Zhukov continued to practically beg Stalin to take steps that would effectively amount to mobilization. After an especially trying meeting, Stalin blew up at his senior military advisors: "Are you suggesting that the country mobilizes, raises troops and moves them to the western borders? But this means war! Do you two understand this or not?"[33]

Finally, Stalin partially relented:

> Moscow, of course, knew the situation on the other side of the border better than we did, and our supreme military command took actions. On June 15th we received orders to begin moving all five rifle corps of the second echelon closer to the border on June 17th. We had everything ready for this since beginning of May. . . . [Each] corps was given two to three days to get ready for the force march. Some of divisions were to set off in the evening of June 17th, the rest—a day later. They were to take with them everything needed for combat operations. As a measure of concealment, the troops were to move only at night. They would need a total of eight to twelve night stages.[34]

In order to prevent the Germans from finding out about these movements, the reserve corps were to take up positions not at the border, but several marches to the east. The XXXI Rifle Corps, leaving Korosten area, was to reach Kovel by morning of June 28. The XXXVI Rifle Corps was to arrive in Dubno-Kremenets area by morning of June 27. The other three reserve rifle corps were also given similar time tables.

On June 19, Major General Ponedelin, commanding the Twelfth Army, requested clarification in which instances he could open fire on German aircraft violating Soviet air space. General Kirponos permitted opening fire only in the following situations: "a) with special permission by the Military Council of the District, b) with announcement of mobilization, c) with activation of covering plan, unless specifically forbidden."[35] This amounted pretty much to "when the war starts." Kirponos also offered a pointed reminder to Ponedelin and his staff: "The Military Council of the Twelfth Army knows that we do not open antiaircraft fire on German aircraft during peacetime."

Also on June 19, a telegram arrived from Zhukov informing them that Timoshenko ordered to redesignate peacetime Kiev Special Military District into wartime South-Western Front. Front's command element was to move to its wartime command post in Tarnopol by June 22. Of course, neither Zhukov nor Timoshenko knew that this command post had not been established as previously ordered. The move was to be carried out in compete secrecy. In order to speed up the process and conceal it from the enemy, command element was to move in two parts—by railroad and by car. Those leaving by railroad were to depart in the evening of June 20, those in the wheeled convoy, in the morning of June 21.

Two days later, as the last day of peace, June 21, drew to a close, a German deserter crossed over to the Soviet side of the Western Bug River border in Ukraine in the area of operations of Major General Fedyuninskiy's XV Rifle Corps. This deserter, with the rank of sergeant, reported that the invasion would begin at 0330 hours the next morning. Information was quickly relayed from Fedyuninskiy's headquarters to the Fifth Army, then to South-Western Front. From there, General Purkayev called Moscow. For the previous several days, personnel at the People's Commissariat for Defense and the General Staff had worked almost eighteen-hour days, with Timoshenko and Zhukov often sleeping in their offices. It took only a few minutes to reach and brief them. In their turn, Zhukov and Timoshenko immediately reported to Stalin, who ordered them to the Kremlin in forty-five minutes.

Timoshenko and Zhukov quickly gathered up their already-prepared drafts of alert orders, picked up Lt. Gen. N. F. Vatutin, Chief of NKO's Operations Section, and went to see Stalin. "On the way there we agreed to convince Stalin by all means possible for permission to bring up forces to combat readiness," Zhukov later recalled. Stalin was alone in his office. After a brief report by generals, several members of Politburo arrived, who remained more or less silent observers without taking any significant part in discussions.

Finally, Stalin asked Timoshenko and Zhukov straight out what they wanted to do. They quickly presented their MP-41 mobilization plan. After hearing them out, Stalin still did not agree with full measures, consenting to a watered-down version, strongly cautioning not to fall for provocations. The three generals excused themselves to another room and hashed out a modified version, which was finally approved by Stalin. Vatutin immediately hand-carried this version to the General Staff for dissemination to border districts. Transmission was completed by 0030 on June 22. The war was three hours away.

Part II:

THE BORDER BATTLE

▶ CHAPTER 6

We Are Under Attack!
What Should We Do?
June 22

MANY OF THOSE WHO SURVIVED THE WAR to talk about the predawn hours of Sunday, June 22, 1941, remembered the multitude of frogs inhabiting this particular swatch of northwestern Ukraine among the wide, swampy banks of the Western Bug River.[1] Their unrelenting croaking provided a cacophony of sounds in the foggy morning up and down the river near a small Ukrainian town of Ustilug.[2]

The sounds of frogs, however, did not mask the growling of vehicle engines on the other, German-occupied, bank of the river. To the young guard pacing across the Soviet end of the highway bridge spanning the river, these sounds seemed to be increasing over the past few nights, with the hooded glare of vehicles' headlights dissipated somewhat in the morning fog.

The fog would melt away in a couple hours of what was promising to be a beautiful Sunday morning. He pulled his green-topped round cap of NKVD Border Guards deeper on his closed-shaved head and pulled the overcoat tighter around himself, keeping alert eyes on the other end of the bridge.

Few minutes later, the young guard became aware of two sets of dimmed headlights as two trucks pulled onto the bridge from the other bank. Wary, but not worried yet, he quickly glanced to his left and right where two heavy machine guns were emplaced to cover the bridge. The three-man crews of Maxim machine guns also saw the two approaching vehicles; the gunners' thumbs rested on the butterfly-shaped triggers of their weapons.

As the two vehicles pulled closer, the young guard was surprised to recognize the shapes of Russian-built GAZ-AA trucks. He pulled his rifle off his shoulder but held it at port-arms, ready to halt them. The cab of the first vehicle, an upgraded clone of an American Ford truck, was occupied by two men in Soviet uniforms, the man in the passenger seat wearing collar tabs of a captain. The truck slowed down and lurched to a stop several steps past the young guard. The captain in the front truck addressed him in a flawless Russian: "Good morning, comrade." Machine gunners in the emplacements, recognizing Soviet uniforms and hearing Russian speech, eased their fingers from the triggers.

The last thing the young guard saw was a seemingly gigantic muzzle of a pistol appearing in captain's hand. He was cut down by several shots even before uttering a sound. The canvas tarp was thrown off the back of the truck, and two pairs of grenades arched high into the morning air, descending onto the machine-gun positions. They were followed by men in Soviet uniforms, bearing Soviet weapons, jumping off the truck and running towards the border guards' emplacements. Dazed survivors of machine-gun crews, crumpled around scattered sand bags, were quickly finished off by point-blank shots.

The second truck raced by them and halted farther down the block, disgorging its own load of German Brandenburg commandos clad in Soviet uniforms.[3] Scarcely a year and a half ago, the Russo-Finnish War ended, leaving ample amounts of Soviet equipment, arms, and uniforms in Finnish hands. The Finns readily provided Germans with a sufficient quantity of captured materiel of their common enemy. Now, the Soviet-dressed German commandos spread out in a skirmish line, hugging whatever cover available, setting up a perimeter around the bridgehead on the Soviet side. A dozen commandos scurried under the bridge, removing pre-positioned Soviet explosives. The bridge thus secured, the captain, in actuality a Brandenburg lieutenant, turned toward the German side and quickly dashed off a prearranged sequence of blinks with his flashlight. A score of headlights came to life on the western bank, and a company of German armored cars and motorcyclists dashed to the eastern side to reinforce commandos.

The same scene repeated itself eight miles farther south, where German commando and reconnaissance troops secured a railroad bridge. They were closely followed by combat engineers, bringing forward prepared wooden planking to make the railroad bridge passable by wheeled vehicles. On their heels more and more *Wehrmacht* troops began flowing onto the Soviet territory, covered by massive German artillery barrage of all calibers. Overhead in the brightening sky, squadrons of aircraft with black crosses darted east, seeking out Soviet airfields, communication centers, and military installations.

At 0330 hours, all up and down the western border of the Soviet Union, the German artillery and air force unleashed punishing strikes on largely still-sleeping Soviet forces. Fearful of provoking Germans into an armed conflict, the Soviet dictator Josef Stalin had expressly forbidden Red Army field forces from taking up defensive positions in the fortified regions along the border. When he finally gave in to frantic pleas of his senior military advisers and permitted partial alert and deployment of Red Army field forces, it was too late. In many instances, the first notification of war the Soviet soldiers received was German bombs and shells exploding among their garrisons.

Repeated stern orders about not provoking Germans into hostile actions robbed many Soviet officers of needed initiative. Even with German shells bursting around them, many frontline Red Army officers sent off desperate inquiries: "We are under attack! What should we do?"

VLADIMIR-VOLYNSKIY DIRECTION

The main brunt of the assault by Army Group South fell onto the Soviet XXVII Rifle Corps of the Fifth Army. This Soviet formation covered the extremely important strategic direction. From the small border town of Ustilug, what passed for a major road lead to Vladimir-Volynskiy, then Lutsk, and on to Rovno, Zhitomir, and, finally, Kiev, the Ukrainian capital. Capturing this vital roadway was paramount in German plans for rapid destruction of Soviet forces in the Ukraine.

Enjoying the initiative of launching the first strike allowed Germany to achieve maximum favorable concentration of forces at the place and time of their own choosing. At the *Schwerepunkt* (point of main effort) of the German invasion in the Ukraine, three under-strength Soviet divisions, plus several border guard detachments and machine gun battalions, were opposed along almost sixty miles of border by eight infantry and two panzer divisions of German first echelon.

As the German commandos were storming the bridges at Ustilug, less than twenty miles away to the east, a little black staff car was bouncing over a potholed road, taking two lieutenant colonels from the staff of Soviet 41st Tank Division fishing. While Lt. Col. Dmitriy Vasilyev was enthusiastic about putting in some quality fishing time, division's Chief of Staff Konstantin Malygin could not shake off gloomy foreboding.

Before they had the chance to cast their fishing lines, the two officers were alerted by their driver pointing towards the border:

Several red and green signal flares go up from direction of the border. Before they burned out, a far-off thunder was heard. Reflecting of lightening sky, flashes from cannon shots began blinking. Somewhere ahead, ricocheting, tracer bullets flew high. In the fortified region the earth rose up, mixed with smoke. We could hear chattering of machine guns, pops of rifle shots, thuds of shells and mortars.[4]

Abandoning their fishing poles and gear, they raced towards their garrison in Vladimir-Volynskiy, a small town with several small Gothic churches. Their base was already a beehive of activity under sporadic bombing and shelling as troops from the 41st Tank Division hurried to get ready to set off for the division's staging areas. As more and more vehicles pulled out the front gates, division's artillery regiment, possessing only four prime movers, sat idle. Its commander, Maj. Nikolai Khizhin, and Malygin put their heads together and came up with a field-expedient solution to get some of the guns moving. The 41st Tank Division possessed fifteen old BT-2 two-turreted tanks, armed only with machine guns and protected by paper-thin armor. Virtually useless other than as training machines, these tanks at the end of their useful lives were detailed to tow some of Khizhin's howitzers.

At the division's headquarters, staff officers attempted in vain to reach headquarters of their parent XXII Mechanized Corps or of the Fifth Army, both located in Rovno. Division's commander, Col. Petr Pavlov, and his political deputy, Commissar Mikhail Balykov, were attempting to piece together the situation. One radio message came in from the division's 41st Motorized Rifle Regiment, located separately some distance away in Lyuboml: "The regiment is fighting on the border under operational control of XV Rifle Corps."[5]

Not receiving any orders from above and with Balykov's agreement, Colonel Pavlov tore open his sealed orders packet. In accordance with the plans developed before the war, all of the XXII Mechanized Corps to which the 41st Tank Division belonged was to concentrate in the Kovel area and protect it against possible attack from northwest. The envelope also contained a map with designated staging areas and routes to them. Following these only orders available to him, Pavlov turned his division northeast to Kovel, *away from the fighting* at the border nearby.

As the 41st Tank Division began rolling out of its base camp, an urgent request for help came from commander of 87th Rifle Division, Maj. Gen. F.

F. Alyabyshev.[6] Alyabyshev's division was responsible for covering thirty-four miles of the border directly west of Vladimir-Volynskiy. As German shells starting raining on his garrisons, General Alyabyshev began moving his units forward to the sound of the guns. On his own initiative, Pavlov detached one tank battalion from the 82nd Tank Regiment to assist Alyabyshev. Placing Malygin in charge of moving to Kovel, Colonel Pavlov stayed behind with the tank battalion to assess the situation.

While the bulk of the 87th Rifle Division, hampered by German air attacks, advanced to the border, the only forces directly available to oppose the Germans around Ustilug were one engineer and three rifle battalions involved in construction of fortifications along the border.[7] They were augmented by several platoon-sized border guard detachments and two machine-gun battalions garrisoning a scattering of bunkers belonging to the fortified region. In addition, just days before the invasion, Alyabyshev, without approval from above and at his own risk, pre-positioned one artillery battalion in the overwatch positions around Ustilug.

A bitter fight flared up all around this tiny picturesque town. Following on the heels of commandos and recce troops, the main forces of the German 298th Infantry Division attempted to bull its way through Ustilug. Vicious fighting developed among the twisted cobblestone streets and muddy banks of the river. For the first two hours, outnumbered Red Army soldiers were able to put up stiff resistance, supported by point-black artillery fire and aided by narrow confines of ancient streets. However, effective German counter-battery fire forced the Soviet artillery battalion to withdraw east. Stubborn Red Army machine gunners manning bunkers along the river were largely neutralized by direct fire of German artillery and assault teams of combat engineers armed with flamethrowers and demolition charges. Left on their own, the depleted remains of 1st Battalion, 16th Rifle Regiment, and few surviving border guards withdrew east to link up with advancing elements of the 87th Rifle Division.

By 0900 hours, as more and more of his units went into the fight directly from the march, Maj. Gen. Alyabyshev was able to somewhat stabilize the situation, temporarily halting the German advance by determined counterattacks north and south of the town. Alyabyshev's riflemen were supported by the point-blank fire of his division's 212th Howitzer Regiment and T-26 tanks from the 82nd Tank Regiment loaned by Colonel Pavlov.

Several miles away to the east, Lieutenant Colonel Malygin was moving the rest of the 41st Tank Division north, parallel to the fighting, through the areas where the 87th Rifle Division was staging for a counterattack. The Germans were heavily bombing and shelling both units. He recalled a direct bomb hit striking a heavy KV-2 tank and setting it ablaze. Another KV-2 became stuck in a swampy patch of ground, common throughout the northwestern Ukraine. Since there was no way to pull it out under fire and with Germans approaching, its crew blew the immobile tank up.

Just south of Ustilug, two other Soviet rifle and one engineer battalion which were employed in construction briefly attempted to prevent *Wehrmacht*'s 44th Infantry Division from crossing the Western Bug River in rubber boats and ferries. Despite stubborn resistance by Red Army troops, the 44th Infantry Division was able to establish a beachhead on the right bank of the Bug River and expand it to the depth of five miles. The 14th Panzer Division, following closely behind infantry, began shifting its main forces there. Finding themselves outflanked in the open, the survivors of the three Soviet battalions were forced to fall back, ceding the disputed eastern river bank to the enemy. A virtually unguarded gap of over twenty miles, thinly held by widely separated bunkers, developed between the 87th Rifle and its sister 124th Rifle Division to the south.

Throughout the day the German 14th Panzer, 44th Infantry, and 299th Infantry divisions advanced into the widening gap, despite dogged resistance of Soviet soldiers in their isolated positions. By 1700 hours the Germans began flanking the 87th Rifle Division approximately ten miles southeast of Vladimir-Volynskiy, with Major General Alyabyshev not having any reserves to plug the gap. His 341st Artillery Regiment used up all cannon ammunition and had to fight as infantry. Alyabyshev also received information from the XXVII Rifle Corps headquarters that on June 23 the 135th Rifle Division would be deployed in the gap between the 87th and 124th divisions. Alyabyshev, therefore, made the decision to maintain his position and continue attacking on the 23rd in the direction of Ustilug.

In the evening of June 22, the bulk of the 41st Tank Division reached its staging area in the vicinity of Kovel. There were still no communications with the XXII Mechanized Corps or the Fifth Army. Whatever meager news Lieutenant Colonel Malygin could gather trickled in over the newly laid telephone line to the headquarters of Colonel Fedyuninskiy's XV Rifle Corps at Lyuboml. The 41st Motorized Rifle Regiment belonging to Malygin's division was by then fully engaged in fighting on the border and was barely holding the gap between the 45th and 62nd divisions of the XV Rifle Corps.

Several hours later, Colonel Pavlov rejoined the main body of the 41st Tank Division with the remains of the tank battalion that was left behind to assist Alyabyshev. This tank battalion was one of the very first Soviet armored formations to engage the Germans in World War II. For a time, they helped hold Vladimir-Volynskiy, but at a steep price. Out of fifty T-26 tanks, almost thirty were destroyed. While advancing in support of Alyabyshev's infantry, the light-skinned T-26s were severely mauled by German antitank artillery. Battalion commander, Maj. A. S. Suin, wiping away blood from a minor head wound, described to Malygin and other staff officers how some tanks were put out of commission even by fire of heavy machine guns. Lacking means to recover damaged vehicles and ceding the ground to the enemy, all the disabled vehicles of Suin's battalion were irretrievably lost. Neither Pavlov nor Suin knew yet that Vladimir-Volynskiy, for which their men paid so dearly, was lost in the late evening after their departure.

As darkness descended over Vladimir-Volynskiy, bursts of automatic weapon fire and sporadic explosions still ripped the night. Here and there, isolated groups of border guards were holding out in basements of their destroyed block houses. Some bunkers of the fortified region grimly hung on for days, waiting for relief that would not come. Border Guard Outpost #13 under Lt. A. I. Lopatin held out for eleven days and died to the last man.

SOKAL DIRECTION

On General Alyabyshev's left flank, the 124th Rifle Division, under Maj. Gen. F. G. Suschiy, was responsible for roughly twenty-four miles of the border. The bulk of its units was stationed over twenty-five miles away to the east, behind a small town called Sokal. This tiny town, located on the east side of Western Bug River, was approximately eight miles from the border. The river, following the border in 87th Rifle Division's sector, veers off southeast in that of the 124th, with less than ten miles of ground between the river and the border. This small land bridge gave the German advance the chance to pick up steam before coming into contact with Soviet field forces around Sokal.

Racing through the thinly held border and bypassing resisting bunkers, forward elements of four German infantry divisions captured Sokal before the Soviet forces could set up effective defenses there. Red Army units, hampered by German air strikes, clashed in a series of meeting engagements east of Sokal with rapidly advancing German infantry, closely supported by the 11th Panzer

Division. Major General Crüwell's 11th Panzer Division went into action around 1000 hours and, with a reconnaissance battalion in the lead, quickly pushed east. Despite sporadic fire from isolated Soviet pockets of resistance, the division made good progress.

The Soviet resistance was rapidly collapsing as the 11th Panzer Division expanded its front and was more of a nuisance than a serious threat. As Sergeant Alfred Höckendorf from the 4th Company of the 15th Panzer Regiment rode his scout motorcycle through the field of tall wheat, a wild artillery shot came from nowhere, rendering the motorcycle a total loss. For a short time, Sergeant Bergander and his panzer stayed behind with Höckendorf and his disabled machine. However, Bergander had to resume the advance, and Sergeant Höckendorf remained alone. From time to time, disoriented and dispirited Soviet soldiers in ones and twos chanced upon the German sergeant. A few shots from Höckendorf, taking cover behind the wreck of his motorcycle, were usually sufficient to convince the Russians to drop their weapons. By the time a German search party located Höckendorf, he was guarding a group of forty Red Army prisoners.[8]

Soviet divisions holding this sector of the border were inadvertently deployed in a sort of checkerboard formation. The spaces between the forward-most divisions were to be occupied by the supporting divisions upon mobilization. In fact, the 135th Rifle division of the XXVII Rifle Corps, part of Fifth Army's reserve, had been on the march since June 20, aiming to take up positions between its sister 87th and 124th divisions. However, when Germans struck at dawn of June 22, the 135th Rifle Division was still over sixty miles away from the border.

By the end of June 22, the ever-present German mobile reconnaissance units found unguarded gaps between the 87th and 124th Rifle Divisions and their neighbors north and south. Quickly exploiting these openings, while pinning the Soviet divisions from the front, German follow-on echelons began flowing around their flanks. Nightfall on June 22 found the two Soviet divisions surrounded on three sides and out of touch with each other, their neighbors, and higher command. The forward elements of the 15th Panzer Regiment belonging to 11th Panzer Division, when halted for the night at 2300 hours, were actually behind the positions of the 124th Rifle Division, approximately twenty miles into Soviet territory, west of Stoyanov. This Soviet division was in especially bad shape. Two of its rifle regiments, when pushed back from their garrisons in small towns of Tartakov and Poritsk, lost their regimental depots and virtually all their supplies there.

KOVEL DIRECTION

North of the XXVII Rifle Corps, the XV Rifle Corps under Col. Ivan Fedyuninskiy also found itself pressed hard.[9] However, not being astride main axis of German invasion, two divisions of the XV Rifle Corps were in a relatively stable position. Nonetheless, an undefended gap of over ten miles developed on its left, southern, flank between its 62nd Rifle Division and the 87th Rifle Division of the XXVII Corps.

Opposing Fedyuninskiy's corps and advancing close behind rolling artillery barrages, Landsers from the German 56th Infantry Division crossed the Soviet border at 0315 hours. Ferried across the Bug River in rubber boats and rafts, German assault parties captured intact the bridges south of Vlodava, and the main body of their division flowed across these vital bridges. Spearheaded by the advance elements, German XVII Army Corps began developing its attack along the Lyuboml-Kovel axis.

As the first German soldiers were splashing into the Bug River, Colonel Fedyuninskiy was smoking at the window of his apartment in Kovel. Looking at dark spires of a small Gothic cathedral, he was tired, but could not sleep. There was a lot to think about. An unpleasant sound of telephone interrupted Fedyuninskiy's worried reverie. His immediate superior, commander of the Soviet Fifth Army, Maj. Gen. Mikhail Potapov, was on the other end of the line. With tension in his voice, Potapov ordered Fedyuninskiy to return to his headquarters and stand by for Potapov's call.[10] With a sinking feeling, Fedyuninskiy did not wait for a staff car to pick him up and practically ran to his nearby headquarters. On the way there Fedyuninskiy could hear sounds of explosions coming from the border.

Upon arriving at his headquarters, Fedyuninskiy found the dedicated military telephone line not functioning. He managed to reach Potapov by a civilian telephone line. Potapov ordered him to sound an alert, keep ammunition at hand, but not to issue it to the men yet, and not to fall for any provocations. Soon communications with Potapov were completely lost.

Sounds of explosions from the border grew into a constant roar. A flight of aircraft with black crosses appeared over Kovel and dropped bombs. Half-dressed, panicked people were running aimlessly through the streets. Needing no more convincing that the real shooting war was upon them, Colonel Fedyuninskiy ordered his divisions to the border. In some places, units from the 45th and 62nd Rifle Divisions were located within seven miles of the border, and by 0500 hours Fedyuninskiy's men were able to reinforce the hard-pressed border guards. (Note: There were both Soviet and German divisions numbered "62nd" operating in the same sector.)

As everywhere else, the Soviet airfields around Kovel were being hammered by German aviation. When the bombs began to fall, the airfields were still on a peace footing, with only one or two aircraft per unit on standby. Dodging explosions and bomb craters, some of Soviet pilots managed to get into the air. In the few first minutes of the war, one of these duty pilots from the 17th Fighter Regiment, a senior lieutenant with the quintessential Russian name Ivan Ivanovich Ivanov, rammed his I-153 fighter into a German bomber, plunging both of them to their deaths.

On the ground, resistance was stubborn, if disorganized at first. Soviet border guards in their bunkers along the Bug River near Volchiy-Perevoz, south of Vlodava, fought to the last man.[11] Advancing German units became intermixed with the Soviet ones. Two battalions of the German 192nd Infantry Regiment from the 56th Infantry Division became cut off and were able to reestablish contact only during the night.[12]

Commanding the Soviet 45th Rifle Division deployed north of the Chelm-Lutsk railroad was Maj. Gen. G. I. Sherstyuk. Already in his fifties, able and reliable, Sherstyuk still maintained the stiff-backed bearing of the former Russian Imperial Army officer that he was. Disputing every meter of swampy ground, the right flank of Sherstyuk's division tenaciously defended defiles among the lakes around Shatsk.

During the late morning, Sherstyuk's headquarters received unconfirmed rumors of a German mechanized attack in the area southwest of Shatsk. Sherstyuk immediately cobbled together a makeshift task force and rushed it to block the perceived threat. Comprised of an armored car company from the 45th Rifle Division's reconnaissance battalion, one artillery battery, one mortar battery, and one infantry company mounted on trucks, this task force easily blocked the German scout detachments from probing closer to Kovel.

While insignificant tactically, this minor German probe proved very important in other ways. Soviet command could not ignore possibility of German outflanking thrust to Lutsk via Kovel, and for the following several days, strong elements from the Soviet XV Rifle Corps remained in static defense guarding against such eventuality.

A more intense battle was developing to the south, along the road from Chelm to Kovel, near the town of Lyuboml. Around 0800 hours, a regiment from the Soviet 45th Rifle Division under Col. G. S. Antonov ran head-on into the advance elements of the German 56th Infantry Division. A stubborn fight ensued, with the Red Army regiment tenaciously holding its own against stronger enemy forces. Additional help came from the already mentioned 41st Motorized Rifle Regiment belonging to the XXII Mechanized Corps.

The second division from Fedyuninskiy's corps, the 62nd Rifle commanded by Col. M. P. Timoshenko and deployed south of the Chelm-Lutsk railroad, found itself in an extremely difficult situation.[13] One of its regiments, the 104th, was detached as the corps' reserves. Another, the 306th Rifle Regiment, had only its 1st Battalion available for defending the border, with another employed on construction works over ten miles away and the third serving as garrison of Lutsk. The third regiment, the full three-battalion 123rd, reinforced with both divisional artillery regiments, was positioned to guard the approaches to Vladimir-Volynskiy from the northwest, south of Mosyr village.[14] And, naturally, this strong three-regiment group sat idle as fierce fighting raged to its north and south, practically within rifle shot.

From the opening shots of the invasion, the lone battalion of the 306th Rifle Regiment was fighting for the area immediately south of the railroad. Outnumbered and outgunned, it was being cut to shreds and pushed southeast from the road. Only the timely arrival of the 41st Motorized Rifle Regiment temporarily shored up the situation along the railroad and reestablished contact with Colonel Sherstyuk's division.

As the day wore on, the 62nd Rifle Division became completely fractured. The survivors of the 1st Battalion/306th Rifle Regiment, along with the left flank of the 41st Motorized Rifle Regiment, were pushed east. This created a twelve-mile gap between it and the group south of Mosyr, the 123rd Rifle and two artillery regiments. Furthermore, as Vladimir-Volynskiy was lost in the evening of June 22, the Mosyr group became surrounded on three sides. Being out of communications and instructions from the 62nd Rifle Division, the two artillery regiments of the Mosyr group sat silent throughout the day, without providing desperately needed fire support, neither north nor south of them.

While XV and XXVII Rifle corps were fighting for their lives, command staffs of their parent Fifth Army and the Kiev Special Military District were scrambling for information about events at the border. From the very start, these senior command echelons operated in a virtual information vacuum.

In the last hour of the last day of peace, June 21, Marshal S. K. Timoshenko, the People's Commissar for Defense (Defense Minister), and Gen.

Georgiy K. Zhukov, Chief of General Staff, finally managed to convince Josef Stalin of the necessity of immediate actions. This was a difficult task, relentlessly carried out in low key by the two most senior Soviet commanders over a period of two weeks. It was not that Stalin was blind to the looming German danger. Desperately realizing his military's unpreparedness for a difficult and protracted campaign with such dangerous foe as Germany, Stalin was playing for time.

Despite numerous indications otherwise, Stalin believed that there still was a cushion of time remaining before full mobilization would be needed. During previous instigated conflicts, Adolf Hitler demonstrated his modus operandi of getting his way by following a process over time of applying political pressures and demands, backed up by show of force. Stalin was quite possibly interpreting the massing of German troops as just such saber-rattling. In keeping with Hitler's past pattern of behavior, it appeared that the Soviet Union still should have had several weeks before the guns would sound. Therefore, Stalin was pursuing a policy of appeasing Hitler for as long as possible.

In line with the above thinking, the Soviet military leadership developed series of plans based on assumption that there would be approximately four weeks of increased political tension, eventually leading to full mobilization. Each military border district, army, corps, and division had their own prepared plans, tailored to their particular theater of operations, outlining specific steps that would be taken once mobilization was announced.

Kiev Special Military District had its own version of such plan, codenamed KOVO-41 (KOVO is the Russian acronym for Kievskiy Osobiy Voyenniy Okrug, meaning Kiev Special Military District). Under this mobilization plan, the forward Soviet units would be brought up to full alert and deployed in a prepared, or, in most cases, partially prepared network of fortified regions. Forces of the second echelon would be positioned to contain possible enemy breakthroughs and to take the fight into enemy territory. Reservists would be called up and units brought up to full strength. Vital equipment, especially tractors and prime movers for artillery units and communication equipment, would be received from civilian economy, and number of specialist support and service units would be unfolded.

However, even with the eleventh hour approaching, the Soviet dictator still resisted full mobilization and consented only to bringing the armed forces to alert status. Shortly after midnight, a terse directive was transmitted from Moscow to all the Soviet military districts lying along the western border:

21st June 1941

Directive to the Military Councils of Leningrad Military District, Baltic Military District, Western Special Military District, Kiev Special Military District, Odessa Military District

Copy to: People's Commissar of the Navy of the USSR

1. During 22nd–23rd of June, 1941, a sudden German attack is possible along the fronts of Leningrad Military District, Baltic Military District, Western Special Military District, Kiev Special Military District, and Odessa Military District. The attack may be preceded by provocations.
2. Mission of our forces—not to fall for any provocations, possibly leading to serious consequences. At the same time, forces of Leningrad, Baltic, Western, Kiev, and Odessa military districts are to be at full combat readiness to meet the possible sudden attack by Germany or its allies.
3. I order:
   - During the night of June 22, 1941, to secretly occupy the firing positions of fortified regions along the state border.
   - Before dawn on June 22, 1941, to disperse and thorough camouflage all aircraft along the field airfields, including army-level aviation.
   - All units to be brought up to full readiness. The forces are to be kept dispersed and concealed.
   - Air defense is to be brought up to full readiness without calling up additional round-out personnel. Prepare all measures for blackout of cities and important objects.
   - Do not take any other measures without specific instructions.

Signed,
Timoshenko, Zhukov

On the crucial night when the above directive was transmitted to Kiev Special Military District, both the district headquarters and headquarters of the Fifth Army were on the move. An earlier directive, received on June 19, ordered these higher headquarters to relocate their operations to their respective field command posts.

The command element of the Fifth Army departed its headquarters in Lutsk after 0100 hours on June 22, headed by its chief of staff, Maj. Gen. D. S. Pisarevskiy. A skeleton crew stayed behind with the army commander Maj.

Gen. Mikhail I. Potapov to continue operations until the alternate post came on line in the woods surrounding Byten collective farm, roughly forty miles northeast of Lutsk. When the alert directive was received in Lutsk around 0230 hours, the convoy bearing Pisarevskiy and the rest of headquarters personnel was just reaching their destination near Byten and was out of touch with Lutsk. With the war being an hour away, General Potapov had no means to reach his command element.

Potapov personally made calls to headquarters of the four corps comprising his Fifth Army, while a duty officer was tasked with calling the army-level support units. The already mentioned XV and XXVII Rifle Corps were deployed directly along the border. Their subordinate units were located anywhere from five to forty miles east of it on roughly north-south axis. The two mechanized corps of the Fifth Army, the 9th and 22nd, were spread out over a significant distance along the west-east axis to the border. The XXII Mechanized Corps was the closest, with its 41st Tank Division being just six miles from the border in Vladimir-Volynskiy. The rest of the corps was over ninety miles east in Rovno. The other mechanized corps, the IX, was farther east, centered on the town of Novograd-Volynskiy, over 150 miles from the border.

Potapov's direct superior, Col. Gen. M. P. Kirponos, was in a similar situation, moving his command post forward from Kiev to Tarnopol. Almost a month earlier, on May 27, 1941, the Soviet General Staff issued orders to all western border districts' headquarters to begin building field command posts with all haste.[15] Despite these instructions, when Timoshenko's orders arrived on June 19 to move Kiev Special Military District's command element to Tarnopol, no such command post was yet prepared. Until Kirponos and his entourage descended on Tarnopol on June 21, the small garrison where his new command post was to be set up was occupied by some minor Soviet rear-echelon unit. It was unceremoniously moved on, and feverish work began bringing the command post to a working condition.

Kirponos and his staff moved in two elements. The first element, carrying the district commander and senior personnel, plus some communications equipment, moved by train in the morning of June 21. They were followed by the rest of headquarters personnel and more equipment in the evening of the same day, moving in a truck and bus convoy commanded by the chief of operations section, Col. Ivan Kh. Bagramyan.

In the early morning of June 22, Kirponos' new command post was not yet fully functional. Thus, commander of the strongest Soviet military district was limited to several telephone lines, routed through the civilian telephone exchanges, and a teletype machine. There were several radio stations set up around Tarnopol, belonging to units garrisoned there, but the use of radio was expressly forbidden until the start of combat operations.[16]

A small staff of several cipher clerks and communications officers was left behind in Kiev to handle all communications traffic until the command post in Tarnopol was set up by the end of June 22. This skeleton crew received Moscow's directive around 0100 hours. After being deciphered, it was then encoded again and forwarded to Tarnopol, were it had to be decoded once more. After Kirponos; his chief of staff, Major General Purkayev; and district's commissar, Nikolay N. Vashugin; evaluated the orders, they were encoded yet again and forwarded down to armies.

This constant conversion of instructions in and out of code resulted in loss of precious time. Notification of first-echelon armies was uneven at best. The Fifth Army received this directive by 0230. However, the Twelfth and Twenty-Sixth armies were notified only around 0400 hrs, when it was already too late. The Sixth Army was not informed of the above directive at all; its commander, Lt. Gen. I. N. Muzychenko sounding an alert based on reports from his own forward troops and border guard outposts. This interim alert order did not filter down to a majority of individual corps and divisions, which had to go directly from peacetime to wartime footing without even a minimal notification period by their commanders.

A major factor in the breakdown of Soviet military communications were pinpoint strikes directed specifically at communication facilities. Up to a week prior to the invasion, small units of German commandos and activated cells of anti-Soviet Ukrainian nationalist OUN organization had been infiltrating the Soviet territory. Now these units struck at vital and vulnerable Soviet installations, adding chaos and confusion behind the Red Army lines. Paramount among these targets were Soviet communications centers. Pending mobilization orders, the Soviet military communications were routed through the civilian telephone and telegraph installations. Now, the German commandos and Ukrainian saboteurs struck at these virtually unguarded soft vital targets, almost instantly blacking out Soviet communications at the main thrust of German invasion. Since the use of military radios were expressly forbidden until the official mobilization orders, and these orders came too late, the loss of regular telephone and telegraph lines left a significant portion of the forward Red Army commands deaf and mute.

As the field-gray masses of German *Wehrmacht* surged across the Soviet border, over four hundred attack aircraft from Luftflotte 4 darted towards the Soviet side overhead. In the period of two hours, the first wave of German aircraft hit twenty-four airfields belonging to Kiev Special Military District.

Even though the total aircraft count of Luftflotte 4 barely reached eight hundred machines, they qualitatively outclassed the 1,939 aircraft in Kirponos' command. The seventeen Soviet fighter regiments numbered 1,296 planes, including 243 new ones. These new models were mainly grouped in the 45th Fighter Division, while the other units had just one or two new aircraft for training. While most of the pilots assigned to the new aircraft had around four hours of flight time on their new machines, a majority of Soviet pilots were well trained on the older I-16 and I-153 fighters.

Bomber aviation of Kiev Special Military District was composed of eleven short-range bomber regiments totaling 349 planes, including 50 new ones. There were also two regiments of ground attack aircraft of older I-153 and I-15 planes. In the reserve of Kiev Special Military District's commander were two fighter regiments, four short range bomber regiments, and two reconnaissance regiments. An additional thirteen combat squadrons and one medical evacuation squadron were assigned directly to covering armies, but most of them were extremely under strength and underequipped and not combat ready.[17]

Even though commander of the air force of Kiev Special Military District, Lt. Gen. E. S. Ptukhin, was more diligent than his counterparts in the other districts about dispersing and camouflaging aircraft, losses were significant. A majority of forward airfields in Kiev Special Military District were dirt strips, often rendered inoperable after rains. There were not enough of reserve airfields. In the spring of 1941, construction battalions began working on improving the existing airfields. However, by the time the war started, not a single airfield had finished its upgrades. Moreover, many of them, due to construction in progress, were rendered even less operable. This caused the aircraft to be bunched up on their airfields without adequate air defense artillery.[18]

Along with orders on June 19 about building field command posts, western border districts received instructions about dispersing and camouflaging aircraft. In addition to this directive, General Ptukhin demanded that aircraft shelters be built at every airfield. However, he neither allotted funds nor resources for this endeavor. And, anyway, there was no time.

Since there weren't sufficient airfields on which to disperse the aircraft, a majority of commanders limited their efforts to spreading the aircraft around the perimeter of their existing airfields, often in squadron formations. On many airfields, the Soviet aircraft lined up almost wingtip-to-wingtip, presenting mouth-watering targets for German fliers. During the first day of war, air force units of Kiev Special Military District lost 301 aircraft.[19] According to various sources, between 174 and 277 of them were destroyed or damaged on the ground. Total losses amounted to roughly 16 percent of available aircraft, a serious but not fatal blow.[20] Success achieved by the German Air Force over its Soviet counterpart resulted not in one devastating opening blow, but in the systematic reduction of Soviet airfields and assets.

Lack of adequate housing near the airfields resulted in majority of Soviet pilots leaving on Saturdays to spend the weekends with their families in bigger towns and cities. Therefore, by attacking in the early Sunday morning, the Germans ensured that the overwhelming majority of Soviet pilots would be away from their aircraft. By the time Soviet aviators began trickling in to their units on June 22, their airfields were already undergoing second, third, or fourth attacks, and significant numbers of their aircraft were destroyed.

On the fateful morning of June 22, the 17th Fighter Regiment from 14th Mixed Air Division was based at Velitsk airfield, near Kovel. Twenty-year-old Lt. Fedor Arkhipenko was the duty officer at the airfield the night of the 21st–22nd. As was normal practice, a majority of married officers from the 17th Fighter Regiment was away from the airfield for the weekend with their families in Kovel. Only one pilot was on flight duty that night—Arkhipenko's section leader, Senior Lieutenant Ibragimov with his I-153 plane. The previous evening was quiet, and Arkhipenko stopped by the officer's club at the edge of the airfield to arrange a date with his girlfriend, a Polish girl named Yadviga, for the next day, Sunday, June 22.

Around 0325 hours, Arkhipenko was contemplating getting off duty shortly and catching up on his sleep. Shattering explosions brought him to a harsh reality as multiple German aircraft descended upon his airfield. Years later, Arkhipenko still remembered that German planes flew so low that he could see one gunner, whom he mistook for a woman because the German's long hair was sticking out from under his helmet.[21] The bombing was heavy. Before there even was a chance to evaluate the damages from the first strike, the second arrived.

Arkhipenko's unit could not oppose the German bombers: a majority of pilots were gone, and there was no air defense artillery at the airfield. As the flight and technical personnel began dribbling in, they began individual sorties by Soviet pilots. Before noon, the air base was bombed four times.

Years later, now a general, Arkhipenko wrote:

> In reality, in this extremely difficult situation there was no leadership at the airfield. I, the duty officer Junior Lieutenant Fedor Arkhipenko, incompetently attempted to organize sporadic individual sorties and evacuate damaged planes. Communications were cut, there were no directions or orders; only the internal telephone lines, laid towards the squadron's parking area, miraculously survived.[22]

Around 1100 hours another regiment of I-153s landed at his airfield, flying in from deeper in the district. Even though there were plenty of officers senior to Arkhipenko in the newly arrived regiment, none of them assisted him in running the airfield. Arkhipenko thought that they were from Zhitomir; however, since the only air regiment based directly in Zhitomir was the 315th Reconnaissance Regiment, this unit was most likely from the 44th Air Division in Vinnitsa-Uman area.

To Arkhipenko's immense relief, deputy commander of the 14th Mixed Air Division, Maj. Gen. I. A. Lakeyev, arrived around 1300 hours. The experienced flier, veteran of wars in Spain and Finland, took over command of the airfield. Arkhipenko's plane was still undamaged, and he requested Lakeyev to permit him to scramble. However, the general did not let him go—the junior lieutenant was the general's whole staff. The regimental command post was now manned by a general, a junior lieutenant, and two privates from communications section.

When Germans attacked the airfield for the third time, a scratch flight of three Soviet fighters were taxiing on the runway. None of them made it into the air.

Around 1400 hours, 17th Fighter Regiment's commander, Major Dervyanov, finally arrived, and Arkhipenko was allowed to leave the command post. [Why did it take regimental commander ten hours to get to his headquarters, less than twenty miles away from his residence in Kovel?] Arkhipenko's plane was still intact, being camouflaged at the edge of the cemetery. He took off by himself, without waiting for orders. At the same time, a flight of fighters from Vinnitsa Regiment was also taking off, and they almost collided in midair. Arkihpenko tucked in behind them. This demonstrates that despite the presence of at least one regimental commander and a general at the airfield, flight operations were still not organized or monitored.

In his memoirs, Arkhipenko remembered that they first flew together north to Brest and then along the border south to Rava-Russkaya. Again, why had they flown so far out of their area of operation, all the way to Brest? Did they have specific instructions, or did they get lost? Arkhipenko does not clarify this detail. He recalled that the whole border looked aflame, as if the very earth itself was burning. West of Vladimir-Volynskiy, they were fired upon by German antiaircraft artillery, and Arkhipenko developed a severe distaste for flack.

After the other three fighters dove into the clouds to escape fire, he broke off and flew east. Soon, Arkhipenko encountered another solo Soviet aircraft like his, and they flew together to Velitsk. They landed among the nightmarish landscape of burning aircraft, collapsed buildings, mangled bodies of the dead, and screaming wounded.

Arkhipenko's first combat sortie is another vivid example of confusion into which the Soviet Air Force was thrown: a flight of fighters manages to get into the air without instructions from any controller; seemingly aimlessly flying in and out their area of operations, and returning without engaging the enemy.

Despite an undoubtedly severely damaging first strike, numbers of Soviet fighters managed to get into the air, especially from the airfields located deeper in the Soviet territory. Upon return, many of them increasingly found their airfields damaged and more aircraft put out of action in consecutive attacks. Russian historian A. V. Isayev writes: "Destruction of significant part of the aircraft park of KSMD [Kiev Special Military District] on the airfields was only a matter of time. If the decisive success was not achieved during the first strike, the German pilots succeeded during second, third, and sometimes, tenth strike."[23]

Soviet reinforcements flying in from deeper in Ukraine were forced to land on the airfields already known to and damaged by the Germans. The already mentioned 17th Fighter Regiment based at the Velitsk airfield was finished off on the third day of war:

> In the morning of the third day, a dozen Me-109 fighters arrived. They formed two circles: six aircraft turning right and six—to the left, and began diving as if on exercises. They shot true, confident, as if at [practice] targets. As the result, there were ten combat-capable I-153 and one MiG-1 remaining, the rest of aircraft, numbering around 150—were damaged. They included . . . aircraft from Zhitomir Regiment [reinforcements].[24]

Since a majority of Kiev Special Military District's fighter regiments, fifteen out of seventeen, were assigned to forward armies, a majority of them were destroyed in the first few days of war, virtually ceding the skies over the border region to the Germans.

The Soviet aircraft that did manage to get airborne were immediately outnumbered by German Bf 109 fighters from Jagdgeschwader 3 under Maj. Gunther Lutzow. OberLieutnant Robert Olenik from the 1st Squadron of this wing scored their first air victory at 0430 hours, shooting down a Soviet I-16 fighter.

German aircraft of the Luftflotte 4 were still to meet large numbers of Soviet aircraft. Further east, aircraft of Soviet 17th, 19th, and 44th Air Divisions began moving closer to the border. Despite definitely gaining initiative, the German Air Force did not achieve complete air domination in western Ukraine, as it did in Byelorussia in the area of operations of Western Special Military District. Already on the very first day of the war, despite terrible odds, the 62nd Air Division of the Fifth Army was attacking advancing German units in the area of Ustilug, dropping 134 50-kilogram bombs.[25]

In the above-mentioned action in the afternoon of June 22, aircraft from 17th and 89th Fighter regiments escorted bombers from 62nd Bomber Division. While they were away, Germans visited their home airfields, destroying thirty-six fighter planes and seven bombers. Another Soviet joint fighter/bomber attack by thirty-six bombers supported by fighters was carried out at 1840 in the same area. This mission cost dearly: fourteen bombers were lost to German fighters.[26]

Despite individual bravery demonstrated by Soviet fliers, their efforts initially came largely to naught due to lack of cohesive actions and coordination. Senior air force leadership was out of touch with its subordinate elements from the very first moments of the invasion. Accompanying the rest of Kiev Special Military District headquarters personnel, General Ptukhin and his Air Force staff were also on the move to Tarnopol at the start of the invasion. Ptukhin's detachment started off in Bagramyan's wheeled column in the morning of June 21. Until they set up shop in Tarnopol, Ptukhin left a small detachment in Kiev, under his deputy chief of staff, Major General Maltsev, along with a small group of staff officers and several cipher clerks. This follow-on element was to maintain communications with all the airfields in Kiev Special Military District until the main air force command post in Tarnopol would be set up.[27]

While Ptukhin's staff was frantically working on setting up their new command post, air units around Tarnopol were taking severe beating. Then-Colonel Nikolay S. Skripko related description of events at the nearby

Buchach airfield, related to him by then-Major I. S. Suldin, commander of the 87th Fighter Regiment belonging to the 44th Mixed Air Division of the Sixth Army.

Even though normally a majority of married pilots and staff went to their families on Saturdays, on this particular weekend, division commander, most likely arriving at correct analysis, did not permit anyone to leave their units. The 87th Fighter Regiment had the following combat-capable aircraft: sixty older I-16 fighters and four new MiG-3s. Ten other I-16s were to be transferred to the 36th Air Division the next day, and pilots from that unit were also at the airfield.

Skripko writes:

> A telegram was received from division [headquarters] . . . at 0430 [hours]: "According to reports, German aviation is bombing border towns of Peremyshl, Rava-Russkaya, and others. Bring the regiment to combat readiness." The duty officer, squadron commander Senior Lieutenant P. A. Mikhailyuk, sounded alarm. Pilots, engineers, technicians, and maintenance crews took their places near the fighters. . . . The pilots from the 36th Air Division took places at their just-received ten planes and started up their engines. It seemed that combat readiness was full. But a serious mistake was made, for which many were made to suffer. Approximately at 0450 hours, barely visible in the raising sun, a two-engine bomber was spotted approaching from the east. Everybody thought that the division commander was coming to check on regiment's readiness. But that was a German Ju-88 bomber. On a strafing run, he attacked the planes lined up in a row. Seeing the crosses on the bomber, the soldiers around the airfield opened rifle fire on him. But it was too late. The German plane accurately dropped small fragmentation bombs and fired machine guns at the personnel: out of ten lined-up aircraft, seven completely burned down, two pilots sitting in the cockpits were killed, and two maintenance crewmen were wounded.[28]

Even though Bagramyan's column managed to get to Tarnopol on time, at least according to Bagramyan's claims, Ptukhin and his staff fell behind and only made it to Tarnopol around 1400 hours on June 22. *This meant that for almost ten crucial hours, the commander of the Air Force of Kiev Special Military District was isolated on the road and out of touch with his command* [emphasis added].[29]

Finally arriving in Tarnopol, Ptukhin and his staff managed to establish communications only with the 14th, 16th, and 17th Air divisions and with Kiev staff. Contact with the other units was possible only by routing communications through the Kiev headquarters. Back in Kiev, General Maltsev's group served as a clearing-house between Tarnopol and those air force units that could be reached.

An unforeseen crucial situation developed at this juncture. The small air force staff element in Kiev strictly adhered to protocol of only sending encoded messages. However, the few cipher clerks left behind in Kiev with Maltsev could not possibly handle the sudden avalanche of reports that needed processing. Nobody could have foreseen that the invasion would catch Ptukhin's element in transit to the new headquarters. There was simply no visible need at the time to leave more cipher clerks with Maltsev.

Now the reports began to bottleneck in Kiev. Received information needed to be decoded, evaluated, and disposition decided. Outgoing reports needed to be encoded and transmitted. Maltsev's small group was not equipped or staffed to cope with their sudden task during the most crucial hours of the invasion and became overwhelmed by the avalanche of communiqués. Only by evening of June 22 was Ptukhin able to somewhat sort things out and ascertain damages inflicted upon his command.

Ptukhin and Maltsev paid the steep price for all oversights, real or imagined. They were relieved of command the following week and shot a month later.

The convoy, in which General Ptukhin started out his trip from Kiev, was constantly suffering mechanical breakdowns. Colonel Ivan Kh. Bagramyan, in charge of the convoy, was becoming concerned that this unplanned loss of time would delay their scheduled arrival in Tarnopol by seven hours. Still, he prudently instituted periodic ten-minute stops to inspect the vehicles and do minor preventive maintenance.

At daybreak, when his convoy was halted just north of Brody, Bagramyan heard an increasing howl of aircraft engines overhead. "Our pilots starting their day a bit early," Bagramyan thought.[30] Soon, shattering explosions and oily clouds of fire rising above Brody made the situation brutally clear. War!

They raced through the waking town and made it the remaining forty miles to Tarnopol. On their way they were strafed by German aircraft once, causing several light casualties. More vehicles broke down, and Bagramyan decided to abandon them on the road, leaving their drivers to do their best to fix the vehicles and rejoin the headquarters. It is unknown but possible that General Ptukhin's delayed arrival in Tarnopol was caused by such breakdown.

Still, in spite of all delays, the mad dash from Brody allowed Bagramyan to make up lost time, even arriving in Tarnopol slightly ahead of schedule.

As Bagramyan's column rolled up to the new location of Kiev Special Military District's headquarters, he was expected. The front door flew open, and worried Major General Purkayev, Bagramyan's boss, ran down the steps. Interrupting Bagramyan's salutation, Purkayev ordered: "Unload quickly and get to work! Use all communication channels to alert commanders of the second-echelon corps to implement plan KOVO-41! Insist on confirmation of orders and report them to me!"[31]

Purkayev was followed by Col. Gen. Mikhail P. Kirponos himself. Bagramyan was taken aback when Kirponos began loudly and angrily lambasting him for arriving late. "Things must have gone really badly," Bagramyan thought, watching red-faced district commander who normally was very calm and collected. The colonel attempted to explain that he actually arrived before schedule, and it calmed Kirponos down a bit. He stomped off, ordering Bagramyan to be ready with a situation report in an hour. Kirponos' unfortunate tendency to lose his head under pressure was remarked upon by other memoir writers as well.

Bagramyan rushed to find General Dobrykin, Kiev Special Military District's chief of communications, whom he found huddled with several junior officers. The telephone lines, routed mainly through civilian exchanges, were constantly suffering breakdowns. While communications with Moscow were relatively reliable, connections with the armies at the border were tentative at best.

As in all other border districts, district-level signal units were supposed to be activated upon mobilization and their equipment was largely to come from the civilian sector. The sudden German attack caught Kirponos without vital communications means and personnel, immediately handicapping his ability to keep in touch with his units.

Dobrykin brought Bagramyan up to speed. Communications with the Twelfth and Twenty-Sixth armies were reliable. The Twelfth Army reported that the border with Hungary was quiet. The Twenty-Sixth Army reported some fighting along its front, but situation stable overall. However, there was virtually no contact with Fifth or Sixth armies. As the sketchy and disjointed reports began coming in, it appeared that the main German attack fell on these two armies.

Chief of Intelligence Colonel Bondarev had very little to add: Germans crossed the Western Bug River on the far right, several small border towns were captured, and Germans were conducting major artillery and air strikes in the areas of Ustilug and Vladimir-Volynskiy. However, there was absolutely no reliable information about German strength or composition. At this point, only several small units moved forward and engaged the invaders.

After listening to Bagramyan's meager report, Kirponos flew into a rage at the lack of communications. General Purkayev interceded on behalf of his subordinate, informing Kirponos that efforts at reestablishing and maintaining communications were given top priority and liaison officers had been dispatched by planes to all army headquarters.[32]

Reports continued slowly trickling in. Around 1030 hours came the first radio report from Fifth Army: "Sokal and Tartakov on fire. The 124th Rifle Division could not fight through to the border and took up defensive positions north of Strumilov Fortified District."[33]

In midafternoon, telegram from Timoshenko in Moscow arrived:

> On June 22, 1941, at 0400 hours German aviation without any provocation attacked our airfields and cities along the border and subjected them to bombardment. Simultaneously, German forces opened artillery fire along many points and crossed our border. Due to this brazen attack by Germany upon the Soviet Union, I order:
>
> 1. Our troops to use all force and means to attack enemy forces and destroy them in the areas where they violated Soviet border. Our ground forces are not to cross the border without specific orders to do so.
>
> 2. Reconnaissance and combat aviation is to identify areas of concentration of enemy ground and air forces. [German] main concentrations of ground forces are to be bombed and [their] aviation destroyed on their airfields by mighty blows of our bomber aviation. Air attacks are to be carried out to the depth of 100–150 km [sixty to ninety-two miles] of German territory. Koenigsberg and Memel are to be bombed. Territories of Finland and Rumania are not to be attacked without special orders.

The staff of Kiev Special Military District was supposed to send its first situation report to Moscow at 1500 hours. Bagramyan later wrote in his memoirs that this document was the most difficult one he had to prepare in his career as staff officer.

> The picture still remained unclear: What was the real situation of the armies? Where was the main push by the enemy? What are his intentions?—we could only guess about these things. And our first combat

report to Moscow was full of generalities and unclarities. Because of this, although guiltless, my aides and I could not but feel ourselves guilty.[34]

From fragmentary data coming in, by evening of 22nd of June the picture began clearing up: the main thrust was in the areas of Ustilug and Sokal at the junction of Fifth and Sixth Armies. The main invasion axis was directed towards Lutsk and Dubno. At the same time, there was heavy fighting in the sectors of Sixth and Twenty-Sixth Armies, especially around Rava-Russka and Peremyshl.

General Kirponos was informed that enemy tanks were rushing for Radekhov. These were the leading elements of the 11th Panzer Division, which was moving through defensive lines of the 124th Rifle Division. Still not knowing the exact strength of German units advancing on Radekhov, Kirponos ordered the main body of XV Mechanized Corps to be moved there to meet the developing threat. Its 10th Tank division was approximately forty miles from Radekhov. Who would get there first? Kirponos and his staff were well aware that even if the 10th Tank Division could reach Radekhov ahead of Germans, the XV Mechanized Corps overall would still enter the fight piecemeal.

Major General Ignatiy I. Karpezo, commander of the XV Mechanized Corps, soon reported that his 10th Tank Division had already set off, but only four tank battalions of the 37th Tank Division were on the move. His 212th Motorized Rifle Division was marching on foot due to lack of wheeled transport. The corps signal and combat engineer battalions and the motorcycle regiment could not move at all—no transport. Karpezo was urgently requesting transportation.

Kirponos told Purkayev to find out what could be done to help the XV Mechanized Corps. Purkayev instructed Bagramyan to find out if any trucks could be taken from local civilian infrastructure. While seeing to this task, Bagramyan found General Morgunov, chief of Auto-Armor Directorate of Kiev Special Military District, and asked him for at least one transportation battalion. Morgunov had nothing at hand. Almost all transportation units under direct command of Kiev Special Military District were already employed moving forward the several rifle corps from deeper within the district. There was a small reserve vehicle park left around Shepetovka, almost two hundred miles away, but it would take some time to move them to Tarnopol.[35] Thus, Karpezo received reply: "Carry on with your orders."

Similar requests came from Major General Feklenko's IX Mechanized Corps and Major General Rokossovskiy's 19th, both located deeper within the district's territory. Since Rokossovskiy's and Feklenko's corps were urgently needed at the border, they were given priority with all trucks coming in from the civilian sector. Also, Kirponos ordered Morgunov to immediately move forty trucks from Shepetovka to Feklenko.

Bagramyan later wrote in his memoirs: "By the evening of 22nd of June nobody at the front's headquarters could think about the possibility of immediate counterattack. We could barely hold! Everybody was convinced that further directives from Moscow would be aimed at defensive actions."[36]

However, when the next directive arrived around 2300 hours, it was a rude shock to the command element of the Kiev Special Military District, renamed into wartime South-Western Front. This Directive #3 from the People's Committee of Defense bore General Zhukov's signature. Years later in his memoirs, Zhukov claimed that he was not the author of this directive, but was ordered to sign it by Stalin.[37]

While correctly determining that the main thrust was at the juncture of Fifth and Sixth armies, this directive was downplaying enemy gains, stating that in most places German attacks have been halted or achieved only minor penetrations. Bagramyan could not help thinking that this optimism in Moscow was partially caused by his staff's overly cautious report. He tried to justify their inadequate reporting by stating that around 1500 hours, when they sent in their first report, they had no information yet about the breakthroughs of two strong enemy panzer forces at Sokal and Vladimir-Volynskiy—they received this concrete news only in late afternoon.

After the war, while writing memoirs and poring over the first intelligence reports, Bagramyan saw how easily the situation was misinterpreted. From the reports issued by Kirponos' staff, it appeared that only five or six enemy divisions were attacking in the area of Fifth Army. This would not have been seen as very alarming by Moscow due to the fact that the Fifth Army had four divisions of its own near the border. The first intelligence summary sent to Moscow by the South-Western Front made the following conclusion estimating the attacking German forces:

> The Lutsk [Fifth Army] direction: four–five infantry and one panzer
> division; the Rava-Russkaya-Lvov [Sixth Army] direction: three–four

infantry divisions with [some] tanks; the Peremyshl-Lvov [Twenty-Sixth Army] direction: two–three infantry divisions; the Chernovtsy [Twelfth Army] direction: four Rumanian infantry divisions.[38]

"It is possible that similar mistakes in evaluating correlation of forces which invaded us took place at the other fronts as well," Bagramyan wrote.[39]

Regardless of the reasoning upon which its decision was made, the Soviet High Command issued its infamous Directive #3:

> While maintaining strong defense of the state border with Hungary, the 5th and 6th armies are to carry out concentric strikes in the direction of Lyublin, utilizing at least five mechanized corps and aviation of the [South-Western] Front, in order to encircle and destroy the enemy group of forces advancing along the front Vladimir-Volynski–Krystonopol, and by the end of June 24th to capture the vicinity of Lyublin.[40]

To Bagramyan and Purkayev these orders were plainly unrealistic: at the present time they would be lucky just to hold on. Lyublin, located roughly eighty miles on the *other* side of the border, was as unreachable as the moon. Purkayev took Bagramyan with him to see Kirponos.

Upon receiving these news, Kirponos immediately called for Vashugin. Predictably, Commissar Vashugin was enthusiastic about attacking. Purkayev plunged into an argument with Vashugin, trying to convince the party hack about the necessity of defense, not attack. Purkayev tried to reason with him, pointing out that against the ten already-identified infantry and panzer German divisions between Sokal and Lyuboml, they could only place four weak rifle divisions. At best, on June 23 two more divisions could come up, the 135th Rifle and, maybe, the 41st Tank Division, of which there were still no news. They did not know yet that without contact with his superiors, the commander of the 41st Tank Division broke open his red envelope and moved his unit from Vladimir-Volynski to Kovel, away from the fighting, where the XXII Mechanized Corps was to concentrate in accordance with pre-war plans.

Therefore, Purkayev continued, by tomorrow they could have six divisions against ten German ones, not even taking into account additional divisions which the Germans were sure to send in to exploit the breakthroughs. Of the approaching reserve corps, the XXXI and XXXVI Rifle Corps would need five or six days to arrive, the IX and XIX Mechanized Corps were still three to four days away. The IV, VIII, XV, and XXII Mechanized Corps could be ready in a day or two. He especially stressed the fact that neither the armies nor the South-Western Front itself had rear echelon support structures, because they had not been mobilized yet.

General Purkayev went as far as making an outrageous suggestion that Kirponos tell Moscow the real situation and insistently request to change the mission. Purkayev wanted permission to organize strong defenses along the pre-1939 border using the second echelon units. Only after halting the Germans along the old border, he argued, any thoughts of offensive could be entertained.

As was fast becoming his habit, Kirponos deferred to Vashugin, who spoke up first. In the dual-command structure of the Red Army, Commissar Vashugin was the dominating personality in this particular symbiotic relationship with Kirponos. While demonstrably a capable division commander, Kirponos was promoted beyond his ability to command the Kiev Special Military District, the most powerful one in the Soviet military establishment. Unfortunately for him, and tens of thousands of Soviet soldiers, this rise in rank was not accompanied by a rise in experience. Additionally, his mild-mannered persona was completely overshadowed by the bombastic Commissar Vashugin.

True to himself, Vashugin pointed out that while Purkayev was correct from the military standpoint, this was the narrow view of a specialist, not taking into account the morale factor: "Did you know what kind of morale damage this would be, when we, after nurturing the Red Army in high offensive spirit, would order a passive defense in the very first days of war?!"

Seeing Purkayev unconvinced and ready to contest the point further, Vashugin calmly played his trump card: "You know . . . if I would not have known you as a tested Bolshevik, I would have thought you panicked!"[41] While Purkayev was ready to explode, Kirponos intervened.

Playing the peacemaker, Kirponos stated that they both were right. According to Kirponos, while correct overall, Purkayev overlooked that fact that the fortified districts along the old border were not ready for defense. He brushed off Purkayev's retort that they could be rapidly brought up to partial readiness by utilizing combat and construction engineer units.

Kirponos continued. While it was obvious that they could not take Lyublin by the end of the 24th, they were still obligated to counterattack. Thus, they now needed to concentrate on rapidly bringing the five mechanized corps towards the developing area of main battle and conduct a coordinated attack. Commander of the Fifth Army, General Potapov, was to do everything possible to hold what he got. The IV, VIII, and XV Mechanized corps would attack from the south, while the IX, XIX, and XXII Mechanized corps would strike from the east and northeast. The XXXVII Rifle Corps was to cover Tarnopol from the northwest with two of its rifle divisions. Its third division would be held in reserve of the South-Western Front near Tarnopol.

This was it, then. While Vashugin expressed his loud and enthusiastic agreement, Purkayev and Bagramyan quietly left and began preparing for an offensive which they believed suicidal. They understood that Kirponos would not change his mind for fear of being labeled as defeatist and panic-monger, even if he knew them to be correct. All Soviet officers knew that the punishment for an even perceived display of inability to carry out orders and accomplish the mission was an arrest by NKVD and swift execution.

The two senior staff officers had to make plans with meager assets available to them. The VIII and XV Mechanized Corps were still out of position. The IV Mechanized Corps became involved in local fighting along the front of the Sixth Army and could not disengage in time to participate in the general counterattack. Therefore, the Fifth Army under General Potapov would have to carry out the counterattack alone.

Year later in his memoirs, *Reminiscences and Thoughts*, Marshal Zhukov acknowledged that instructions about carrying the war into enemy territory were *premature* [emphasis added]. He, however, defended these orders by stating that nobody in the senior Soviet command echelons knew the main direction of enemy's push nor the German strength. Zhukov attempted to distance himself from the fiasco, stating that this directive was composed and disseminated according to a decision by Stalin and People's Commissar for Defense S. K. Timoshenko, without Zhukov's input.

Major General Potapov's Fifth Army, which was to be the leading force in the counterattack, was in woefully inadequate shape for the task. It is the clear indication of terror under which Stalin held his military commanders that Kirponos was willing to knowingly commit inadequate forces rather than even to attempt to change or postpone the mission. The four forward rifle divisions of the Fifth Army were pinned down by the enemy, plus the 41st Tank Division was out of contact at Kovel and feared lost. Consequently, the three divisions of the Fifth Army which had not been engaged yet would have to form the strike force of the counteroffensive. These units were the 135th Rifle Division of the XXVII Rifle Corps and two divisions of the XXII Mechanized Corps, the 19th Tank, and the 215th Motorized Rifle. However, even the participation of the 135th Rifle Division was still questionable. In its Situation Report #1, forwarded to Moscow at 2000 hours on June 22, Major General Purkayev stated that as of 1800 hours location of the above division was still unknown.[42] This rifle division was advancing to the border incommunicado, and it was Kirponos' wishful thinking that it would be informed of its mission in time to participate in the offensive the next day.

The jump-off time for the counterattack was set for 2200 hours on June 23. However, while advancing towards the border, these three divisions were discovered by German reconnaissance aircraft and subjected to severe air attacks. Besides inflicting casualties and destroying invaluable vehicles and equipment, the air attacks caused significant time delay. Thus, the counterattack was later postponed until 0400 hours on June 24.

After receiving his marching orders, Major General Potapov, in turn, had no doubts that the proposed counterattack was doomed to failure. His chief of staff, Major General Pisarevskiy, suggested that they at least keep the motorcycle regiment of the XXII Mechanized Corps as their last reserve since committal of the three above-mentioned divisions on June 23 would leave them without any unengaged major units. Potapov approved his suggestion, wondering if the Moscow leadership had lost their collective mind.

During the night of June 21–22, a majority of officers at the General Staff and People's Committee for Defense in Moscow were ordered to remain at their posts. Timoshenko and Zhukov were constantly on the phone with border district commanders, receiving information updates. Everybody was tense from incoming multiple reports about increasing German activity along the border.

At 0307 hours, Timoshenko received a call from the Black Sea Fleet commander, Adm. F. S. Oktyabrskiy, informing him that naval forward listening posts were reporting an approach of a large number of unidentified aircraft from the sea. The fleet was standing by, and Oktyabrskiy was requesting instructions. Zhukov, who was in Timoshenko's office, asked him what he wanted to do. The admiral replied: open fire on the unidentified aircraft. After a quick consultation with Timoshenko, Zhukov gave Oktyabrskiy permission to open fire.

Things started happening fast after that. From 0315 hours calls began coming in from commanders of Baltic, Western, and Kiev military districts with reports of air attacks by German aircraft.

At 0430 hours Timoshenko and Zhukov met with Stalin and selected members of Politburo (Politburo, short for Political Bureau, was the Soviet supreme governing body) in Kremlin. After a short discussion, a call was placed to the German embassy with request for explanations. As the reply, the German ambassador Count von Shulenburg requested an urgent meeting with the Soviet foreign minister, Vyacheslav Molotov, which was immediately granted.

The Soviet leadership awaited Molotov's return amid further disjointed news from the western frontier. Every passing minute added to the list of more and more Soviet cities subjected to German bombing and Red Army and Air Force units coming under attack. At last Molotov arrived. His opening statement dispelled any doubts as to German intentions: "The German government declared war on us."[43] Back at their headquarters, Zhukov and Timoshenko were struggling with lack of communications:

> Without having communications, army commanders and some district commanders went directly to forward units to find out the situation for themselves. But because the events unfolded so rapidly, this method of command further complicated situation. District headquarters were receiving the most conflicting information from various sources, often inflammatory and panicked in character. . . .
>
> Until 9 a.m. we were not able to find out anything of significance, because the [Districts'] headquarters and [their] commanders could not receive concrete information about the enemy from headquarters of armies and corps. They simply did not know where and in what strength the German units were advancing, where the enemy was striking main blows and where the secondary ones, where his armored and mechanized units were operating.[44]

At noon all the staff officers gathered around the radio. Amid slight crackling, Molotov's voice, minutely shaking, but strong, came through:

> Citizens of the Soviet Union! The Soviet Government and its head, Comrade Stalin, authorized me to make the following statement:
>
> Today at 4 a.m., without making any demands upon the Soviet Union, without declaration of war, the German forces invaded our country, attacked our borders in many locations, and their aircraft bombed our cities: Zhitomir, Kiev, Sevastopol, Kaunas, and some others, killing and wounding over two hundred people. Air attacks and artillery bombardment were also conducted from Rumanian and Finnish territories.
>
> This unheard-of attack upon our county is an unprecedented travesty in the history of civilized countries. The attack on our country

was perpetuated despite the fact that a treaty of nonaggression had been signed between the USSR and Germany and that the Soviet Government most faithfully abided by all provisions of this treaty. The attack upon our country was perpetrated despite the fact that during the entire period of operation of this treaty, the German Government could not find grounds for a single complaint against the USSR as regards observance of this treaty. Complete responsibility for this treacherous attack upon the Soviet Union completely and totally falls upon the German Fascist rulers.

After the attack took place, at 5:30 a.m. Von Schulenburg, the German ambassador in Moscow, made the statement to me, as the People's Commissar for Foreign Affairs, in the name of his government, that the German Government decided to enter into war against the Soviet Union in connection with the concentration of Red Army units near the eastern German border.

In reply to this, in the name of the Soviet Government, I stated that until the last moments the German Government did not make any demands upon the Soviet Government, that Germany attacked the Soviet Union despite the peaceful stance of the Soviet Union, and in this the Fascist Germany is the aggressor.

On instruction of the government of the Soviet Union I also stated that at no point had our troops or our air force committed a violation of the frontier and that the statement made this morning by the Rumanian radio to the effect that Soviet aircraft allegedly had fired on Rumanian airfields is a sheer lie and provocation.

Likewise, the whole declaration made today by Hitler is a lie and provocation by Hitler, who is trying belatedly to concoct accusations charging the Soviet Union with failure to observe the Soviet-German pact.

Now, when the attack against the Soviet Union is an accomplished fact, the Soviet Government orders our troops to repulse the treacherous attack and drive the German forces from our territory.

This war has been forced upon us, not by the German people, not by German workers, peasants, and intellectuals, whose sufferings we well understand, but by the clique of bloodthirsty Fascist rulers of Germany who have enslaved Frenchmen, Czechs, Poles, Serbians, Norway, Belgium, Denmark, Holland, Greece, and other nations.

This is not the first time that our people have had to deal with an attack of an arrogant foe. At the time of Napoleon's invasion of Russia our people's reply was war for the fatherland, and Napoleon suffered defeat and met his doom.

It will be the same with Hitler, who in his arrogance has proclaimed a new crusade against our country. The Red Army and our whole people will again wage victorious war for the fatherland, for our country, for honor, for liberty.

The Government of the Soviet Union expresses its unshakable confidence in that our glorious Army and Navy and the brave falcons of the Soviet Aviation will honorably carry out their duties to the Motherland, the Soviet people, and deliver a crushing blow upon the aggressor.

Our whole nation now must be united as one as never before. Each one of us must demand from ourselves and others discipline, order, and self-sacrifice worthy of the real Soviet patriot in order to ensure that all the needs of the Red Army, Navy, and Air Force, in order to ensure the victory over the enemy.

The Government calls upon you, the citizens of the Soviet Union, to even tighter close ranks around our Soviet Bolshevik Party, around our Soviet government, around our great leader Comrade Stalin.

Our cause is just. The enemy will be defeated. Victory will be ours.

Late at night on June 22, as the western Soviet frontier continued to be ripped apart by flames and explosions, Colonel General Kirponos' staff sent off another report to Moscow. Like the first report, intentional or not, and most likely lacking the actual knowledge of the situation, it was another sketchy one. It estimated German strength facing the South-Western Front at somewhat between twelve to fifteen divisions, including several armored and mechanized. Kirponos and his staff were oblivious as to the depth of German penetration or even where the most threatening incursions occurred. Most significantly, they did not know that a major gap was kicked open between the flanks of Fifth and Sixth armies, and the German mechanized forces were rapidly probing in depth.

In his memoirs, Zhukov stated that he arrived at Kirponos' headquarters around midnight on this first night of war. Alarmed by lack of cohesive actions at the border, Josef Stalin sent out several high-ranking military personages to the front in order to oversee the matters and report back directly to him. General Georgiy Zhukov, chief of staff of the Red Army and former commander of Kiev Special Military District, was the natural choice to as an emissary to the South-Western Front. However, it is highly unlikely that Zhukov was able to reach Kirponos' headquarters by midnight. He definitely had time to arrive there the following night, June 23. Zhukov was accompanied by Nikita Khruschev, the future Soviet premier. Up until the start of the war, Khruschev was Stalin's appointee as the first secretary of the Central Committee in Ukraine, the highest Communist Party assignment there. Now, Khrushchev put on a uniform and was assigned by Stalin as another member of Military Council of the South-Western Front.

General Franz Halder, chief of German General Staff, was much better informed about the situation along Soviet border. At the end of the day, he wrote in his now-famous war diary:

> The enemy was surprised by the German attack. His forces were not in tactical disposition for defense. The troops in the border zone were widely scattered in their quarters. The frontier itself was for the most part weakly guarded. As a result of this tactical surprise, enemy resistance directly on the border was weak and disorganized, and we succeeded everywhere in seizing the bridges across the border rivers and in piercing the defense positions (field fortifications) near the frontier.[45]

▶ CHAPTER 7

Creaking to the Sound of the Guns, June 22

IN THE EVENING OF JUNE 22, summoned by orders from headquarters of the South-Western Front, Soviet forces began concentrating towards their staging areas for the counterattack. On paper, the Soviet mechanized forces slowly advancing to meet the German armored thrust looked very formidable. However, the six mechanized corps earmarked for the offensive on June 24 were a mixed bag of older and new combat vehicles, experienced soldiers and raw recruits, suffering shortages of vital equipment, supplies, and armament.

Some of these formations belonged to combined-arms armies covering the border. The XXII Mechanized Corps belonged to the Fifth Army; the IV and XV Mechanized, to the Sixth Army; the VIII Mechanized, to the Twenty-Sixth Army. Two more mechanized corps, the IX and XIX, were part of reserves of South-Western Front and were moving up from the areas of pre-1939 border.

In addition to the above units, six more large formations were on the move: the 1st Anti-Tank Artillery Brigade and five rifle corps: XXXI, XXXVI, XXXVII, XLIX, and LV. Out of these five rifle corps, only two, the XXXI and XXXVI, were approaching the area of operations of Soviet Fifth Army. The other three were aimed farther south. In accordance with orders received from Moscow on June 15, the reserve rifle corps of Kiev Special Military District began marching towards the border on June 17. In order to ensure that Germany was not aware of their move, these corps upon arrival at their designated areas were to be deployed in concealed positions, usually in the woods, within several days' march from the border. They were to move only at night, needing eight to fifteen days to arrive at their predetermined locations. The XXXI Rifle Corps was to concentrate near Kovel, behind the right flank of the Fifth Army; the XXXVI Rifle Corps, around Dubno, behind the left.[1]

XXII MECHANIZED CORPS

As previously mentioned, the 41st Tank Division was located relatively close to the border and lost contact with its parent XXII Mechanized Corps right at conflict's opening. In addition to being away from its parent formation, the division itself was widely separated. Its main body, comprised of two tank regiments, the artillery regiment, and division's support units, was located in Vladimir-Volynskiy, while the motorized rifle regiment was at Lyuboml.

From the very beginning, the division began being pulled apart. Its 41st Motorized Rifle Regiment entered the fight near Lyuboml in support of the XV Rifle Corps, and its survivors were eventually absorbed into the 45th Rifle Division of that corps. A tank battalion was detached to support Soviet infantry fighting west of Vladimir-Volynskiy, losing over half of its combat vehicles in the process.

Out of touch with each other, the 41st Tank Division and the rest of the XXII Mechanized Corps began converging on Kovel. Colonel Pavlov, commander of the 41st Tank Division, wrote in an after-action report:

> Since morning, the 41st Tank Division was subjected to heavy artillery fire, but despite being under heavy fire and [suffering] heavy casualties . . . division reached its assigned staging area . . . by 1400 hours after completing 50–55 km march along wooded and swampy roads. Division did not receive instructions from commander of 22nd Mechanized Corps for four to five days, even though he knew location of our staging area. Division was under direction of commander of 5th Army and commander of 15th Rifle Corps.[2]

In the evening of the same day, commander of the Fifty Army, Major General Potapov, directly involving himself in managing a division, detached two tank companies to chase down alleged small groups of German parachutists. Potapov also assigned the heavy tank battalion containing all the

KV-2 tanks, minus several that became disabled during the march to Kovel, to set up defensive positions across the Brest-Kovel road to guard against enemy advance from that direction. Lacking ammunition for their cannons, the KV-2s were nothing but giant slowly moving machine-gun–armed pillboxes.

In the same report, Pavlov mentioned that his howitzer regiment, armed with 122mm and 152mm cannons, did not have a single tractor to move them. He is silent on the subject of whether any of them were moved by any other means or left behind in their garrison in Vladimir-Volynskiy. Judging from the fact that he no longer mentioned his artillery regiment in the report, it is a safe assumption that these powerful weapons were left behind and subsequently lost when the Germans took Vladimir-Volynskiy by the end of June 22.

The rest of the XXII Mechanized Corps was on the move west along the Vladimir-Volynskiy–Rovno highway. The 19th Tank Division, leaving behind 12 percent to 15 percent, or roughly twenty, vehicles inoperable in its garrison, led the way. From the very beginning, divisions began experiencing a large number of mechanical breakdowns. Many of these disabled tanks were older models, for which no spare parts were available. With mobile repair shops and recovery vehicles in short supply, many of those tanks that suffered breakdowns were left abandoned at the side of the road.

The 215th Motorized Rifle Division, being "motorized" in name only, largely marched on foot. Its tank regiment was experiencing similar problems with its tanks, albeit on much smaller scale.

VIII MECHANIZED CORPS

Commander of the VIII Mechanized Corps in Drogobych, Lt. Gen. Dmitriy I. Ryabyshev, returning home shortly after midnight on June 22, still tired from his two days of commander's reconnaissance, fell asleep as soon as his head touched the pillow. He wasn't allowed to rest long. Around 0400 hours he woke from pounding on his apartment door. The duty runner, a young private, out of breath, reported: "Comrade General, you are urgently asked to come to the telephone at the headquarters."

Ryabyshev rushed to his headquarters. While waiting for the call from the Twenty-Sixth Army's headquarters, he sent out the word for his staff officers to gather in his office.

Like Ryabyshev, commissar of the VIII Mechanized Corps, Nikolai Popel returned to his apartment late. He was tired after a long day and decided to take a shower. As the warm water washed over him, weariness began leaving his body. His mind kept wondering what the Germans were doing at this very moment, there on the other bank of the San River.

A call from corps headquarters interrupted his relaxation. The duty officer informed Popel that Ryabyshev asked him to come to headquarters right away. These late-night recalls were commonplace enough as of late that Popel did not become concerned.

"What's going on?" His wife was worried nonetheless.

"Nothing much. Dmitriy Ivanovich [Ryabyshev] is calling me in for prayers."

The headquarters of the VIII Mechanized Corps were located in a former church and Popel thought his joke would cheer up his wife.[3]

As staff officers gathered in Ryabyshev's office, he informed them that he just received a telephone call from Lt. Gen. F. Y. Kostenko, commander of the Twenty-Sixth Army, advising them to "be ready and wait for orders."[4] Not sure what was going on, Ryabyshev ordered his divisions to "stand to" and move out to their staging areas.

He called Maj. Gen. T. A. Mishanin, commander of the 12th Tank Division, first. This unit was located in Striy, a small town twenty-five miles east of Drogobych. Ryabyshev's message was short.

"Hello. There is lighting in the sky."

"I understand," replied Mishanin.

"Good luck," wished Ryabyshev and rung off.

Colonel Gerasimov, commander of the 7th Motorized Rifle Division, also located in Striy, was next.

"Gerasimov here."

"Hello, my friend. Do you hear the sounds the forest is making?"

"It is indeed making sounds, but the forester knows what he is about," Gerasimov replied.

Major General Vasilyev, commander of 34th Tank Division in the village of Sadovaya Vishnya, thirty miles west of Lvov, was the last one. Their exchange was even shorter.

"Hello. Mountain! Good Luck!"

"I understand."

Shortly prior to the start of the war, Ryabyshev prearranged with his division commanders, for security purposes, code phrases which would notify them to open their sealed orders with war-time deployment areas. "Lightning," "forest," and "mountain" were the code phrases for the three divisions.[5]

Roughly at 0430 hours, Colonel V. S. Varennikov, chief of staff of the Twenty-Sixth Army, called with grim news: Germans were bombarding forward Soviet positions, city of Peremyshl was under direct fire of German artillery, and in some places German infantry had crossed the border. Varennikov's instructions were not to fall for any provocations, not to open fire on German aircraft, and wait for orders.[6]

While the command staff of VIII Mechanized Corps waited for orders, the city of Drogobych was bombed twice by German aviation. As the second wave of bombers was just starting its run, Ryabyshev pulled Popel into his office. On the way there he ordered the duty officer:

"Connect me with commander of air-defense artillery brigade!"

Without saying another word, Ryabyshev looked at Popel. Besides being colleagues, the two men were friends. Popel knew that Ryabyshev was asking him, his commissar, for approval to violate the explicit orders not to open fire on German aircraft. Fully knowing the gravity of his decision, Popel nodded agreement.

After a second's pause, Ryabyshev dropped instructions into the telephone:

"Open fire on enemy aircraft!"[7]

A minute later, barking of antiaircraft guns punctuated the sound of exploding German bombs.

Telephone lines, cut by German bombs, commandos, and Ukrainian nationalists, were working only intermittently. News began trickling in: casualties among units were light; however, there were casualties among officers' families, victims of German bombs.

Ryabyshev also received reports that two small groups of enemy paratroopers were dropped in the area between Drogobych and Striy. He sent out two battalion-sized task forces made up of motorcycle companies, companies of BT-7 tanks, and companies of motorized infantry to track down and destroy the German commandos.

Reports, good and bad, continued trickling in. German bombing around Drogobych and Striy hit the rear echelon units and installations of the VIII Mechanized Corps hard. Both groups of enemy paratroopers were located and wiped out. A small airfield near Striy was bombed, and a squadron of Soviet reconnaissance aircraft, destroyed. Twelfth Tank Division finished leaving its garrison and proceeded to staging area without incident. One regiment from the 7th Motorized Rifle Division did not get moving orders in time and was hit hard by German aircraft in its camp; the casualties were heavy: 70 killed and 120 wounded.[8]

When around 1000 hours a liaison officer from the Twenty-Sixth Army at last brought orders, Ryabyshev and Popel could breathe easier: they finally had clear instructions after five hours of inactivity. The VIII Mechanized Corps was to concentrate by the end of the day in the vicinity of town of Sambor, roughly twenty miles to the west. Hastily prepared orders for subordinated divisions were sent out with liaison officers and over the radio when possible.

Ryabyshev with his headquarters element accompanied the 12th Tank Division to Sambor. Even though it was only twenty miles from Drogobych to Sambor, the trip there was extremely difficult. Other large units were on the move as well. While the 12th Tank Division was moving west from Striy and Drogobych to Sambor, another formation, the XIII Rifle Corps under Maj. Gen. N. K. Kirilov, belonging to the Twelfth Army, was moving east along the same road from Sambor to Drogobych.

The narrow two-lane unpaved road became a nightmare of entangled tanks, wheeled vehicles, tractors, wagons, men, and horses. Swearing, shouting, occasional bursts from air-defense machine guns were all enveloped in a thick cloud of dust. There were constant traffic jams. Some vehicles slipped off the narrow roads and became stuck in the marshy ditches. The roadbed did not hold up to the pressure of multitudes of men and machines and became a thick morass of soft earth. Ancient small bridges over many streams constantly broke under the weight of heavy vehicles.[9]

Popel, who was a good friend of the commander of the 34th Tank Division, Colonel I. V. Vasilyev, volunteered to go along with the liaison officer sent to that division. As Popel's staff car and an armored car escort raced along the road to Lvov, a flight of German fighters spotted them and began hunting them along the rutted road. Drivers of both vehicles began series of evasive maneuvers, accelerating and stopping in order to foil the aim of German pilots.

Relief came unexpectedly in the shape of a single Soviet I-16 fighter. Without hesitation, the Soviet fighter threw himself against half-dozen German aircraft. Several moments later the I-16 went spiraling to the ground trailing a thick plume of smoke and crashed in front of Popel's eyes. The name of the pilot who selflessly sacrificed himself to save strangers on the ground will never be known. But where was the rest of the Soviet Air Force?[10]

Popel found the 34th Tank Division well hidden in its assigned place in the woods west of Drogobych. Being able to leave its garrisons in time and disperse in the woods, Colonel Vasiliev's division hardly suffered any casualties from German bombing. However, the division's officers saw that the Germans were dropping bombs on the garrisons where their families remained and were extremely anxious for any news about safety of their loved ones.

After receiving updated instructions, the 34th Tank Division set off towards the border. This division contained a large portion of the new T-34 and KV-1 tanks, and Popel now proudly observed these new machines heading off to war.

As the 34th Tank Division approached the border, the sounds of fighting grew louder and more intense. Refugees, first in ones and twos, then in streams, appeared heading away from the border. The lucky ones found places on trucks, cars, or horse-drawn wagons. Many fled on foot, clutching their meager belongings. Almost every truck contained wounded soldiers.

By 2100 hours the VIII Mechanized Corps concentrated in the woods around Sambor. The corps headquarters were set up near the headquarters of the Twenty-Sixth Army.

Ryabyshev called for a staff meeting to get a situation report. All of his combat elements were in their assigned staging area. Roughly 700 of his 932 tanks were present and ready for action. In his memoirs Ryabyshev mentions that the missing 232 tanks were left behind in the garrison areas due to the need of major overhaul. However, the major portion of the missing tanks fell prey to various noncombat causes: broke down on the march, became stuck in difficult terrain, or suffered the prosaic indignity of running out of fuel.

Shortly thereafter, Col. A. K. Blazhey from the staff of the Twenty-Sixth Army hand-delivered to Ryabyshev orders from the front headquarters. The VIII Mechanized Corps was ordered to turn around and by noon on 23rd of June concentrate in the area fifteen miles east of Lvov and report to the commander of the Sixth Army, Lt. Gen. I. N. Muzychenko.

These orders completely nullified the fifty-mile road march westward accomplished by majority of Ryabyshev's corps on this day. Now the VIII Mechanized Corps had to move seventy-five miles to northeast.

Popel bitterly thought about worn-out men and equipment, used-up fuel, and combat vehicles that broke down and had to be abandoned by the side of the road due to lack of recovery means. But he kept his thoughts to himself, more concerned how to best break the news to his men.

In order to meet the new time schedule, the VIII Mechanized Corps was forced to depart almost immediately, practically without any rest. They would have to retrace their steps back from Sambor to Drogobych to Striy, then north to Nikolaev and Lvov.

By 2300 hours the corps was on the move again. The road from Sambor to Drogobych again became choked with men and machines. The 12th Tank Division led off, then the 34th Tank, followed by 7th Motorized Rifle Division. While the 12th Tank Division moved off around 2300 hours, the rear-most units of the 7th Motorized Rifle did not get under way until dawn. The long column kept telescoping onto itself, in spurts of stop-and-go in the accordion fashion familiar to most military men. The soldiers in units towards the end of the long column could at least catch quick catnaps in their vehicles.

IX MECHANIZED CORPS

Working in his office right through the last night of peace, commander of the IX Mechanized Corps, Konstantin K. Rokossovskiy, was still awake when a duty officer knocked on his door at 0400 hours.

In an unconscious gesture which became his habit, Rokossovskiy rubbed his jaw. Four years earlier, in 1937, Rokossovskiy was swept up in the horrible wave of purges that all but swamped the Red Army. Arrested for close association with the discredited and executed Marshal Blukher, Rokossovskiy had undergone severe beatings at the hands of NKVD interrogators, and all of his teeth were knocked out. Now the fiery general of Russo-Polish ancestry sported a mouthful of metal teeth. After three years of incarceration, in May 1940 Rokossovskiy was freed, reinstated in rank, first appointed to command a cavalry corps, and, later, the IX Mechanized Corps, still in process of being formed.

The duty officer handed Rokossovskiy a message from headquarters of the Fifth Army: he was to immediately open the secret operational packet. The message was signed by the deputy chief of operations section of the Fifth Army. This was very irregular, since only two people were allowed to give this order: Stalin or Marshal Timoshenko.[11] Instructing the duty officer to authenticate the message through either the headquarters of the Fifth Army, the Kiev Special Military District, or the Defense Ministry, Rokossovskiy called together his senior officers.

The duty officer soon reported that communications were out; neither Moscow, Kiev, nor Lutsk were answering. On his own initiative, Rokossovskiy opened the secret packet. He was directed to bring his corps to combat readiness and deploy in the direction of Rovno, Lutsk, Kovel. Rokossovskiy immediately ordered general alert. The IX Mechanized Corps was still in its peacetime garrisons, spread out in the areas of Novograd-Volynskiy and Shepetovka, and it took time to pull the units together. While his divisions were getting on the way, Rokossovskiy's staff officers hurriedly, but calmly, were preparing orders and dispositions for individual units.

Although the people were getting organized smoothly, the problems with equipment were immediately apparent. Only limited amounts of fuel, ammunition, and vehicles were on hand. Rokossovskiy ordered storage depots opened and necessary supplies and equipment distributed. After the war, Rokossovskiy ruefully recalled how he was almost thwarted in this endeavor by the supply officers. Unwilling to take responsibility for opening the emergency stores depots, the supply officers demanded Rokossovskiy's personal signatures for every action. Rokossovskiy later joked that he never signed his name as much as he did on this first day of war.[12]

Chief of staff Maj. Gen. A. G. Maslov, was constantly trying to establish contact with higher headquarters. Around 1000 hours he succeeded in talking for a few minutes with the headquarters of the Fifth Army in Lutsk. A harried staff officer on the other end of the line told Maslov that Lutsk was being bombed for the second time; there were no reliable communications and no news of what was going on at the border.

Around 1100 hours Novograd-Volynskiy was overflown by a group of German bombers. Again, on his own authority, Rokossovskiy ordered his air-defense artillery to open fire, but no German aircraft were knocked down.

This particular enemy flight apparently was on the way somewhere else, and the city was spared bombing for a time.

At 1400 hours, the IX Mechanized Corps set off toward Lutsk along three separate routes. Traveling along the southern route was the 131st Motorized Rifle Division under Col. N. V. Kalinin, a former cavalry officer. Wheeled vehicles were worth their weight in gold, and Rokossovskiy, again acting on his own authority, took almost two hundred trucks from the district's reserve at Shepetovka and gave them to Kalinin.[13] Severely overloading his transport and having some of his infantrymen ride onboard tanks, Kalinin managed to get his division completely mounted and on the road. Being fully mobile, Kalinin's division began making good time and moved ahead of the rest of the corps.

Kalinin later lamented that he should have attempted to split his division along two roads to facilitate movement.

> The 489th Motorized Rifle Regiment under Lieutenant N. D. Sokolov was the first one to leave camp. The columns moved off along one road. The division immediately spread out to the length of 15–20 miles. By the time the leading units reached Rovno, the tail of the column was just leaving Novograd-Volynskiy. This clearly was a mistake. The march to Lutsk, of course, needed to be accomplished simultaneously along two roads. Then we would have arrived in Lutsk much sooner.[4]

Following Kalinin's unit was the 35th Tank Division under Maj. Gen. N. A. Novikov and 20th Tank Division under Col. V. Chernyaev, also traveling along one road each and experiencing similar congestion problems. Colonel Chernyaev was in temporary command of the 20th Tank Division, while its permanent commander, Col. Mikhail Katukov, who himself only took command of this division in early June, was sick in a hospital. Katukov was to catch up to his division within a week, still feeling effects of his illness. He rose to distinction during the war, commanding the 1st Tank Army during the Battle of Kursk, and was awarded the rank of marshal in 1959.

As many other memoirists, Rokossovskiy mentioned a recurring fact appearing in practically all memoirs of the first days of war: an almost total lack of presence by Soviet Air Force. Most of these memoirists mentioned that the majority of the Soviet aircraft that they saw were either burning on the ground or scrambling from the airfields being bombed. Rokossovskiy remembered encountering several Soviet airfields where burned and destroyed aircraft were lying almost wingtip to wingtip.[15]

Riding in his staff car, Rokossovskiy sadly observed long columns of his infantrymen struggling alongside the roads in intense heat, walking through clouds of dust and carrying on their backs all their personal equipment and extra ammunition. The men resembled the pack mules, hauling machine guns, mortar tubes, and plates and ammunition for them.

Each of his two tank divisions contained a motorized infantry regiment. However, these regiments were "motorized" in the name only. They were still very early in the formative stages. Being called "motorized," Rokossovskiy's infantry regiments did not have draft horses or wagons assigned to them while possessing roughly 30 percent of their assigned wheeled vehicles. Therefore, his men had to trudge toward the front under the weight of their equipment. During the first day of the war, the men of the two motorized infantry regiments of the tank divisions covered almost thirty miles, laboring under the weight of their equipment in the stifling heat. The tank divisions were forced to slow down in order not to outrun their infantry.

His main worry, however, was the fact that he received operational orders as if he were commanding a fully manned and operational mechanized corps, not the weak facsimile of one. He was appalled that orders given to him treated his corps as a fully combat-ready formation.[16]

Rokossovskiy described events of the first day of the war:

> After completing a 30-mile march during the first day, the main body of the corps, represented by infantry, was completely exhausted and lost all combat capability. We did not take into consideration that the infantry, for the lack of any transportation, besides personal equipment had to carry light and heavy machine guns, 50mm and 82mm mortars, and spare ammunition. This development forced us to reduce the infantry marches to 30–35 kilometers (18–22 miles), which resulted in 20th and 35th so-called "tank divisions" to move on ahead. The motorized rifle division, having ability to load its infantry on trucks and tanks, albeit with an extreme overloading, proceeded at normal pace.[17]

Even though the 131st Motorized Rifle Division had 595 trucks, it was only a paltry 37 percent of authorized 1,587 vehicles. Ironically, this division made the best progress and, after covering almost sixty-five miles, halted for the night near Rovno. In the tank divisions, all available trucks were allocated to carry supplies and ammunition, leaving the "motorized" infantry to march on foot.

In the evening, while his exhausted men rested, Rokossovskiy called together his tank division commanders, Colonels Nikolay Novikov and Vasiliy Chernyaev. Together they worked out movement plans for the next day. They would send forward all the tanks with as many infantrymen they could pile aboard and part of artillery which had mechanized vehicles. This mobile group would be followed by infantry marching on foot and horse-drawn artillery. The mechanized echelon would leapfrog, moving forward and halting, waiting for marching infantry to catch up. Then they would repeat the maneuver. While waiting for the infantry, the tankers would perform preventive maintenance on their vehicles and refuel.

One thing that Rokossovskiy was happy about so far was that he managed to maintain good communication with all three of his divisions and was well aware about the situation in his corps. However, throughout the day, Rokossovskiy was extremely concerned about the total lack of communication with the South-Western Front's headquarters.

XIX MECHANIZED CORPS

Unlike Major General Rokossovskiy, who moved his corps as a cohesive unit, Feklenko's XIX Mechanized moved in two echelons: the "mobile" echelon, comprising almost all operational tracked and wheeled vehicles, and the "dismounted" echelon, comprising troops marching on foot and some horse-drawn supply wagons and artillery. Colonel Tsibin described his 43rd Division's departure:

> By the start of combat, operations division was made up of two groups: a) mobile group—tank regiments, each of two-battalion composition . . . and two battalions of motorized regiment on trucks; b) dismounted group of approximately 1,500 men, composed of parts of motorized rifle regiment and other specialists without vehicles (reconnaissance troops, combat engineers).[18]

Lack of mobility of reconnaissance detachments was endemic among Soviet forces at the beginning of the war, and their effectiveness was largely negated. With their mobility severely reduced, Red Army recce troops could not provide their commanders with sufficient information about German strengths and dispositions or scout out their own routes of advance. In the similar manner, combat engineers were usually absent from locations that required their specialist attention.

The 43rd Tank Division, in the manner similar to other divisions of the IX and XIX Mechanized Corps, experienced shortages of all kinds and operated virtually without instructions:

> During the march . . . division experienced major difficulties obtaining spare parts and petroleum/oil/lubricants, which had to be foraged for, with the [foraging parties] ranging out to 60-80 miles away from their units. During the march, up to June 26, 1941, there was no information from higher headquarters about situation at the front. Lack of intelligence information and situation reports did not allow us to correctly appraise the situation, especially about situation on the flanks. There was mostly conflicting and contradictory information about the enemy.[19]

Ironically, and almost defeating the purpose, these foraging parties, while looking for resources, were, in turn, using up valuable resources themselves.

1ST ANTITANK ARTILLERY BRIGADE

Another person whom Potapov's urgent telephone call ripped out of bed was Maj. Gen. K. S. Moskalenko, commander of the 1st Antitank Artillery Brigade. He was supposed to meet with Potapov in the morning of the 22nd and spent the night in Lutsk in a temporary apartment which Potapov provided for him.

After Potapov informed him that they were under attack, Moskalenko immediately called Kivertsi to his political deputy, Battalion Commissar N. P. Zemtsov, and ordered an alarm sounded. Interestingly, Moskalenko did not inform Zemtsov of the nature of emergency.

As Moskalenko's car sped along the road to Kivertsi, he witnessed a German air attack on a small airfield housing about thirty Soviet aircraft. Not a single one of them was able to take off, with most of them burning on the ground.

When Moskalenko arrived at his brigade's base camp, he found everything quiet: soldiers were still largely in their bunks, no efforts to get the brigade ready to move were taken. As it turned out, Commissar Zemtsov, not sure of what to make of Moskalenko's vague phone call, delayed taking any actions until the latter's arrival.

As Moskalenko rushed up the flight of stairs to his headquarters office, he was greeted by a smiling Zemtsov.

"What, maneuvers started already? I keep hearing explosions and shooting, but our brigade is not taking part."

Moskalenko curtly cut him off:

"The hell you say, maneuvers! WAR! The Germans attacked us! Can't you hear they are bombing the airfield!"[20]

Moskalenko and Zemtsov rushed to the safe containing secret mobilization packet. Hurriedly, Moskalenko ripped the envelope open. According to instructions, the 1st Antitank Artillery Brigade was to proceed southwest to Lvov vicinity, in the area of operations of the Sixth Army.

Despite being directly subordinated to the Reserves of Supreme Command, Moskalenko had developed cordial relations with Potapov before the war. Naturally, not knowing what the secret mobilization orders would proscribe, both Potapov and Moskalenko assumed that the 1st Antitank Artillery Brigade would operate in the Potapov's Fifth Army area of responsibility.

Moskalenko immediately called Potapov with this unexpected development. Potapov was shocked:

> The situation along the front of the 5th Army is extremely serious: German troops forged the Western Bug River in the area of Ustilug-Sokal and are advancing on Vladimir-Volynskiy. Therefore, I am asking you, no, demanding, that you set off for Vladimir-Volynskiy and, together with the 22nd Mechanized Corps, destroy the enemy units which crossed our border and stabilize the situation![21]

While Moskalenko was very sympathetic to Potapov's plight, he had to politely remind him that his brigade was subordinated directly to the Reserve of Supreme Command and had to carry out its instructions. Potapov requested that Moskalenko wait while he contacted Moscow or Kiev. Since the brigade was still mobilizing and not ready to move in any direction yet, Moskalenko agreed to wait for clarifications.

General Potapov called back within twenty minutes to tell him that he could not contact either Moscow or Kiev. Moreover, they received news (which turned out to be false) that the 41st Tank Division from the XXII Mechanized Corps was hit hard by German aviation and suffered severe casualties. Therefore, Potapov on his own authority overruled Moskalenko's original orders and ordered him to proceed to Vladimir-Volynskiy, which was about to fall into enemy's hands. Moskalenko agreed with Potapov. After holding a meeting with his subordinate commanders, he ordered departure time set for 1000 hours.

Both Potapov and Moskalenko very well knew that the punishment for deviating from the mobilization orders could cost them their heads. Courage to face their superiors was in far shorter supply on that fateful day than courage to face the enemy. Had more Soviet commanders, above and below them in rank, displayed similar qualities, the events of the border battle would have most likely unfolded differently.

Moskalenko was pleased that his brigade was ready to move ahead of schedule. After a short speech, he gave a terse command: "Mount up!" Unlike the rest of the antitank artillery brigades still in the process of forming, Moskalenko's units received all of its allocated wheeled and tracked vehicles. Therefore, he began making good time towards Vladimir-Volynskiy.

Once across the bridge over Styr River, German aircraft carried out its first attack on Moskalenko's columns. In his memoirs he wrote that despite very intense bombing and strafing, his units suffered only light casualties. Noting the unpaved nature of the roads, he remembers how the German bombs raised such huge clouds of dust as to completely obscure the moving Soviet columns. Even though the casualties were light, valuable time was lost reorganizing Moskalenko's units and getting them moving again.

By the end of the day, despite all the difficulties experienced while deploying forward, an impressive array of Soviet armor began converging on the threatened sector of the border. Panzer Group 1, commanded by General Oberst Ewald von Kleist, the strike force of German Army Group South, numbered less than eight hundred operational tanks in its five panzer divisions. Opposing them, the armored forces of the Soviet South-Western Front numbered over 4,500 tanks and 1,000 armored cars. Even allowing for the common disclaimer of roughly 15 percent non-operational vehicles, over 3,800 Red Army machines were converging on the German spearhead. The clash of the iron avalanches was promising to be a loud one. Halder's diary seconded this:

> In Army Group South, Group Kleist was able to get its northern and central corps moving in the midday hours. If, as seems likely, they reach the Styr River still today, they will have to fight it out with the enemy motorized group east of Styr tomorrow and the day after. The outcome will be decisive for their operational freedom of movement.[22]

CHAPTER 8

Hold What You've Got!
June 23–24

JUNE 23, 1941

DURING THE NIGHT OF JUNE 22–23 almost no one slept at the South-Western Front's command post. There was still no reliable telephone communications, and most of liaison officers sent to the major commands had not returned yet. News that did get in were often either discouraging or confusing. Colonel Bagramyan remembered: "Meager reports were coming in without any rhyme or reason."[1]

Mobilization efforts were producing poor results in the chaotic environment. For example, the 2nd Antitank Artillery Brigade did not receive its allotment of tractors from the civilian sector and could only send one artillery battalion to the border.

Only by the evening of June 23, the command group of the South-Western Front developed relatively clear picture of the situation at the border. It became obvious that the main German effort fell on the Soviet Fifth Army, and the fate of the border battle would be decided on its front, in the area from Vladimir-Volynskiy to Sokal.[2]

After the 87th and 124th Rifle Divisions became cut off and surrounded, the Soviet defenses in the Vladimir-Volynskiy area collapsed. The town itself was taken, and a strong German panzer group advanced along the highway to Lutsk.

Another German panzer force became engaged around Radekhov with the forward elements of XV Mechanized Corps under General Karpezo. The Soviet commander had to leave his motorized rifle division, the 212th, in Brody due to lack of transport. His 37th Tank Division and one tank regiment from the 10th Tank Division became delayed by marshy terrain. Only two regiments from the 10th Tank Division, under Maj. Gen. S. Y. Ogurtzov, one rifle and one tank, met the Germans at Radekhov. Moving around Ogurtsov's unprotected flanks, the Germans advanced toward Berestechko, completely unprotected by Soviet troops.[3]

Meanwhile, the Sixth and Twenty-Sixth armies, while heavily engaged, were hanging onto their positions for time being. The Twelfth Army, guarding the border with Hungary along Carpathian Mountains, reported practically no enemy activity.

In the evening of June 23, the Military Council of the South-Western Front gathered to work on the counteroffensive plans. After a short situation report by General Purkayev, they began figuring out what assets could participate in the counteroffensive on June 24: the XV Mechanized Corps and one division from XXII Mechanized Corps, supported by 135th Rifle Division and 1st Antitank Artillery Brigade. The VIII Mechanized Corps was still on the march from Lvov, under constant air attacks. The IV Mechanized had been diverted to fight in its parent army's area of operations. The IX and XIX Mechanized Corps were still at least two days away. The XXXI, XXXVI, and XXXVII Rifle Corps were at least four to five days away.[4]

As usual, Commissar Vashugin began spouting the offensive-minded philosophy demanding stronger attacks against the Germans. Purkayev soberly opposed him, pointing out that if they attacked right now, they would be committing their forces piecemeal. He insisted that it was absolutely crucial to maintain defensive posture for at least two more days, allowing three more mechanized corps and parts of two more rifle corps to concentrate for a large-scale offensive. Still, Kirponos supported Vashugin, and the argument was over.

Thus, the plan for the next day's counterattack was worked out. The two-pronged attack would be aimed at Vladimir-Volynskiy in the north and Berestechko in the south. Three divisions were to advance on Vladimir-Volynskiy: 135th Rifle from the XXVII Rifle Corps and 215th Motorized Rifle and 19th Tank from the XXII Mechanized Corps. They were to be supported by the 1st Antitank Artillery Brigade. The initial time for the first large-scale counterattack by the Fifth Army was set for 2200 hours on the 23rd of June. However, the German aviation so severely hampered the advance of the 135th Rifle

Division and the XXII Mechanized Corps that the offensive was postponed until 0400 hours on the 24th.

The southern pincer would be comprised of the 10th and 37th Tank divisions of the XV Mechanized Corps. Both forces were not in communication with each other and would be attacking on their own timetables.

After finalizing the plan, Colonel Bagramyan brought it to Kirponos' office for final approval. He found a grim atmosphere there. In addition to Kirponos, Purkayev, and Vashugin, two more people were there. Chief of General Staff Colonel General Zhukov and Member of Military Council Nikita Khrushchev had just returned from their inspection of the situation closer to the border.

Bagramyan's entry interrupted Zhukov lambasting Kirponos for what he considered the latter's lackluster efforts to bring sufficient forces to bear on the German panzer and mechanized group of forces. Zhukov was particularly upset that Kirponos allowed the commander of the Sixth Army, I. N. Muzychenko, to use the powerful IV Mechanized Corps in local fighting, instead of shifting it north to support the XV Mechanized Corps.[5]

By the end of June 23, 1941, despite stubborn resistance by the Soviet forces, the Germans achieved significant inroads, up to forty miles, into the Soviet territory. The nightfall found the 14th Panzer Division halted in the woods three miles northwest of Voinitsa, with orders to reach the Styr River in the area of Lutsk on June 24. The 298th Infantry Division was firmly in control of Vladimir-Volynskiy. The 44th Infantry Division, after leaving few units pinning down the remains of the 87th Rifle Division, moved off to within six miles southwest of Voinitsa. The 299th Infantry Division was moving through a small town of Lokachi in the direction of Lutsk. The freshly committed 13th Panzer Division, leapfrogged them, also moving to Lutsk. Another follow-on unit, the 16th Panzer Division, was advancing on Radekhov in the wake of hard-charging 11th Panzer.

Kovel Direction

Throughout the night of June 22–23, commander of the XV Rifle Corps, Col. Ivan I. Fedyuninskiy, continued receiving disturbing reports about increasing German activity along Brest-Kovel road. Especially disturbing was news that a significant number of German tanks were descending upon his right flank. However, none of these reports were true. Paralyzing "tankophobia" afflicting the Soviet troops in the early days of the war made the ever-present German motorcycle scouts and armored reconnaissance cars to be major panzer formations. Lacking his own effective reconnaissance assets, Fedyuninskiy had not way of verifying the false reports. Therefore, he kept the bulk of his reserve 41st Tank Division and 104th Rifle Regiment aimed at defending the Kovel area from the threat that wasn't there.

Fedyuninskiy was in an unenviable position. Knowledge that he was responsible for holding the right flank of the entire South-Western Front weighed heavily on him and robbed the colonel of the ability to interpret the events unfolding to his front. The real threat was in the center of his position, along the railroad tracks leading from Chelm to Lyuboml. Realizing that Germans had punched gaps between and in their units, both commanders of Fedyuninskiy's rifle divisions spent the night preparing for their counterattacks in order to eliminate German penetration of their lines.

During the night, virtually no resupply reached Timoshenko's 62nd or Sherstyuk's 45th Rifle divisions. However, the 253rd Rifle Regiment from the 45th Division finally arrived during the night and took up positions for the attack in the morning. Colonel Timoshenko, commanding the 62nd Rifle Division, having his units widely scattered, was forced to put his reconnaissance, combat engineers, and signal battalions in line to fight as infantry. Intent on maintaining even a semblance of linkup with the 87th Rifle Division from the XXVII Corps to his south, Timoshenko kept a strong group of his forces at Mosyr. This group, as mentioned previously, composed of his 123rd Rifle Regiment and two artillery regiments, remained idle in its positions throughout June 23.

The 41st Motorized Rifle Regiment from the 41st Tank Division was deployed between the two divisions, partially linking them together. This regiment, which fought as part of Fedyuninskiy's corps throughout June 22, was composed mostly of almost-untrained recruits and suffered disproportionately heavy casualties. With the commitment of the 253rd Rifle Regiment, the only immediately available reserve was a makeshift battalion of border guards. These men, survivors of destroyed outposts, gathered around the core of the 98th NKVD Border Guards Detachment and formed themselves as the reserve behind the 45th Rifle Division. However, numbering only several hundred men, the heaviest weapons in their possession were a dozen light machine guns salvaged from their destroyed blockhouses.

At 0900 hours on June 23, both rifle divisions began their counterattack after a short preparatory artillery fire. The short duration of supporting fire was not intentional. Within ten minutes, German aircraft located Soviet artillery positions and subjected them to severe bombardment. A majority of XV Rifle Corps' artillery was put out of action. Those that survived ceased fire so as not to invite deadly German reply.

The infantrymen of the XV Rifle Corps were supported by two companies of tanks from the 41st Tank Division attacking in the area of operations of 45th Rifle Division. When the Soviet tanks were within two hundred meters of the enemy's positions, Germans met them with practically point-blank artillery fire. The soft-skinned T-26s were brutalized. Lieutenant Bochakoshvili, commanding one of the tank companies, ordered his unit to pull back after losing seven tanks in quick succession. By the time his company returned to its starting position, Bochakoshvili had only three tanks left. The other company suffered similar fate. After their attack halted, both gutted tank companies numbered five tanks out of thirty-two they started with. Later in the day, dismounted tank crewmen were organized into a makeshift rifle company, armed mainly with pistols and light machine guns removed from disabled tanks and lacking bipods. Because of their black tanker uniforms, they were nicknamed the "black infantry."[6]

The two weak Soviet rifle divisions did not fare any better. The attack of the 45th Rifle Division faltered almost immediately, except on its left flank, where its 61st Rifle Regiment made minor initial progress, pushing Germans back about a mile before running out of steam in face of mounting casualties. Advancing on its left flank, the 41st Motorized Rifle Regiment also made a good showing before being similarly halted.

South of the Chelm-Lyuboml railroad, the 62nd Rifle Division made only a token attempt to counterattack. Immediately met with withering artillery and machine-gun fire, Colonel Timoshenko's division halted and treaded water in place throughout the day, absorbing heavy casualties in the process.

In their turn, the Germans counterattacked their counterattackers. The 62nd Infantry Division slammed into both Soviet divisions with a vengeance. Very soon the Germans recovered the ground lost in the morning and began pushing the Soviets east. By the end of the day, the XV Rifle Corps held the line roughly ten miles east and paralleling the border. Its south wing around Mosyr, the relatively quiet sector of Soviet lines, remained slightly forwards. Germans expanded the gap between the 45th and 62nd Rifle divisions to almost four miles wide and ten miles deep.

The Soviet counterattack did have some small measure of success, however. During the day's fighting, the pressure on the surrounded 1st Battalion, 306th

Rifle Regiment, and the 201st Machine-Gun Battalion lessened, and the survivors of both units managed to fight their way out of the encirclement. A two-train detachment of Soviet armored trains significantly contributed to the day's fighting, alternatively supporting the Red Army riflemen in attack and retreat.

Vladimir-Volynskiy Direction

As difficult as Fedyuninskiy's situation was, the one facing his counterpart, commander of the XXVII Rifle Corps, Maj. Gen. Pavel D. Artemenko, was simply nightmarish. Bearing the brunt of attack by Army Group South, the two frontline rifle divisions, 87th and 124th, found themselves practically surrounded by the end of June 22. However, receiving the word that their sister division, the 135th, would be deployed between them on June 23rd, both divisions remained in place. Believing themselves to be reinforced and going onto offensive, the Soviet soldiers prepared only the most rudimentary defensive positions during the night.

Throughout most of the day, Major General Alyabyshev's 87th Rifle Division attempted retaking Ustilug, only to be drawn further into the trap. Two of its rifle regiments made no headway against the town, while the third regiment, reinforced with a tank regiment from the 41st Tank Division, fought its way to the southeastern outskirts of Ustilug by 1400 hours. The price paid by the tank regiment, equipped with T-26 tanks, was disproportionally high when compared against gains achieved.

The steep price paid by Soviet riflemen and tankers was for naught. German response came around 1600 hours when units from *Wehrmacht's* 298th Infantry and 14th Panzer divisions counterattacked the winded Soviet formations from the west and northwest. At the same time, the German 44th Infantry Division attacked the left flank of the 283rd Rifle Regiment and forced it to retreat with heavy casualties. The pullback exposed the left flank of the 96th Rifle Regiment, which in turn was forced to abandon the fight for Ustilug and retreat.

The Red Army units were thrown back from Ustilug in disorder, and victorious Landsers broke into Vladimir-Volynskiy on the heels of retreating Soviets. So swift was the German attack that the Soviet soldiers did not have a chance to prepare the small town for defense. After a series of running street fights lasting several hours, disorganized units from the 87th Rifle Division were pushed out of town. One small group of die-hard Red Army men made a suicidal stand on a hillock east of town, amid the remains of earthen ramparts of a ruined fourteenth century castle.

Attacking just south of them, the 299th Infantry Division of the German XXIX Corps found the going much easier. Other than two border guard block-houses and two bunkers from the fortified district, there were no Soviet troops readily available to oppose them. After surrounding and bypassing the Soviet strong points, the 299th Infantry Division continued its dash eastward.

Throughout day this division continued a two-pronged effort. As the bulk of 299th pressed forward, its rear echelons continued to systemati-cally isolate and destroy the Soviet bunkers which continued to resist in its rear. By evening, the main body of 299th Infantry Division concentrated in the vicinity of Yanevichi railroad station, ten miles south of Vladimir-Volynski. Its forward elements reached Lokachi but were furiously attacked and severely mauled by the approaching 396th Rifle Regiment from the Soviet 135th Rifle Division.

By the nightfall of June 23, situation of the 87th Rifle Division looked bleak. As the result of the 14th Panzer Division's breakthrough, its defensive front was broken in two. The main body of the 87th Rifle Division, flanked on both sides, became cut off and surrounded and suffered punishing casualties. Ammunition was running low, and there was no communications with head-quarters of the XXVII Rifle Corps or the Fifth Army or with the neighboring divisions. In these circumstances, commander of the 87th Rifle Division, Maj. Gen. F. F. Alyabyshev, decided to begin a pullback east during the night. His intent was to rejoin the Fifth Army, which he believed was to begin a counter-attack in the direction Vladimir-Volynski at any time.

When the 87th Rifle Division attempted to break out during the night, its 283rd Rifle Regiment was cut off and annihilated. During the retreat, Alyaby-shev's command became fragmented from brushes with German troops. In one of these countless skirmishes in the early morning of June 25, General Alyabyshev himself was killed. Division's Chief of Staff Colonel Blank replaced the fallen general and led the unit in the northeast direction through the wooded and swampy area between rivers Turya and Stokhod.

Sokal Direction

Throughout the day, the Major General Suschiy's 124th Rifle Division continued its stubborn fight as well. Containing its spirited, but ineffec-tive, counterattacks from the front, the Germans shifted their attention to the flanks of the 124th Rifle Division. Slowly, the Soviet division was being completely surrounded. On their way to their goal of Radekhov, the 15th Panzer Regiment of the 11th Panzer Division passed through and around the left flank of the beleaguered division, pinning it in place. Following closely in the wake of panzers, German 57th Infantry Division surrounded Suschiy's division and began tightening the noose. Not having prepared adequate defensive positions during the night, the 124th Rifle Division suffered heavy casualties before being able to halt the Germans.

Being out of communications with higher echelons, Major General Suschiy still expected to be relieved by the counterattacks of the Soviet reserves. Without orders to withdraw, Suschiy decided to continue holding his positions and established all-around defense. By this time, the 124th Rifle Division has been pushed almost forty kilometers east of the border. He ordered evacuation of as many supplies as possible from the divisional depots in Gorokhov and the destruction of what could not be evacuated.

Soviet Reserves Moving to the Border

While the forward Soviet units fought for their lives, reserves of the Fifth Army and the South-Western Front were ponderously moving forward. The 135th Rifle Division, detached from its parent XXVII Rifle Corps to be Fifth Army's reserve, bivouacked in a forest west of Torchin, ten miles west of Lutsk. Its forward-most unit, the 396th Rifle Regiment, as mentioned previously already had a brush with advance German elements. After expelling a reconnaissance unit from the German 299th Infantry Division from Lokachi, it set up defensive positions there for the night.

The 1st Antitank Artillery Brigade, after a night march from Kivertsi, in the morning of the 23rd deployed west of Zaturtsi, approximately eighteen miles west of Lutsk, straddling the Vladimir-Volynskiy–Lutsk road.

The main body of the XXII Mechanized Corps, after completing a thirty-mile night march from Rovno, was concentrating approximately twelve miles northeast of Lutsk. It was preparing to leave in the evening for Kovel area to link up with its 41st Tank Division, which was covering the city from northwest.

The XIX Mechanized Corps, setting off in the late evening of the 22nd from Zhitomir-Berdichev area, since the morning of June 23 was resting in the woods east of the river Slutch, still 125 miles southeast of Lutsk. The corps was preparing to leave in the late evening of the 23rd to the area of Klevan, northwest of Rovno.

Two rifle corps from reserves of the South-Western Front were moving into the area of operations of the Fifth Army as well. The XXXI Rifle Corps, consisting of three weak rifle divisions and some minor corps assets and marching on foot, was still over seventy miles east of Lutsk. The XXXVI Rifle Corps, of similar composition and moving in similar fashion, was even further away, its struggling units centered on Shepetovka. Both divisions were preparing to move out again at night. While the XXXI Rifle Corps was advancing roughly due west, the XXXVI Rifle Corps was aiming southwest towards Kremenets, on the left flank of the Fifth Army.

IX Mechanized Corps, Maj. Gen. K. K. Rokossovskiy Commanding

During June 23, Rokossovskiy's corps continued moving towards Lutsk. Due to exhaustion of his troops during the first day of march, he was forced to reduce movement during consecutive days to approximately twenty miles.

Rokossovskiy's motorized division, the 131st Motorized Rifle under Colonel Kalinin, was better supplied with wheeled vehicles and outpaced the rest of the corps, reaching the vicinity of Lutsk. There, Major General Potapov, commander of the Fifth Army, subordinated this division directly under his command. Kalinin's new orders were to take up defensive positions along the Styr River between Lutsk and Mlynuv and prevent any enemy breakthroughs.[7]

Colonel Kalinin remembers:

> [Lutsk] was on fire. The small local garrison was staunchly resisting the enemy, especially on the southwestern outskirts. Our forward detachment, after crossing Styr, immediately attacked a German unit. The Fascist antitank artillery knocked out several of our combat vehicles. The enemy was pressing hard towards the bridge we held. . . . The main body of the division after arriving at Lutsk took up defensives along the eastern bank of the river. The tank regiment provided fire support from beyond the river. To its right, by the river, was the 743rd, and to its left—the 489th Motorized Rifle Regiments. Each of them was reinforced by an artillery battery, two antiaircraft guns, and a tank company. Division command post deployed at the tree line, two kilometers east of the bridge across Styr. The reserves, the 3rd Battalion/743rd Regiment, deployed there as well. The firing positions

of the artillery regiment were established two–three kilometers beyond the river. The front of our defenses stretched to almost twenty kilometers.[8]

Corps' Chief of Staff Maj. Gen. A. G. Maslov sent ahead a platoon of combat engineers to set up a temporary command post along the route of advance of the 35th Tank Division. This division experienced a slight delay crossing Goryn River by ferries, and Rokossovskiy ordered part of it diverted through the town of Goscha to utilize the bridges there.

After ensuring that the crossing was being carried out in an orderly manner, Rokossovskiy with his command group moved ahead. As an afterthought, he ordered a battery of 85mm guns to accompany him.

Rokossovskiy's convoy drove west alongside extensive wheat fields, with stalks as tall as a man. After a while, they began noticing strange individuals in the wheat fields. These people, single or in small groups, would hide upon seeing Rokossovskiy's group. Some of these people were dressed in a mixture of military and civilian clothing, some only in underwear. After rounding up and questioning few of those men, Rokossovskiy's staff found out that they belonged to the units who had already engaged the Germans and had been routed by them.

Rokossovskiy wrote that these panicked soldiers attempted to "masquerade" themselves as civilians. Those who could not obtain civilian clothes remained in their underwear, shedding the uniform and boots. He noted that this naive trickery did not fool the Germans—at a later time he encountered bodies of Red Army men executed in their underwear.[9]

Among this panicked group in the wheat fields, Rokossovskiy's officers found two soldiers from the engineer platoon sent ahead by Maslov. They relayed that their platoon was ambushed by German motorcyclists and truck-mounted infantry and wiped out.

In those early days of the war, often whole large units would panic even at the slightest surprise attack by Germans and run. The panicked men would see German parachutists, panzers, and saboteurs around every corner and under every bush. Some officers attempting to stem the panic were shot down by their own men, afraid to return to the front. Some men committed suicide. Rokossovskiy recalled a suicide note left behind by an officer from his 20th Tank Division: "The feeling of fear that I would not measure up in combat drove me to commit suicide."[10] Rokossovskiy noted that when the newspapers wrote articles about increasing vigilance in spotting saboteurs dressed in police, army, and NKVD uniforms, they also spread fears and rumors.

Rokossovskiy relayed a sad anecdote from those hectic first days of war. One day a general was brought to Rokossovskiy's command post. He was in a shredded uniform blouse, tired, and without weapon. This unnamed general was a liaison officer from the staff of South-Western Front to Fifth Army's headquarters. West of Rovno this general encountered several truckfuls of Red Army men driving at breakneck speed east to Rovno. The liaison officer attempted to stop one of the vehicles to find out what was going on. When one vehicle did stop, he was unceremoniously pulled into the truck and roughly interrogated by soldiers who decided that he was a saboteur. The men took away his pistol and his ID and decided to execute him at first opportunity. Luckily, the general managed to jump out of the truck and duck into the thick rye field. He was not chased by soldiers intent of getting away themselves. There were many similar cases.[11]

During the day, Rokossovskiy and Maslov continued sending out reconnaissance parties and liaison officers to find out situation ahead and around them. Many times Major General Maslov would himself jump on a motorcycle and speed off to find news.

Despite their best efforts, only meager unconfirmed news filtered in through the chaos. They heard that Kondrusev's XXII Mechanized Corps already entered the battle north of Lutsk. Feklenko's XIX Mechanized Corps was heading towards Dubno.

Maslov reported that he briefly established communications with General Purkayev. South-Western Front's chief of staff had enough time to inform him that IX Mechanized Corps was being subordinated to the Fifth Army. It was to continue concentrating around the town of Klevan, roughly fifteen miles northwest of Rovno.

In the evening Rokossovskiy's convoy traveling just east of Zdolbunov, less than ten miles south of Rovno, encountered a German reconnaissance element of several armored cars and truck-mounted infantry. As Rokossovskiy's 85mm howitzer battery began deploying for a fight, the German scouts exercised the better part of valor and withdrew without engaging the Russians.

Cautious about blundering into Germans in descending darkness, Rokossovskiy set up his command post for the night in the immediate vicinity south of Rovno.

VIII Mechanized Corps,
General Ryabyshev Commanding

Throughout the night and into late morning of June 23, the VIII Mechanized Corps covered almost seventy-five miles to their designated area east of Lvov. During the night, German aircraft found the corps on the road. Aided by air-dropped flares, German planes strafed and bombed the strung-out Soviet columns. While the casualties from air attacks were not significant, valuable time was lost. After men would scatter for cover, it would take some time to round them up and account for them. Corps Commissar Nikolai Popel remembered that on many occasions, the men, newly subjected to the howling death from above, would be reluctant to leave whatever shelter they found and mount up again.[12]

After each attack, the rate of march kept decreasing. The drivers, most of whom had not slept for day and a half, kept falling asleep at the wheel. This was the time before power steering, and it took significant physical effort on part of drivers to handle their heavy tanks and trucks. Forced to observe strict light discipline, the vehicles were driving into ditches and ramming each other in the dark. Before nightfall, many officers had their men draw a large circle in white chalk on the back of their vehicles in order to see the preceding vehicle in the dark. This trick worked while the drivers were awake.[13] Sometime during the night, the VIII Mechanized Corps moved through Drogobych, the town they left the morning before, and a lifetime of road marches ago. Those officers who were stationed in town had a chance to briefly visit their families and grab a bite to eat. Popel was grateful for the opportunity to check on his wife and two daughters. He was immensely relieved to see that his wife, who suffered a concussion during the bombing morning before, was feeling better.

The main body of the corps left Drogobych with the break of dawn. Its commander, General Ryabyshev, accompanied the 7th Motorized Rifle Division. Commissar Popel went with the 12th Tank Division. The route of this division went through the town of Striy, the very town where division was stationed. Now for the second day in the row, the town was subjected to heavy German air attacks, and large parts of it were burning. Popel recalls how difficult it was for the men of the 12th Tank Division to maintain their disciple and keep driving in convoy through town while not knowing the fate of their families who lived just a few blocks away. After moving through Striy, the 12th Tank Division halted in the woods east of it. While men rested, those officers who lived in town were given an hour's break to run back to town and check on their families.

Instructing General Mishanin to get his division moving as soon as possible, Popel set off for Lvov, accompanied by his driver and an adjutant. On the way there, his car was strafed several times by German aircraft, which were hunting down even individual Soviet vehicles. Popel credited his driver Mikhail Kuchin's skills for saving their lives.

Ryabyshev was already waiting for him at the command post of the Sixth Army, in a small forest northwest of Lvov. Lieutenant General I. N. Muzychenko, commander of the Sixth Army, gave Ryabyshev and Popel their immediate mission. They were to support the VI Rifle Corps under Maj. Gen. I. I. Alekseyev at Yavorov in its attack on June 24. A messenger has been sent to Ryabyshev already, but, obviously, he did not find Ryabyshev while still on the road.

By noon, the forward elements of the 8th Mechanized arrived at their staging areas near Lvov, with the bulk of the corps was still strung out along the roads. In order not to lose time concentrating his divisions near Lvov, Ryabyshev attempted to intercept his straggling units on the march and turn them towards Yavorov. He sent out his senior staff officers to ensure that the majority of his units received new directives. Corps commissar N. K. Popel went to the 34th Tank Division, and corps Chief of Counterintelligence M. A. Oksen to the 7th Motorized Rifle Division. One of the tank regiments from the 12th Tank Division was already at its designated area near Lvov, and Ryabyshev gave its commander new instructions in person. After arranging to meet Popel in Yavorov, at the command post of the VI Rifle Corps, Ryabyshev himself set off to find the main body of 12th Tank Division.[14]

They managed to divert the main body of VIII Mechanized Corps while still on the march and sent them along the dirt roads to Yavorov. The roads leading away from the borders were now chocked with multitudes of refugees, on foot and in vehicles, by trucks evacuating property, by wounded. Mixed in with the wounded and refugees, apparently able-bodied soldiers could be spotted.

At one road intersection, Popel spotted a team of draft artillery horses, without cannon, with soldiers mounted on them. The panicked soldiers told Popel about how their 45mm artillery battery was overrun by German panzers. These few men abandoned their weapons and threw away most of their gear. Popel ordered these men arrested and turned over to military police.

Around 1700 hours, Popel arrived in Yavorov at the command corps of the VI Rifle Corps under Maj. Gen. I. I. Alekseyev and began getting acquainted with the situation. Shortly thereafter, Popel and Alekseyev received a disturbing report that the highway, which Popel just used to get to Yavorov, was cut off by German motorcycle troops. Popel became concerned that Ryabyshev might blunder into Germans while attempting to reach him in town.

The situation in Yavorov was quickly becoming chaotic. As nearby explosions rocked the command post, reports came in that German tanks were already in the city. Popel decided to make a break for it and rejoin the VIII Mechanized Corps at their designated staging area. After spending most of the night driving around the unfamiliar town and its vicinity, Popel and his two companions managed to find their corps south of Yavorov. Ryabyshev was already there.

Popel could not believe the news Ryabyshev had for him. Around 2200 hrs, while Ryabyshev was en route to Yavorov, his chief of intelligence, Lieutenant Colonel Losev, caught up with him. Losev brought new orders from headquarters of the South-Western Front. Not believing his eyes, Ryabyshev read that he was to turn east yet again and concentrate in the area of Brody by the end of June 24. He was to establish contact with the commander of the XV Mechanized Corps and, after ensuring close cooperation, attack together in the morning of June 24 in general direction of Berestechko and destroy enemy tank forces there "as situation develops."[15] Not wanting to use up any time, Ryabyshev drove directly to his corps' assigned staging area south of Yavorov, instead of checking in with the VI Rifle Corps and linking up with Popel there. There was no way to inform General Alekseyev that the VIII Mechanized Corps would not be supporting him on the morrow, and the beleaguered infantrymen were left on their own.

Once again, Ryabyshev and his staff officers had to search for their scattered units at night along the dirt tracks. Only two tank battalions, one from 12th Tank Division and the other from the 34th, were within immediate reach. Ryabyshev ordered them to make haste to Brody after refueling in Lvov. These two battalions were to take up defenses along the west, north, and east outskirts of Brody, establish communications with any Soviet force already there, and conduct reconnaissance.

A majority of combat units of the corps did not receive their instructions while on the march and concentrated near Yavorov by morning of June 24. As quickly as possible, Ryabyshev briefed division commanders on their new mission and ordered them to make haste preparing to move out as soon as possible. The two tank divisions were to lead off, followed by corps support elements. Corps headquarters was to set up on the west outskirts of Brody. The 7th Motorized Rifle Division was to stay in reserve in the woods two miles southwest of Brody.

Meanwhile, straggling units of the VIII Mechanized Corps continued crawling into Yavorov. It took until 1000 hours on June 24 before the main body of the corps set out to follow their lead two battalions.

XV Mechanized Corps,
Maj. Gen. I. I. Karpezo Commanding

Approaching Radekhov from the southeast, Major General Karpezo's XV Mechanized Corps marched to the sound of the guns. This small, dusty town became the sight of the first significant tank battle in Ukraine. Since the previous day, Radekhov was occupied by a task force of two tank battalions and one motorized rifle battalion from the IV Mechanized Corps. This scratch formation was headed by commander of the 323rd Motorized Rifle Regiment, Lt. Col. Georgiy E. Lysenko. North of Radekhov, between it and the equally small and insignificant town of Stoyanov, was the leading two-battalion element of 10th Tank Division from XV Mechanized Rifle Corps.

Continuing its progress south and east towards Radekhov at 0330 hours, the leading battalion from the 15th Panzer Regiment of the 11th Panzer Division briefly traded shots with several of 10th Division's tanks south of Stoyanov. Brushing the small Soviet detachment aside, the regiment continued south to Radekhov and approached it around 0530 hours. As the panzers drew near the small town, German aerial reconnaissance reported approach of significant numbers of Soviet armor advancing from the east. This was the main body of Soviet 10th Tank Division. The whole of 15th Panzer Regiment halted and deployed into line, supported by strong elements of divisional field and air-defense artillery. This pause allowed the forward detachment from the 10th Tank Division to fall back into Radekhov and join Lysenko.

As the panzer regiment and its supporting elements were finishing taking up their positions, the hum of multiple aircraft engines was heard approaching from the west. Soon, approximately a regiment-worth of heavy bombers flew over the German unit. Believing them to be their own aircraft, the German flak gunners did not even unlimber their cannon. However, very soon red stars became clearly visible on the wings of the large aircraft. Fortunately for the surprised Germans, they were not the intended target of the Soviet bombers, who continued droning on towards the east as if not even noticing German forces concentrated directly below them.[16] It was also possible that the Soviet bomber force was returning to their home airfield after expanding their entire payload on other targets.

Advancing with its two battalions abreast in line, the 15th Panzer Regiment moved on to Radekhov. As the German panzers crept closer, they were met with intense defensive fire of several batteries of Soviet artillery, drawing out the noise of tank engines. Supporting their infantry, a dozen Soviet tanks entered the fray:

> Overall, majority of [15th] Regiment for the time being had only the hostile infantry opposing it; however, part of the 1st Battalion . . . had to contend with the Russian tanks. Soon, three enemy vehicles went up in flames. Unfortunately, a [tank] of the 1st Kompanie had its turrett shot away. Feldwebel Hans Albrecht was mortally wounded during this incident.[17]

Still, despite spirited opposition, the Germans broke into Radekhov. Under mounting German pressure, the survivors of the Soviet force abandoned town and retreated south and southwest.

Pursuing the Soviets out of the town, the main body of the 15th Panzer Regiment halted between Radekhov and a hill to its southwest. Schrodek picks up the story:

> The area to the south continued to rise gently and was visible for a couple of kilometers. A group of volunteers went forward to scout out the intentions of enemy forces. Lieutenant von Renesse, Commander of 2nd Platton/5th Company led the scouting party composed of all five [tanks] of the 2nd Plt, three of them armed with 5cm (Short) cannons, and the other two with 3,7cm cannons. One of the 3,7cm KwK cannons was non-operational, but to participate was everything. They formed up in wedge and moved forward. . . .
>
> Less than 100 meters before the highway, which runs transverse to it and is not visible from the staging area, the 2nd Platoon halted and sent out its first situation report. There was nothing special to report; so far everything was running smoothly, and apart from several enemy infantrymen, nothing was seen. The transmission hardly over, engine noises [arose] from right of the road leading into a small forest.
>
> Watch out!—then the Soviets come.

A tank comes in sight and a second one perhaps 50 meters behind it, than a third and finally a fourth follow. It is not clear what type of tank it is. Watching the tanks, the men of the scout detachment completely get off the road. . . .

The Russians did not see the German vehicles and continued down the road without decreasing speed. Can our combat vehicles hold against them? As an enemy panzer came exactly opposite vehicles from 2nd Platoon, Sergeant Schrodek, the gunner on platoon leader's vehicle (vehicle #21) sent off his first armor-piercing round with his best regards at the Russians. All other vehicles of the platoon also opened fire.

Even though at this short distance every shot was a hit, the Russians drove on without much visible effect. For God's sake, were the Russians so superior that they could only be affected by their own tank guns?

Only the rapid fire and repeated hits got the reactions from Russians, who turned around and quickly retreated from where they come from.

"Second platoon, come on!—Second platoon, come on!"

While the one-sided combat was fading away and the enemy tanks were still followed by some shells, the platoon leader received a call over the radio. He finally acknowledged it and reported: "Found ourselves in combat with four enemy tanks. Type unknown, not indicated on recognition tables. Despite repeated hits, our fire had no effect. It appears as if shells are simply bouncing off. The enemy tanks disengaged without fight and retreated. Are we to push on? Please advise."

The 2nd Platoon received instructions to return as soon as possible. The men of the reconnaissance detachment were only happy to follow the instructions, because it did not appeal to them to follow the enemy who shrugged off the well-placed hits without effect.

Significant in this minor exchange of gunfire was the appearance of the new Soviet T-34 tanks. This was one of the earliest references to the arrival of T-34s. Amazement and anxiety experienced by German tankers at the sight of these new machines was clearly demonstrated in Sergeant Schrodek's description.

The Soviets did not pursue Lieutenant von Renesses's detachment, and his men had a chance to refuel their tanks and replenish the ammunition, and even catch a quick cat-nap. The lull in action did not last long, shredded by a Soviet artillery barrage, as short as it was ineffective. Coming on the heels of the artillery was the main Soviet push of the 10th Tank Division from the XV Mechanized Corps. Once again, Sergeant Schrodek tells the story:

> A divisional reconnaissance plane—a Fiesseler Storch—flew over the regiment and threw out a message in the proximity of regimental commander Lieutenant Colonel Riebel's car. Afterwards, the entire regiment received orders: "Clear for combat!"
>
> Soon everyone down to the last man knew that behind the heights before Radekhov a large concentration of enemy tanks set itself to intercept the regiment's direction of march and could emerge any moment.
>
> Hardly quarter of an hour passes before one can see them coming. Ten—twenty—thirty—and still more coming, beginning to roll over the crest of the hill and open fire immediately. However, their fire is landing short, without seriously impacting the regiment.
>
> It is better to let the Russian tanks get closer still, because it is best for our tank cannons to fire from less than 400 meters. A shallow dip in the ground temporarily hides the first wave of the enemy vehicles from the view. However, if they emerge from it again, they will give the men in the combat vehicles of the regiment an ideal firing position. The gunners on all cars re-sighted their guns in such a manner as to take the enemy tanks under fire the moment they emerge from the dip.
>
> Then it's time, and shell after shell flies towards the Russians. Most of the first shells were hits, some even direct hits. Others tear away whole sections of armor from the enemy combat vehicles. One can see damaged enemy tanks everywhere, with their crews dismounting the best they can. But still, tank fights tank, with new targets emerging. The Russians did not succeed [in] breaking down or breaking through the German lines anywhere, however.
>
> When . . . in the afternoon of June 23rd, approached the end of the first large-scale acid test of the regiment in the Russian campaign, and the opponent withdrew to the south with heavy losses, 46 of his tanks remained destroyed on the battlefield.[18]

This was the litmus test for the Soviet tanks as well, the one in which they did not perform well. This attack was a microcosm of the deficiencies which were to plague the Soviet mechanized formations throughout the early period of the war. The difficulties could be summarized by an excerpt from a Soviet report:

At 1500 hours, the 20th Tank and 10th Motorized Rifle regiments, carrying out mission of capturing Radekhov, went onto attack in the direction of Radekhov-Sokal. The 10th Artillery Regiment by this time was [still] on the march, since at the time of sounding of alarm it was in the camps at Yanov, and the 19th Tank Regiment, due to difficulties experienced on the march, did not reach staging areas and did not take part in the attack. Attack of the motorized rifle and 20th Tank regiments (each without a battalion), without artillery support, and faced with clearly superior enemy forces deployed in an advantageous position, was unsuccessful.[19]

Besides bringing only partial forces to bear, commander of the 10th Tank Division, Maj. Gen. Sergey Y. Ogurtzov, conducted the attack in the most unimaginative manner. Wave after wave, the Soviet tanks crested the hill, and they went down into a dip, all the while exposing vulnerable sides and under-bellies to German artillery fire. Then, coming out of the low ground, the Soviet tanks exposed their thinly armored undersides for the second time. Even the T-34 tanks, not having their equal among the 15th Panzer Regiment, were neutralized by concentrated German point-blank fire, heavily supplemented by the versatile 88s. The fight at Radekhov demonstrated what would be a major recurring factor during the next week of fighting—Soviet armor attacks, unsupported by their own artillery, dashing themselves to pieces in front of German antitank defenses.

The other tank division of the XV Mechanized Corps, the 37th, was already within twenty miles of Radekhov by 1400 hours when it was intercepted by corps commander Karpezo and sent chasing ghosts. Commander of the 37th Tank Division, Colonel F. G. Anikushkin, later described the events:

> Commander of 15th Mechanized Corps, Major General Karpezo, informed [me] that in the vicinity of Adama there were up to 100 enemy tanks and ordered the 37th Tank Division to [destroy them]. Recon-naissance was sent towards Adama, and the tank regiments were turned 90 degrees from their routes of march. . . . It later turned out that there were no enemy tanks in the vicinity of Adama. The tank regiments, after delaying for five–six hours in Adama vicinity, continued [their] previous mission. This resulted in 37th Tank Division not being able to reach its staging area in time.[20]

Had Karpezo utilized his motorcycle regiment in its proper reconnais-sance role, he would have quickly established the fact that there were no

German tanks in the vicinity of Adama. Instead, he immediately diverted a whole tank division in reaction to rumors. As the result, close to 250 tanks of the 37th Tank Division which could have altered the outcome of the clash at Radekhov did not reach the town until early morning of June 24.[21]

The Germans claimed forty-six Soviet vehicles destroyed at Radekhov, while losing only one of their own tanks damaged beyond repair.[22] Here, a curiosity in reported losses is demonstrated. The Germans reported as lost only those tanks that were damaged beyond repair. The Soviets claimed any German tank disabled on the battlefield as a kill. However, since the Germans, at least in the beginning of the war, generally remained in possession of the battlefield, they were able to evacuate and repair their damaged combat vehicles. On the same note, since the Soviets retreated from the same battlefields, their damaged tanks were irretrievably lost to them.

Still, in this situation, both sides' estimates of Soviet losses were close. While the Germans claimed forty-six destroyed Soviet tanks, just the Soviet 10th Tank Division stated losing twenty-six tanks, including six T-34s. We need to remember that besides the 10th Tank Division, a task force of the 32nd Tank Division from the IV Mechanized Corps fought at Radekhov as well. Given people's tendency of lowering their own losses and inflating those of the enemy, German claims seem reasonable. On the other hand, 10th Tank Division's claims of destroying twenty German tanks look a little high.

As the black, oily smoke still rose from the destroyed Soviet armor near Radekhov, the Germans did not rest on their laurels. Reinforced by the 2nd Battalion of the 15th Panzer Regiment, the 110th Infantry Regiment raced on and by the end of the day established a bridgehead on the Styr River, approximately fifteen miles east of Radekhov.

JUNE 24, 1941
Vladimir-Volynskiy and Lutsk Direction

Being late for the attack the previous evening, the morning of June 24 found the 135th Rifle Division deployed two miles east of Voinitsa, a small village located roughly halfway between Vladimir-Volynskiy and Lutsk. Its commander, Maj. Gen. F. N. Smekhotvorov, while preparing for the attack, did not posses information that Germans were already flowing around both flanks of his unit. Smekhotvorov's division was deployed on the north-south axis across the Vladimir-Volynskiy–Lutsk road, its left flank resting on the

Lokachi village. Behind the 135th, a powerful Soviet artillery task force was taking up its positions astride the road leading to Lutsk. This task force consisted of the 1st Antitank Artillery Brigade, the 406th Artillery Regiment of the XXVII Rifle Corps, and the artillery from the 135th Rifle Division, all headed by the chief of artillery of the Fifth Army, Maj. Gen. V. N. Sotenski. Opposing the Soviet forces were the German 298th Infantry and 13th and 14th Panzer divisions.

The two divisions from the XXII Mechanized Corps, the 19th Tank and 215th Motorized Rifle, had a busy night moving into attack positions. They were subject to constant German air strikes and mechanical breakdowns, which were severely draining the Soviet offensive capability. Part of the route of the two divisions took them cross-country, through the marshy wetlands unsuitable for mechanized formations. The 19th Tank Division was the closest to their assigned positions, but still late. The 215th Motorized Rifle fell hopelessly behind the timetable. Therefore, attack on Vladimir-Volynskiy was postponed from 0400 hours until the time both divisions would be ready to go. Moreover, commander of the XXII Mechanized Corps, Major General Kondrusev, became separated from his command and moved forward with the headquarters element of the 1st Antitank Artillery Brigade.

However, the time for the Soviet attack came and went at 0800 hours, and the 14th Panzer Division, supported by aviation, preempting the Soviet forces, attacked the 135th Rifle Division and pushed it three miles east. There, the advancing Germans ran into defensive positions of two artillery battalions from the 1st Antitank Artillery Brigade. The furious fire of the Soviet gunners finally halted German advance. Still, while stopped in the center and on the northern flank, the Germans began working around the southern flank of Soviet positions.

Around 1300 hours, the 19th Tank Division finally arrived in the woods north of Shelnov. This division only had forty-five operational tanks and twelve armored cars remaining after losing vehicles on the march due to German air strikes and mechanical breakdowns. They were combined into a provisional regiment. After a short preparatory artillery barrage and supported by the 135th Rifle Division, the provisional tank regiment went into the offensive. By 1630 hours the Soviet troops forced the enemy to fall back towards the Voinitsa-Lokachi line.

But the Germans were not done for the day yet. Around 1800 hours they hit back at the 135th Rifle and 19th Tank divisions and mauled them. The 19th Tank Division was particularly severely brutalized. The butcher bill of senior commanders was particularly impressive: Lt. Col. B. G. Bibik, commander of the 37th Tank Regiment—taken prisoner; Lieutenant Colonel Samsonov, commander of the 38th Tank Regiment—killed in action; Lieutenant Colonel Sokolin, commander of the 19th Motorized Rifle Regiment—mortally wounded. The division commander, Major General Semenchenko, suffered a light arm wound and narrowly escaped death after his tank was knocked out. The mauled 19th Tank Division broke, and people began streaming back in disorder, sweeping division's rear echelons along with them. Panic and despair afflicted not just lower enlisted. Many officers were affected just as badly as their subordinates and were unable or unwilling to rally their men. When division was finally rallied and shaken to order on June 26, it mustered only four tanks, four cannons, and two under-strength motorized infantry battalions.[23] However, while the 19th Tank Division was spilling its lifeblood into marshy ground at Voinitsa, its sister 131st Motorized Rifle Division, assisted by some of Moskalenko's gunners, arrived south of Lutsk and stabilized the situation. The action was costly, leaving Major General Kondrusev, commander of the XXII Mechanized Corps, hors de combat.

Commander of the 1st Antitank Brigade, Major General Moskalenko, described these events in his memoirs:

> Halfway between Lutsk and Vladimir-Volynskiy our advance element caught up to a small convoy of several armored cars and two tanks. It turned out that we met up with commander of the 22nd Mechanized Corps and command group of his headquarters. Introductions were quick. I informed Major-General S. M. Kondrusev and his corps Chief of Staff Major General V. S. Tamruchi about my assigned mission.
>
> In his turn, Kondrusev confirmed that he received orders to attack the enemy in the area of Vladimir-Volynskiy. . . . We continued forward together, and I climbed into his tank.
>
> We were close to Vladimir-Volynskiy when we heard rapid artillery fire. They were coming from somewhere up ahead of us. We left the tank and climbed to the top of a small hill near the highway, from where we saw that coming towards us, to the left and right of the highway, large number of tanks and motorized infantry were advancing in combat formation. The brigade's advance guard, located a little ahead of us, was firing upon them.

"Please cease fire immediately," Major General Kondrusev asked me worriedly. "It is possible they are from our 41st Tank [Division], retreating under enemy pressure."

The distance between us and approaching tanks was approximately [one mile], and I could clearly see through my binoculars the crosses on their sides. . . .

Conditions of our entry into the fight were extremely unfavorable. First of all, this was a meeting engagement of artillery units on the march against enemy's superior combined arms forces.

In this first battle, the brigade's gunners knocked out and burned almost seventy tanks and armored cars, many motorcycles, and other materiel of the 14th Panzer Division. Significant casualties were also inflicted upon the 298th Infantry Division. Our losses were heavy as well. The brigade lost four artillery batteries with all personnel and equipment. Major-General S. M. Kondrusev was mortally wounded by a shell fragment."[24]

At the time of Kondrusev's death, he was completely out of touch with his mechanized corps and did not realize that it was his 19th Tank Division, and not the 41st, that was being decimated.

The Soviet losses were not in vain. German units could not advance into the face of heavy fire from entrenched Soviet artillery. While it is highly unlikely that Germans lost seventy combat vehicles, as claimed by Moskalenko, their casualties were serious nonetheless. More significantly, they were unable to quickly break through to Lutsk along the highway and were forced to probe east along less-desirable roads.

Still, the ever-present German reconnaissance elements found suitable roads, and strong elements of the 13th and 14th Panzer Divisions began flanking Moskalenko's positions. By nightfall, the Germans reached so far around Moskalenko's southern flank that he had to abandon his positions, heavily paid for in blood, and pull back to the western outskirts of Zaturtsi. His men spent the night busily preparing new positions.

During the night, Moskalenko deployed his brigade in three lines astride the highway to Lutsk. His last defensive positions were in the immediate vicinity of Lutsk itself. He left his reserves in the city: two of the brigade's own battalions plus several artillery batteries and battalions that became separated from their units.[25]

At the same time, a new threat developed north of Lutsk, in the vicinity of a small town of Rozhysche. At this location, German reconnaissance elements were spotted probing for fords across the Styr River. Fifth Army's commander, Lieutenant General Potapov, ordered Moskalenko to shift part of his force there to prevent Germans from establishing a beachhead. Several other Soviet units from XXII Mechanized Corps and the 135th Rifle Division began pulling back there as well.

Throughout June 24, the 215th Motorized Rifle Division, completely out of contact with the higher echelons or engaging the enemy, slugged on foot through the poor terrain in the triangle between Kovel-Lutsk and Vladimir-Volynskiy–Lutsk highways.

Kovel Direction

While furious battle raged along the Vladimir-Volynskiy–Lutsk highway, the situation north of it was more stable. In morning of June 24, the XV Rifle Corps under Colonel I. I. Fedyuninskiy, after suffering heavy casualties the previous day, was maintaining its positions. By midafternoon, after German advance along the Lutsk highway exposed Fedyuninskiy's left flank, commander of the Fifth Army, Major General Potapov, ordered Fedyuninskiy to pull his corps back to place it on line with Kovel. The Soviet troops began steadily giving ground, not allowing the Germans to achieve a breakthrough of these positions.

The 41st Tank Division from the XXII Mechanized Corps sat largely idle immediately north of Kovel, still protecting it from a rumored attack from northwest. In his memoirs, Fedyuninskiy bitterly claimed that the commander of the 41st Tank Division, Colonel Pavlov, was more concerned with preserving his combat vehicles than actively supporting actions of the XV Rifle Corps.[26]

Small reconnaissance elements of the 41st Tank Division probed almost thirty miles northwest to a town of Ratno, located along the Brest-Kovel highway. Not finding any German tanks advancing on Kovel, the Soviet patrol was fired upon by their German counterparts. Without engaging in a fight, this patrol blew up the only bridge across the Pripyat River north of Ratno capable of supporting tanks.[27]

While the command of the XV Rifle Corps was aware of lack of German armor presence north of Kovel, this information was not passed to headquarters of South-Western Front. Thus, even as late as 2000 hours on June 24, the South-Western Front was still reporting to Moscow the presence of large mechanized enemy formations in that area.[28]

Fedyuninskiy remembered that it cost his corps dearly to maintain their positions. At the end of June 24, one of his regiments from the 45th Rifle Division mustered less than one third of its men from just three days previous. Colonel Fedyuninskiy ordered that stragglers from other units be rounded up and absorbed into his corps. One such unit was the shuttered remains of the 75th Rifle Division, which retreated into Fedyuninskiy's area of operations from the northwest. This particular division ended up far from home, belonging to a completely different group of forces, the Fourth Army of the Western Front located north of the Pripyat Marshes.[29] As the XV Rifle Corps began pulling back closer to Kovel, its rear echelon units began evacuating materiel and servicemen's families.

At his airfield near Kovel, Lieutenant Arkhipenko's 17th Fighter regiment, plus the fighter regiment that flew in from Vinnitsa, were caught on the ground and virtually finished off on this third day of the war. This was a perfect illustration of how Germans achieved the air superiority by systematically reducing Soviet airfields by follow-up attacks. In the evening of June 24, with the Germans already southeast of Kovel, Arkhipenko's superiors made the decision to relocate their surviving aircraft to a reserve airstrip near Rovno. By this time, the two regiments numbered only ten I-153s and one MiG-1 as still-operational aircraft.

As these planes took off, the "unhorsed" pilots were loaded into a truck and sent to Rovno as well. In his memoirs, Arkhipenko mentioned that he was one of these pilots without aircraft, but did not mention how his plane was damaged. Most likely it was put out of commission in the same morning attack that did so much damage to the two fighter regiments. The plane-less pilots did not get much rest at Rovno, being immediately shuffled farther east to Zhitomir.[30]

IX Mechanized Corps,
Maj. Gen. K. K. Rokossovskiy Commanding

Since coming to the rescue of the 135th Rifle Division at Voinitsa and Lokachi in the morning of June 24, the 131st Motorized Rifle Division was under heavy pressure from the Germans. Division's commander Kalinin remembers:

> During the night [of June 23–24] units dug in. . . . Almost everything was conducted in full view of the enemy: the western bank of Styr was

dominating the eastern one, and Germans had the ability to see in depth of our defenses. During the previous night, they attempted to cross Styr in the area of 743rd Motorized Rifle Regiment, but unsuccessfully. At dawn their aviation was bombing our front lines and rear echelons. Throughout the 24th of June, division fought against tanks and infantry, sometimes hand-to-hand.[31]

In 2003, a Russian history magazine called *The Moscow Journal* printed excerpts from unpublished memoirs of Cpl. Ivan K. Yakovlev, who fought during those days as a machine gunner in the 593rd Motorized Rifle Regiment of the 131st Motorized Rifle Division. Yakovlev described the events of June 24:

> Day began sunny, free of clouds. . . . Soon the "Junkers" planes attacked positions of the neighboring regiment. We listened nervously, sitting in [our] trenches and feeling the earth under us begin to shake. The [Germans] advanced directly upon us. . . . Who's going to die, who will live this time? Our friends are already fighting near us. After lunch the 1st Battalion received orders to form up in the neighboring forest in full gear. Five light BT tanks, 45mm [cannons], and 76mm cannons were already there. Battalion was heading to support the neighboring regiment, which was retreating east under pressure from overwhelming German forces. Our company, at the head of the column, climbed on the tanks and artillery vehicles, and the battalion force-marched after us along the forest road.
>
> Soon, around one bend in the road we saw how several Red Army men, upon seeing the tanks, hurriedly dove in the forest. Company [Commissar] Ignatov halted his vehicle, jumped to the ground, and ordered: "Cowards and panickers, fall in!" Retreating soldiers began coming out of the thickets: dirty, without equipment. They formed up along the road in one line. Upon questioning by [commissar], they replied that the Germans bombed them heavily, destroyed artillery batteries and trenches; then, after crossing the river, [their] tanks breached defenses and moved east. . . . [Commissar] and a squad of soldiers stayed behind to collect [other] retreating soldiers. . . .
>
> As we moved on, we could more clearly hear mortar explosions and machine-gun bursts. The leading tank slowed down, its commander periodically sticking his head out of the turret to peek and listen. Suddenly, two soldiers blocked our way. One of them, a junior lieutenant,

informed us that just ahead, beyond the tree line, the 3rd Battalion of the retreating [743rd Motorized Rifle Regiment] was setting up temporary defensive positions.

Commander of this battalion, Captain Muzychenko, was planning to conduct only a holding action until the arrival of reinforcements.[32] Now, the arrival of a full-strength battalion with tanks and artillery allowed him to conduct successful local counterattacks as well.

Grim realities of war were taking place already on this third day of combat. Yakovlev described the aftermath of a Soviet counterattack: "[Germans] would not raise hands, shooting back until the last; however, we did not coddle them, either—not more then ten men were taken prisoner."[33]

Also, this early in the war, the Soviet soldiers taken prisoner, often through circumstances beyond their control, did not know what to expect when other Soviet units freed them. Yakovlev again:

> In the barn we found Red Army men taken prisoner by the Germans. Their glances, happy, and at the same time guilty and cautious (it was terrible to receive the tag of "coward and traitor"!), were mutely asking: "What will happen to us?" Our [commissar] Ignatyev, did not know what to decide: his compassion was struggling with duty. Captain Muzychenko [intervened]: "Wounded to the hospital! Healthy—go eat and reorganize. . . . You will fight in my battalion." He addressed the liberated soldiers, "You will redeem your guilt in combat." The battalion's low murmur approved [his decision].[34]

While the advance elements of the 131st Motorized Rifle Division engaged the enemy, bulk of the IX Mechanized Corps, the 20th and 35th tank divisions, were still coming up, strung out between Lutsk and as far back as Klevan.

XIX Mechanized Corps, Maj. Gen. Nikolay V. Feklenko Commanding

Around 2100 hrs on June 24, forward elements of XIX Mechanized Corps began arriving in the area of Mlynuv, roughly ten miles north of Dubno. Pressing farther west, a reconnoitering tank company of sixteen tanks under Senior Lieutenant Ivashkovskiy ran into its German counterparts scouting for crossings over a narrow and muddy Ikva River. In a sharp clash, Ivashkovskiy's company lost two tanks and was forced to withdraw.

As the forward elements of XIX Mechanized Corps arrived in the Mlynuv-Dubno area, they linked up their left flank with the right-flank 228th Rifle Division of the XXXVI Rifle Corps. This rifle corps from the reserves of the South-Western Front was taking up positions along the Dubno-Kremenets road. Thus, while XIX Mechanized Corps' left flank was relatively secured, a gap developed between its right flank and Rokossovskiy's IX Mechanized Corps.

XV Mechanized Corps, Maj. Gen. Ignatiy I. Karpezo Commanding

The early morning of June 24 found the XV Mechanized Corps firmly in control of vicinity of Brody, with its defensive positions facing northwest to Radekhov and north to Berestechko. Since German reconnaissance units were already operating in the vicinity of Berestechko, corps commander Major General Karpezo received orders to destroy these forward German elements. He was to cooperate with Lieutenant General Ryabyshev's VIII Mechanized Corps in carrying out this mission.

However, the two tank divisions of the XV Mechanized Corps spent the day constantly shifting their positions. Amid the summer heat, dust, and air attacks, the 10th and 37th tank divisions changed directions several times, without engaging the enemy. Both steadily continued losing vehicles to difficult terrain and technical difficulties. This was to have a significant effect on the course of battle during the next few days. Without pressure from the XV Mechanized Corps on June 24, Germans were able to bring up two infantry divisions to support the vanguard 11th Panzer Division.

True to its doctrine, the 11th Panzer Division was moving forward along three routes in three battle groups. One battle group was formed around the 15th Panzer Regiment, the other two around the two panzer grenadier, or mechanized infantry, regiments. Each battle group had its allotment of field and air-defense artillery and combat engineers. One of these battle groups, formed around the 110th Panzer Grenadier Regiment, supported by one panzer company from the 15th Panzer Regiment, reached Berestechko in the evening of the previous day.

The only effective means to slow down the 11th Panzer Division was the Soviet Air Force. According to Isayev, the Air Force of the South-Western Front conducted 523 sorties between June 22 and 24 and dropped 2,500 bombs.[35] Isayev is seconded by Gustav Schrodek: "At dawn of June 24, the [15th Panzer] Regiment underwent its first attack by Russian bombers. It shall not be the only one this day; completely the opposite. Hour by hour, number of hostile attacks increases. As the result of this, the regiment now has several dead and wounded."[36]

Schrodek himself experienced a close brush with the attacking Soviet aircraft. As the rest of 15th Panzer Regiment continued driving east, German aerial reconnaissance identified strong enemy armor concentration coming north from direction of Lopatin around 0700 hours. Detaching Schrodek's 5th Company, under command of Lieutenant von Renesee, as flank security, the regiment drove on.

As dispersing German panzers grabbed whatever scare natural conceal-ment camouflage was available, Lieutenant von Renesse was stuck with hiding his tank in an ancient, dilapidated barn. In order to have a clear field of fire, the lieutenant ordered his driver to simply push out a few boards in the wall of the barn with tank's cannon. Unfortunately, the whole of barn collapsed on top of von Renesse's tank. After considerable efforts, and aided by other crews, they dug out the trapped vehicle only to discover that panzer's torsion bar and suspension system were damaged, putting the vehicle out of commission. While von Renesse commandeered another tank, Schrodek and the rest of the crew took the damaged panzer on a slow, lumbering, and bumpy trek back to division's rear for repairs.

As they traveled west along the traffic-choked dirt road against the tide of other advancing units from 11th Panzer Division, three Soviet bombers dove at the road, spreading a thick carpet of bombs: "The Russian air attack, aided by that continuously beautiful favorable weather, proved to be quite a hindrance to the further advance." Schrodek's damaged tank could not maneuver out of the path of oncoming bombs: "There was no chance of avoiding the bombs, only living through it." While Schrodek and other crew members dove for cover in the ditches, several Russian bombs landed close behind the tank. Fortunately, despite some scratches and bruises, no one on Schrodek's crew was hurt.

In spite of Soviet air attacks, combat engineers for the 11th Panzer Division succeeding in repairing a damaged bridge over Styr River east of Berestechko, and advance continued in direction of Dubno. By the end of June 24, the 15th Panzer Regiment covered another thirty miles, despite the difficult road.

While the two tank divisions from the XV Mechanized Corps moved from place to place, its sister division, the 212th Motorized Rifle, received orders directly from headquarters of the South-Western Front. It was ordered to take up positions north of Brody and hold the area until arrival of the VIII Mechanized Corps.

VIII Mechanized Corps,
Lt. Gen. Dmitriy I. Ryabyshev Commanding

As the other Soviet units were fighting Germans, the VIII Mechanized Corps was bouncing around inside the Stiy-Peremyshl-Lvov triangle. After covering almost two hundred miles, the VIII Mechanized Corps now had to move an additional seventy-five miles east to Brody. The meaningless miles used up fuel at an alarming rate and caused severe stress on men and machines.

Shortly after 0500 hours, the corps set off east. The roads around Lvov were choked with refugees and military units, some moving towards, the others away from the border. As much as Ryabyshev disliked the idea, he had to move his corps through the town, painstakingly negotiating its narrow medieval streets.

Corps Commissar Nikolai Popel accompanied the motorcycle regiment in its vanguard position. He remembered seeing unending streams of refugees flowing through the main thoroughfare. Single rifle shots were heard. As the regiment moved deeper into the city, shooting intensified, turning into regular skirmishes.[37]

Popel quickly found out the source of shooting. Up to a week before the war, armed Ukrainian OUN (Organization of Ukrainian Nationalists) nationalists began infiltrating the city. Now, this "fifth column" began sniping at the Soviet troops moving through Lvov. The garrison of the city found itself not able to contain the situation, and passing regular Soviet units were pressed into lending a hand in eliminating pockets of resistance. Several companies from Popel's motorcycle regiment found themselves involved in a series of confusing running fights along the rooftops and through the alleys.

The OUN saboteurs and snipers began with creating an atmosphere of chaos and panic in the city, setting fires to buildings and picking off individual Soviet soldiers. As the German troops moved closer to Lvov, OUN fighters became bolder and began engaging Soviet regular army troops.

The Soviets exacted more than their share of vengeance upon the citizens of Lvov, however. From almost the very first hours of the war on June 22, the NKVD prison guards throughout western Ukraine began executing their civilian prisoners held in local jails. Majority of these prisoners were people deemed unreliable or potential enemies of the Soviet state. Now, with the

Germans pressing close to Lvov, the wholesale slaughter of political prisoners began. By the time the Soviet forces finally abandoned Lvov, over twelve thousand of these prisoners were shot by NKVD in Lvov alone.[38]

As the main body of the VIII Mechanized Corps entered Lvov, its movement sometimes slowed down to a crawl. The flow of civilian refugees severely interfered with the progress of the Soviet units. Ryabyshev was forced to set up road blocks, sometimes consisting of tanks, to ensure proper movement of his corps.

In the afternoon, the main body of the VIII Mechanized Corps gathered in a small town of Kurovitse, approximately twenty miles east of Lvov. Three men in civilian clothes approached Popel. To his surprise, he discovered that these men were film director Kovalchuk with two assistants. They had been looking for Popel now for two days: "I was, of course, flattered by such a distinguished attention to our corps, but how could I have been of service to [movie people] in these chaotic days! I could only shake their hands, express my sincere hope for a productive cooperation and advise them . . . to go rest."[39]

As the tired units of the VIII Mechanized Corps continued pulling into Kurovitse, it became painfully obvious that the corps was not in any shape to reach Brody the same day. Too much time was lost moving through the bottlenecks in Lvov and fighting the Ukrainian nationalists.

Still, the vanguard 2nd Motorcycle Regiment under Maj. V. F. Trubitskiy continued moving forward. At the small town of Busk, roughly halfway between Lvov and Brody, it ran into an ever-present German reconnaissance element made up of armored cars and motorcycles and exchanged gunfire with them.

Once again, Popel jumped into his car and raced off to check the situation up front. Traveling along the darkening road, he described a surreal feeling: "When, after the hustle and bustle of headquarters, reports, lambasting, and howling of engines, you find yourself on a quiet road, soaked by the early evening sun, a strange feeling comes over you. Is it possible that nothing happened—no bombings, dusty tanks, unshaven officers, a woman cradling a bloodied head of her child? Maybe it's a dream, some nightmare?"[40]

He caught up to a strange procession:

A lieutenant and two privates, all armed with rifles, are escorting a heavy-set man with raised hands, his uniform blouse unbelted. The prisoner is barely moving his feet—apparently, he already gave up on life.

"Who is that?"

"A spy, Comrade Brigade Commissar. We are taking him to be shot." The "spy" turns towards me:

"Nikolai Kirillych, my dear . . ."

The chief of artillery of our corps, Colonel Chistyakov, runs towards me. He is so flustered that he can not talk. The lieutenant explained for him. "No documents, no car. Was asking about some howitzer regiment. He's got colonel's rank tabs, but his gut is as big as bourgeois'."

"And who are you?" The lieutenant names a regiment of railroad escort troops, presents his ID card. He is fully convinced in righteousness of his actions.

Several minutes later, taking the still-shocked Colonel Chistyakov away from the over-zealous lieutenant, Popel found out what happened. While traveling through Lvov in a lone car, Chistyakov was ambushed by either Ukrainian nationalists or German commandos. He had to jump out of the car, leaving his field bag with documents behind. While making his way out of town, the good colonel ran into the lieutenant and his two men.[41]

As Popel was moving with the advance units corps and rescuing lackluster colonels, Lieutenant General Ryabyshev was chivvying forward the main body of the VIII Mechanized Corps.

> The columns were moving at top speed. Unfortunately, the tractor-towed corps artillery was falling severely behind; the difference in speed was slowing down the overall concentration of forces. Since [I] wanted to go into combat supported by artillery, [I] had to call for halts. Often, we were forced to stop because our columns were subjected to enemy air attacks.[42]

Shortly after 2000 hours, after passing Busk, General Zhukov's car caught up with Ryabyshev's headquarters. After listening to Ryabyshev's brief situation report and plans for the next day's battle, Zhukov departed for Tarnopol and headquarters of the South-Western Front.

Unbeknown to the command of the VIII Mechanized Corps, German aerial reconnaissance spotted its concentration in the evening of June 25. The next morning it would have to attack into alerted and prepared antitank defenses.

Tarnopol, Headquarters of the South-Western Front

Since his arrival at the South-Western Front in Tarnopol, General Zhukov was constantly on the move, cajoling and bullying commanders into getting their troops to the front faster. At around 1700 hours, when the outcome of the fight around Voinitsa and Lokachi still hung in the balance, he telegraphed Potapov and requested the update on the situation.

Potapov reported that while the situation around Kovel was stable, the XXVII Rifle Corps was practically shuttered east of Vladimir-Volynskiy. Its 87th Rifle Division was fighting largely surrounded, and there was no news at all about the 124th Rifle Division. Approaches to Lutsk were being held for now, but there were no reinforcements available to shore up threatened sectors. Potapov was especially concerned that the Germans would attack Lutsk from the south, forcing him to fight on two fronts. Potapov was urgently requesting reinforcements, especially in aviation.[43]

In his turn, Zhukov informed General Potapov of the overall situation on the South-Western Front, with particular emphasis being given to the German breakthrough at the juncture between the Fifth and Sixth armies and their push to Brody. He added that the VIII and XV Mechanized Corps would be attacking the German spearhead from the south. The intent of this maneuver was to destroy the enemy group of forces operating around Berestechko. This would allow the Soviet forces to reestablish the integrity of the border and, in their turn, to attack in the direction of Lyublin.

Furthermore, Potapov was to ensure that Kovel was firmly defended, the encircled 87th Rifle Division was to be assisted by any means possible, liaison officers were to be sent to all major subordinate units, and situation reports were to be submitted every two hours. Also, in response to Potapov's report that the 152mm cannons of his KV-2 tanks did not have armor-piercing ammunition, Zhukov advised him to use the concrete-piercing ammunition. In conclusion, Zhukov expressed his belief that Popatov and his commissar, Member of the Military Council Nikishev, would accomplish their task.

The Military Council of the South-Western Front now had to decide whether to continue the attack on June 25 with just the XV Mechanized Corps or halt operations for one day and wait for complete arrival and concentration of IV, VIII, IX, and XIX Mechanized Corps. However, with Zhukov being present at the headquarters of the South-Western Front to ensure that Moscow's attack orders were being carried out, there wasn't much decision-making leeway available to Kirponos, Purkayev, and

Vashugin. The XV Mechanized Corps and whatever units from the IV and VIII Mechanized Corps that reached vicinity of Brody were to attack on the 25th.[44] Kirponos and his staff were not aware yet that the IV Mechanized Corps became largely entangled in fighting along the front of the Sixth Army and would not be able to take part in the general counterattack. Only one of its divisions, the 8th Tank, would make the belated entry into the fray south of Berestechko.

Kirponos' orders read:

> The main mission of the right-flank armies of the South-Western Front for June 25th, 1941—destruction of the mobile enemy group of forces . . . and for the 8th, 15th and 4th Mechanized corps to reach the region of Voinitsa-Milyatin-Sokal. Besides destroying the main (Sokal) enemy group of forces, this maneuver [will] neutralize the threat of encirclement of the main body of our 5th Army by the enemy.
>
> The units of 8th, 15th and 4th Mechanized Corps are to take up starting attack positions during the night of 24th–25th of June. . . . At exactly 0700 hours on June 25th, 1941, the mechanized corps are to go onto offensive and, destroying the mechanized and infantry enemy units, by 1200 hours accomplish the immediate mission.[45]

This attack was to be supported by three Soviet air force divisions.

CHAPTER 9

Piecemeal Forward, June 25

JUNE 25 WAS A DIFFICULT DAY for the South-Western Front, resulting in the loss of the important cities of Lutsk and Dubno.

The command group of the South-West Front recognized the danger which the German armored group operating in the area of Berestechko and Dubno posed to its sector. There was a real danger that after passing Dubno, the German mechanized forces would turn south, attempting to envelope the bulk of the armies of the South-Western Front still holding the Lvov salient.

Therefore, Kirponos ordered Potapov to vigorously attack towards Dubno with the IX and XIX Mechanized Corps. The IX and XIX Mechanized Corps would be attacking Dubno from north and northeast, while the VIII and XV Mechanized Corps would be attacking towards Dubno and Berestechko from south and southwest. At the same time, Kirponos deployed the XXXVI and XXXVII Rifle Corps and bulk of the 2nd Antitank Brigade in line anchored on Kremenets and facing north to parry the expected German attack south. The offensive was planned for 0900 hours on June 26.

The attack of the VIII and XV Mechanized Corps against the Radzekhov enemy group of forces was designated as primary. The IX and XIX Mechanized Corps were delegated the supporting role. In a follow-up move, after destroying the Dubno enemy group of forces, Potapov was to turn northwest and attack the Lutsk German group of forces.[1]

After General Zhukov returned from his inspection tour of the Fifth Army, he approved Kirponos' overall plan. However, Zhukov also wanted the XXXVI and XXXVII Rifle Corps to take part in the offensive, instead of remaining in static positions against the possibility of German flanking move.[2]

Kirponos' staff spent the whole of the 25th gathering information about the status of the mechanized corps that were supposed to take part in the attack. Lieutenant General Ryabyshev, commanding the VIII Mechanized, reported that he would be ready for the offensive in the morning, but with only his two tank divisions. His motorized rifle division fell behind and would not be ready to start off on time.

Major General Karpezo, commanding the XV Mechanized, reported that only small part of his depleted corps would be able to participate in the offensive. He also requested that the time of the attack be postponed to allow the 8th Tank Division from the IV Mechanized Corps to link up with him. Karpezo was disappointed when informed that the 8th Tank Division would need at least another day to arrive. He was ordered by Kirponos to attack at the assigned time with whatever forces available.[3]

Potapov reported that the bulk of the IX and XIX Mechanized Corps would not be completely ready for attack until the afternoon of June 26. Like Karpezo, Potapov was ordered by Kirponos to attack with whatever was available.

Potapov's reconnaissance finally confirmed that there were no large mobile enemy forces north of Kovel. With the loss of Lutsk, the center of the Fifth Army's front lines was deep behind its right flank. In order not to have more of his forces suffer the fate of 87th and 124th Rifle divisions, Potapov ordered the troops holding Kovel to begin retreating east. All too happy, the 41st Tank Division and its supporting 285th Howitzer Regiment started pulling back.

At the same time, the XXIV Mechanized Corps began moving towards positions of the XXXVI Rifle Corps at Kremenets.[4] However, this weak formation did not arrive in time to take part in the fighting at Dubno.

LUTSK DIRECTION

While the situation on Potapov's right flank in the area of the XV Rifle Corps was holding, his left flank was in tatters.

The forces which carried out the feeble initial counterattack the previous day, the 135th Rifle, 215th Motorized Rifle, and 19th Tank Divisions and 1st Antitank Artillery Brigade, not only were unable to destroy the Vladimir-

Volynskiy enemy group of forces, they themselves were threatened with being cut off from Lutsk by the 13th Panzer Division. The Germans steadily advancing on Kovel from the west were beginning to work around the right flank of the XV Rifle Corps, threatening it with encirclement. Likewise, after collapse of the XXVII Rifle Corps, the XV Corps was also threatened on the left flank as well.

With the destruction of the 87th and 124th Rifle Divisions, 135th Rifle Division was holding the area of operations of the XXVII Rifle Corps. The rear echelon support services of Potapov's army were in disarray. Many round-out units were not mobilized due to the suddenness of the German attack. Numerous supply depots that were positioned too close to the border fell into German hands.

Realizing the severity of the Fifth Army's situation, command of the South-Western Front approved Potapov's request to begin pulling troops from Kovel, at the same time transferring the IX and XIX Mechanized and XXXI Rifle Corps under his direct command. The 193rd and 200th Rifle divisions of the XXXI Rifle Corps began taking up positions along the Ikva River, from Dubno to Kremenets. These two divisions had been marching to the border on foot since June 18 and were thoroughly physically exhausted. In addition, as they got closer to the front, their strung-out columns were subjected to numerous air attacks and suffered casualties and loss of equipment. This corps, under Comcor (Corps Commander, an older Soviet rank, roughly equivalent to Lieutenant General. By the start of the war, some Soviet commanders had not yet received their new rank designations.) A. I. Lopatin, received its orders on June 16 to start moving to the border and concentrate in the area roughly five miles northwest of Kovel by June 28.[5] The third division of the corps, the 195th Rifle, remained in the reserve of the South-Western Front.

Like probing pincers, three battle groups of the 14th Panzer Division were extremely active in the vicinity of Lutsk during June 25. Representing a mission-oriented balanced all-arms task forces, each of these combat groups was capable of carrying out independent tasks:

- Kampfgroup Stempel. 108th Panzer Grenadier Regiment (minus 2nd Battalion), 36th Panzer Regiment (minus one tank company), one battalion from the 3rd Artillery Regiment, one battery from

607th Mortar Battalion (corps assets, 210mm mortars), one battery from 60th Artillery Regiment (corps assets, 100mm cannons), one company of 4th Antitank Battalion, 2nd Company of 13th Motorized Engineer Battalion, and several smaller support detachments.

- Kamfgroup Falkenstein. 103rd Panzer Grenadier Regiment, one tank company of 36th Panzer Regiment, 2nd Battalion of 4th Artillery Regiment, 4th Antitank Battalion (minus one battery), and several small platoon-sized detachments.

- Kampfgroup Damerow, holding defensive positions near a bridge at Rozhysche. One battalion of 108th Panzer Grenadier Regiment, one battalion of 4th Artillery Regiment.

- Division was reinforced by corps artillery: 511th Artillery Regiment (150mm howitzers), 2nd Battalion of the 60th Artillery Regiment (100mm cannons), 607th Heavy Artillery Battalion (210mm mortars, minus one battery), 731st Heavy Artillery Battalion.[6]

Other German panzer divisions were similarly formed into mission-oriented combat packages, generously sprinkled with corps artillery. This would prove to be an all-important factor in the upcoming straggle over the next several days.

While pulling back the XV and XXVII Rifle Corps, Potapov began preparing plans for IX and XIX Mechanized Corps' attack on June 26. Severe shortage of staff and communications officers prevented Potapov from setting up a command group to coordinate the activities of the two corps involved in the counterattack. To better exercise control of the attacking mechanized corps, Potapov moved his headquarters closer to the front line. He set up his command post roughly six miles north of Klevan, not far from the headquarters of Rokossovskiy's IX Mechanized Corps.

Since the area west of Lutsk, assigned to the IX and XIX Mechanized Corps as starting positions, was already captured by the Germans, they were instructed to stage in the area roughly southeast of Lutsk. The two mechanized corps, along with units of the arriving XXXVI Rifle Corps, were to destroy the enemy in the area of Mlynuv and Dubno and capture those towns. Rokossovskiy's two tank divisions began shifting there from their positions along the Lutsk-Rovno highway. The XIX Mechanized Corps under Feklenko was closer than Rokossovskiy to their new areas of concen-

German soldiers manning an assault boat. Most of the large rivers in northern Ukraine run north-to-south, aiding the Red Army in defense. After the initial phase of the invasion, when the Germans captured border bridges intact, the retreating Soviet troops became more adept at destroying bridges behind them, requiring Germans to force river crossings frequently.

Red Army POWs. Caught in cauldrons created by fast-moving panzers and mopping-up infantry, Soviet soldiers were being captured by the hundreds of thousands. By the end of 1941, the prewar Red Army was virtually destroyed.

Display of captured Soviet outdated war materiel: I-153 biplane fighter and 152mm howitzer Model 1910/1937. Nicknamed Chayka ("seagull," after the shape of its upper wing), the I-153 fighter was at the top of the biplane fighter class. However, its time had passed, and Chaykas proved to be no match for German Messerschmitt Bf 109s. The howitzer was an upgraded World War I version, suffering from slow towing speeds and limited traverse and elevation.

Wehrmacht soldiers were eagerly welcomed by Ukrainian civilians early in the war, civilians who believed that the Germans were coming to save them from the Bolsheviks. Ukrainian nationalists provided invaluable aid to the Germans as scouts and saboteurs against the Red Army. However, the honeymoon was soon over, once the Ukrainians realized that the Germans were coming not as liberators, but as a different kind of slave master.

T-26 light tanks, year 1933 model. The reversed turrets indicate that this unit was engaged from the rear. The two tanks in the foreground appear abandoned, rather than damaged. However, one of the tanks in the center background has its turret knocked off, which is seen lying on the ground.

T-28 medium tank, a three-turreted machine designed for an infantry-support role. Its main turret mounted a 76.2mm cannon, while the two smaller ones each had one 7.62mm machine gun. It performed reasonably well during the Winter War with Finland in 1940. While outdated by 1941, it was the first vehicle of its class in the world to go into serial production in 1933.

German soldiers inspecting a Soviet 120mm mortar and its limber. Almost completely lacking air defense means, the strung-out Soviet columns became easy prey for German aircraft. Especially hard hit were Soviet artillery units, which greatly reduced the Red Army's ability to support its armor on the attack and deal with attacking German panzers. This particular limber team has its dead horses still in their traces.

Soviet dead lie on one of the nameless roads in Ukraine. Their weapons appear to have been picked up, possibly by their own side. Note the unwound bandages spilling from the head of the figure in the foreground.

Red Army reservist POWs. Very often called-up reservists were sent into combat without being properly equipped and outfitted, many still in their civilian clothes, as demonstrated by the two figures in the foreground. Note several other men wearing the budyonovka, a high-peaked broadcloth hat. These hats were supposed to be phased out in the mid-1930s, but large quantities of them still remained in many depots.

BT-7 light tank. The BT series of tanks, literally meaning "fast tank" (bystrokhondiy tank), was developed to conduct break-through operations in depth. The basis for the BT series was the work of an American engineer, John Walter Christie. BT tanks operated in tracked and wheeled modes. This particular machine had its tracks removed to allow for faster movement on the road.

This BT-7 tank bears a distinctive white triangle marker, identifying it as belonging to the 34th Tank Division of the VIII Mechanized Corps. A similar triangle can be seen on one of the turret hatch covers. Due to its distinctive profile with the oval hatch covers raised, the Germans nicknamed the BT-7 "Mickey Mouse."

German soldiers posing on a KV-1 heavy tank belonging to the VIII Mechanized Corps. The appearance of new Soviet tanks like heavy KVs and medium T-34s was shocking to German troops. However, once the fighting was over, the multitude of abandoned and destroyed Soviet tanks provided a convenient and desirable background for German soldiers posing for keepsake photos..

KV-2 heavy tank. This tank, with a 152mm howitzer in a naval turret mounted on the same chassis as the KV-1, was designed to assist Soviet infantry in breaching enemy fortifications. With its howitzer's high trajectory, the KV-2 was never envisioned to operate in an antitank role and had no armor-piercing ammunition. During the few times KV-2s came to grips with German panzers, Soviet tankers were forced to use concrete-piercing rounds against the German machines.

A sad end for this T-34 medium tank. Often regarded as the best tank of World War II, the highly maneuverable T-34, with its thick sloping armor, was more than a match for any German machine. However, poor Soviet command and tactics negated the tremendous advantage afforded by this excellent tank. Gen. Heinz Guderian was so impressed with this machine he insisted that a team of engineers be dispatched to the eastern front to study this model.

T-38 amphibious reconnaissance tank with its turret reversed. In the swimming mode, this tank was propelled by a three-bladed propeller mounted in the rear. This tank was designed to operate as a scout. However, due to the very small number of radios actually installed in them, the T-38's performance in its reconnaissance role was very limited. After 1941, it was rarely used in combat, most often relegated to the role of artillery tractor.

T-35 heavy tank. The two German soldiers in the photo illustrate the scale of this machine. The huge tank weighed in at fifty tons, mounting five turrets and operated by crew of eleven. Only sixty-one of these machines were produced, with the majority of still-operational vehicles concentrated in the VIII Mechanized Corps. Plagued by a multitude of mechanical difficulties, almost all of these tanks were abandoned before coming to grips with the enemy.

tration. However, as it moved into positions north of Mlynov, it became engaged with the forward German units and could not adequately prepare for the offensive on June 26.

Since the morning of June 24, the 1st Antitank Artillery Brigade had had a difficult fight on its hands in the direct vicinity of the western suburbs of Lutsk. During the previous night, Moskalenko deployed his brigade in three defensive lines. They made the enemy pay dearly, and as the Germans overcame each successive line, the surviving Soviet gunners fell back to the next one.

During the night of June 24–25, Moskalenko's depleted brigade was ordered to abandon its positions on the southwest outskirts of Lutsk and fall back north to the town of Rozhysche. This small town on the Styr River was becoming a focal point of Soviet defenses on the northern flank of Potapov's Fifth Army. Pushing the XV and XXVII Rifle Corps ahead of them, the Germans were attempting to pierce a gap between the two beleaguered corps at Rozhysche and capture beachheads across the Styr River. The shattered XXII Mechanized Corps and the 135th Rifle Division were falling back on this town as well, and Moskalenko's units were to form the keystone of the antitank defenses around town.

As the 1st Antitank Artillery Brigade arrived at the bridge near Rozhysche, which it intended to use to cross to the eastern side of the Styr River, it found the bridge destroyed under orders of General Artemenko, commander of the XXVII Rifle Corps. In the general chaos of the retreat, the Soviet demolition detachment charged with destroying the bridge was not informed to wait for Moskalenko's crossing before blowing up the bridge. Now the brigade was trapped on the western side of the river.[7]

Fortunately, Moskalenko's scouts soon located another bridge nearby. This one was a railroad bridge. While it was possible to move the artillery across the cross ties and rails of this bridge, it would take time. The Soviet gunners began digging in near the bridge's western end, forming a crescent with the flanks resting on the river. At approximately the same time, some rear-echelon support units from the 27th Rifle and XXII Mechanized Corps arrived at the railroad bridge as well.

As the Soviets began frantically digging shallow trenches and foxholes, sporadic German artillery and mortar fire began falling among them. They were quickly followed by determined German infantry and armor attacks around 0600 hours. The Germans pressed very hard, hoping to rush the bridge and trap as many Soviets as possible on the west bank. During one attack, the German panzers broke through the first Soviet line of shallow trenches. In the ensuing close-quarters fighting, one Soviet battery was destroyed, but Germans were forced to fall back.

Utilizing the lull in fighting, Moskalenko began hurriedly transferring his units to the eastern side of the railroad bridge. He barely had enough time to send one battalion over when an unexpected delay took place.

The rear echelon units of the XXVII Rifle and XXII Mechanized Corps rushed the bridge in panic. Several hundred men and horses, pushing and shoving, tried to force their way to the eastern side. In the ensuing panic, men and animals trampled over each other in the narrow confines of the bridge. Wagons, people, and horses lost their footing or were shoved over the sides and plunged into the water. The draft horses began breaking their legs between railroad ties, creating ungodly tangles of overturned artillery pieces, crushed men, flying hooves, splintered wagons, and stalled vehicles. Adding to the panic, German artillery shells began falling among the crowds at the bridge.[8] The whole scene resembled Napoleon's disastrous retreat over Berezina River in 1812.

An indescribable panic ensued. Drivers began unhitching horses; some men jumped in the river and tried to swim across. The debris on the railroad bridge completely blocked the passage and created such an obstacle that it would have taken several hours to clear it. In order to quickly remove the obstacle, Moskalenko sent two heavy KV-1 tanks from 19th Tank Division to bodily push the obstruction off the bridge. The huge tanks flattened, crushed, and pushed the debris off the bridge, and those units that maintained their cohesion began crossing at once. After the rear-guard motorcycle regiment from the XXII Mechanized Corps crossed the bridge, it was blown up.[9]

North of Moskalenko's location, Maj. Gen. I. I. Fedyuninskiy's XV Rifle Corps was retreating as well. Falling back with Fedyuninkiy's corps, the 41st Tank Division fought several sharp rear-guard actions, keeping the hard-pressing German reconnaissance units at arm's length. The rear echelons of the 41st Tank Divisions suffered heavily from German air attacks during the daytime retreat. Meager antiair defenses of this tank division amounted to only four antiaircraft cannons and could not prevent the German planes from getting in close to the strung-out Soviet columns.[10]

Following on the heels of retreating Soviet units, German III Corps deployed a fresh panzer division, the 13th, which looped around Lutsk and entered the town in late afternoon on the 25th.

DUBNO, 11TH PANZER DIVISION

After crushing the left flank of Soviet XXVII Rifle Corps and brushing aside the elements of XV Mechanized, the 11th Panzer Division continued advancing towards Dubno.

Even though several shattered and disorganized Red Army units put up feeble resistance, the Soviet Air Force was present in strength. The Soviet bombers, almost always unprotected by their fighter brethren, launched numerous attacks against the German division. Gustav Schrodek informs us of fifty such attacks recorded during the day; this number seems a little inflated. German fighter aircraft falling upon virtually defenseless Soviet bombers took a terrible toll on these valuable aircraft, often shooting down whole squadrons as they helplessly and unwaveringly droned on to their targets.

Pushing aside weak Soviet defenses and shrugging off air attacks, 11th Panzer Division continued forward:

> While the [15th Panzer Regiment was] continually entangled and stopped by new fights with enemy detachments, the 11th Panzer Division continued its advance on Dubno under cover of a small forest in two columns.
>
> The Recon Battalion 231 (motorized) [attacked] towards Mlynov from the north. The 110th Infantry Regiment, which spent the whole night destroying the weaker enemy units while advancing, [reached] Dubno with its advance elements south of the city and [continued] to penetrate the area at 0730 hours. By 1100 hours, Dubno could be attacked from both south and the north. After defeating a flank attack during which the Russians also used tanks, the 11th Panzer Division announced in the early afternoon on June 25th that Dubno was firmly in their hands at 1400 hours.

In the evening, a rumor of Soviet armor units advancing from Ostrow caused big confusion with the supply units in the rear, and they [returned] to Lopatin. Some columns [turned] back, [causing] major jams on the route of advance. However, the retreat was stopped and intended hasty burn of the timber bridge of Styr at Merva [was] prevented.[11]

IX MECHANIZED CORPS, MAJ. GEN. K. K. ROKOSSOVSKIY COMMANDING

Throughout June 25, the IX Mechanized Corps continued fighting south of Lutsk-Rovno highway against German 13th and 14th Panzer divisions. The Germans were pushing hard to cut the highway and encircle Lutsk from the east. Instead of preparing for the offensive the next day, Rokossovskiy's corps was forced to fight a defensive battle.

At the end of the day as Lutsk was abandoned, Colonel Kalinin's 131st Motorized Rifle Division waited until the last organized Soviet unit retreated across the river, then blew up the bridge. Casualties were heavy. Even though Kalinin's division absorbed small groups of retreating soldiers from other units, they were nowhere enough to make good his losses.[12]

Stragglers and survivors of the XXII Mechanized Corps began arriving in the positions of the IX Mechanized in increasing numbers. One of them was Maj. Gen. Kuzma A. Semenchenko, whose 19th Tank Division was shuttered in the fighting the previous day. As already mentioned in the previous chapter, this attack cost the 19th Tank Division all the regimental commanders hors de combat. Semenchenko himself, narrowly escaping a brush with death, was quite depressed, telling Rokossovskiy the story of the defeat of the XII Mechanized Corps. He was closely echoed by an unidentified regimental commissar from the same corps. Never one to mince words, Rokossovskiy pointedly told the two officers to stop whining, find their units, and rejoin them. In his memoirs, Rokossovskiy did not actually name Semenchenko, stating that this was "commander of a tank division from XXII Mechanized Corps." It is easy to establish Semenchenko's identity, however. There were two tank division commanders in the XXII Mechanized Corps, colonels Semenchenko and Pavlov. Since Pavlov's 41st Tank Division was still at Kovel on June 25, this disheartened division commander had to be Semenchenko.[13]

Still, Rokossovskiy realized that the XXII Mechanized Corps suffered heavily, and morale was low among its survivors. He was very explicit in describing one episode of his interaction with the survivors:

> In the area of Klevan we gathered many [such] sad-sack warriors, among whom were many officers. Majority of these people did not have weapons. To our shame, they all, including the officers, removed their rank insignia.
>
> In one such group my attention was caught by an elderly man sitting under an elm, whose appearance and bearing did not resemble that of a common soldier. A young female medical orderly was sitting next to him. Addressing the sitting men, roughly one hundred in number, I ordered the officers to come to me. Nobody moved. I approached the elderly [man] and ordered him to stand up. Then, addressing him as an officer, I asked for his rank. His forced reply of "colonel" was said so indifferently and his demeanor so arrogantly challenging that I almost exploded at the sight of him and his tone of voice. Pulling out a pistol, I was ready to shoot him where he stood. Apathy and grandstanding immediately left the colonel. Realizing the likely outcome of this, he fell to his knees and began begging forgiveness, swearing to wash off his shame with blood. The scene was not the most pleasant one, but that's how it happened.
>
> I ordered the colonel to gather all the [stragglers] by morning, organize them into a detachment, and personally report to me in the morning of June 26th. My orders were carried out. The newly formed unit numbered over 500 men. They were all used as replacements in the motorized rifle units of the corps.[14]

XIX MECHANIZED CORPS, MAJ. GEN. N. V. FEKLENKO COMMANDING

While its two advance companies were operating east of the Ikva River, the main body of XIX Mechanized Corps was approaching its assigned areas of operations around Rovno in two echelons, mounted and dismounted. All the working tanks, combined into one regiment per tank division, as well as other elements of the corps that could be transported in trucks, constituted the first echelon. Everybody else, marching on foot or with the horse-drawn vehicles, made up the second echelon.

The units available to Major General Feklenko for the attack on the 26th hardly resembled a mechanized corps. His 213th Motorized Rifle Division and the motorized rifle regiments of the tank divisions, being essentially the regular foot-slogging infantry, hopelessly fell behind, needing at least two more days to catch up. Feklenko's meager artillery, whatever could be towed by truck, tractor, or horse, straggled as well.

The two tank divisions, the 40th and 43rd, suffered such horrendous attrition during the march that each division had to be combined into a provisional regiment. Thus, Major General Feklenko would be attacking on the morrow with the equivalent of roughly two tank regiments, unsupported by infantry or artillery. However, orders given to him from above continued to refer to his formation as a full-strength mechanized corps.

VIII MECHANIZED CORPS, LT. GEN. D. I. RYABYSHEV COMMANDING

In the morning briefing on June 25, acting chief of staff, Lieutenant Colonel Tsinchenko (a week before the war, Chief of Staff Colonel Katkov went on leave), outlined their mission for the next day. The VIII and XV Mechanized Corps were to form a mobile group and attack the southern flank of the advancing German armor force.[15]

The XV Mechanized Corps under Major General Karpezo was to attack from Toporov area (approximately twenty-five miles west of Brody) towards Radekhov and Berestechko. A division of fighter aircraft, which failed to materialize, was allocated to support Karpezo's attack. While the right flank of the 15th Mechanized and the left flank of the 8th's were supposed to be in contact with each other, so far the command group of the 8th Mechanized was not aware of XV Mechanized Corps' exact location. There was no neighbor on the right and wasn't going to be one. The area over which the two corps were to advance was wooded and swampy, very unfavorable for tank maneuvers. There were four small rivers running across the axis of advance: Slonovka, Syten'ka, Styr, and Plyashevka. Although narrow, they had wide, muddy banks.

During the meeting, Tsinchenko reported about dozens of vehicles, broken down, damaged by enemy, out of gas, that were abandoned along the roads leading to Brody. Along with the vehicles, they had to leave people behind to repair and salvage whatever possible. Hinting at desertion, Popel writes: "Some commanders could not always account why people were missing."[16]

Especially hard hit by mechanical breakdowns were the older vehicles, like the five-turreted T-35 tanks. According to Ryabyshev:

> Large numbers of older tanks broke down and could not reach the staging area. T-35 tanks, for example, were all left behind on the roads. The flame-thrower tank battalion (T-26s) of the 24th Tank Regiment/12th Tank Division arrived far from full strength. Other older tanks were left behind as well. By this time we found out about major defects in KV tanks. Their brake belts, due to frequent turns during protracted continuous movement, would overheat and break down.[17]

Ryabyshev and his senior staff officers faced a daunting task of planning a major offensive with limited information available. He wrote:

> There was no enemy in Brody, but neither were our troops. We did not receive any information about the enemy from [South-Western] Front HQ. There was no information either about the neighbors on the left and right. We did not know with whom we [would] be cooperating and which air units [would] be supporting corps combat operations. However, we received reports from our reconnaissance, sent out when we were still on the march. When we consolidated information by midnight on June 25th, we reached conclusion that in the area of proposed corps' offensive, the enemy, covering its main tank force operating in the Lutsk-Rovno-Kiev directions, took up defenses along the Ikva River facing east and along the Sytenka River facing southeast. By this time additional reconnaissance reports informed us that to the right and left of the Brody-Berestechko road, along the east bank of Sytenka River, 212th Motorized Rifle Division from Maj. Gen. I. I. Karpezo's 15th Mechanized Corps took up positions and made contact with the enemy.[18]

In the afternoon, corps' commissar Nikolai Popel drove to the vicinity of Toporov, attempting to find the headquarters of the XV Mechanized Corps, and located it after spending several hours bouncing around deep-rutted roads. Upon arrival there, Popel was struck by how different the command posts of the two corps looked.

The VIII, not yet subjected to severe bombardment and precise German artillery strikes, still established its command post as it did before the war by setting up their white canvas tents. Karpezo's headquarters, on the other hand, had already undergone two severe air attacks and adapted the dugouts and slit trenches. Popel recalled a female typist who worked in a slit trench, placing her "Underwood" typewriter on the trench's top lip. Upon hearing the whistling of the incoming German artillery shells, she would pick up her typewriter and duck down into the trench.[19]

Lieutenant General Karpezo, his commissar Ivan Vasilevich Lutai, and Popel conferred about the upcoming attack. Popel was shocked to find out that on the 26th, only one division from the XV Mechanized Corps could participate in the attack. Karpezo's other two divisions suffered such heavy casualties during the previous three days that they could barely hold their defensive positions. In conversation with Popel, Karpezo expressed his concern that the headquarters of the South-Western Front was not aware of his situation and was giving him a mission as if for a full-strength corps. He was right.

During the night of June 25–26, Maj. Gen. T. A. Mishanin conducted a local counterattack using the motorized rifle regiment from his 12th Tank Division. He managed to eliminate a small German beachhead on the southern, Soviet-occupied, side of Slonovka River and set up several observation posts on the northern, German, side of the river. Despite expending large amounts of energy, Mishanin recon patrols could not find out locations of German main defensive positions or their strength.[20]

Also late at night, Ryabyshev's staff was able to establish direct contact with the 212th Motorized Rifle Division under Major General Baranov from Karpezo's corps.

> Headquarters of this unit informed us that the division was located
> on the right flank of the 15th Mechanized Corps, whose troops were in
> combat contact since the beginning of the war with the enemy para-

troopers in the area of Radekhov. After eliminating several airborne groups, the corps became involved in combat with enemy's tank group, which penetrated our border. . . . Forces of the 15th Mechanized Corps were forced to go on the defensive along the line of over forty miles.[21]

Lieutenant General Ryabyshev was forced to plan his attack based on fragmented information. Headquarters of the South-Western Front did not pass down any usable information about the enemy. No liaison officer from the air force fighter division showed up, and there was no telephone or radio contact with it, either.

> Even though the received information did not create a clear picture about the enemy, it still allowed us to more or less get our bearings and begin preparing for combat. Working on the plan for the upcoming battle, I took into consideration that the enemy is not occupying fortified defensive positions and decided to suddenly attack the forward Hitlerite units at dawn of June 26th and, continuing with the offensive, by the end of the day reach the line of Volkovye-Berestechko-Mikolayev. Each division commander received a concrete and clear mission. The corps was deployed in one echelon; the 34th Tank Division was to advance on the right, with the mission of breaching the enemy position in the sector of Sytno-Sytenka River. The 12th Tank Division, advancing in the center, was to breach the enemy in the sector from Sytenka River to Leshnyuv. On the left, acting in concert with the 212th Motorized [Rifle] Division and securing corps' left flank, the 7th Motorized [Rifle] Division will begin its advance.[22]

XV MECHANIZED CORPS, MAJ. GEN. I. I. KARPEZO COMMANDING

The XV Mechanized Corps spent most of June 25 engaged in heavily see-saw fighting and was unable to prepare for the next day's offensive. The 10th Tank Division under Maj. Gen. S. Y. Ogurtzov experienced particularly heavy fighting.

Around 1600 hours, Major Govor, chief of staff of the 20th Tank Regiment, led a task force of fifteen tanks in a local counterattack. They ran straight into strong German antitank defenses and were brutalized, losing eleven out of fifteen tanks, including four new T-34s and seven light BT-7 machines. Personnel losses in this task force were heavy, with Major Govor himself missing and presumed dead.

The Germans continued pressing 10th Tank Division, slowly flowing around its flanks. In order to improve its position, 10th Motorized Rifle Regiment counterattacked, supported by several tanks from 20th Tank Regiment and two batteries from 10th Howitzer Regiment. The attack was bloodily repulsed, resulting in one rifle battalion being completely gutted.

While 10th Tank Division was spilling its lifeblood, its sister 37th Tank Division was slowly moving towards Radekhov. They were advancing practically blind, being unaware of locations of the main German positions near Radekhov. Karpezo ordered its commander, Colonel Anikushkin, to locate the enemy and find fords on the Radostavka River.[23] By the end of the day, its two tank regiments were in position.

The 212th Motorized Rifle Division fought several small clashes with the German reconnaissance elements moving south from Leshnov.

SITUATION AT THE END OF JUNE 25

The suddenness of the German attack and their rapid advance, coupled with heavy Soviet losses, produced many cases of breakdown in morale among the Soviet troops. While on the move to their new command post during the night of June 25–26, the command group of the Fifth Army witnessed a disorderly retreat of units from 135th Rifle and 19th Tank Divisions from XXII Mechanized Corps and 460th Artillery Regiment of XXVII Rifle Corps.[24] Only personal involvement by Potapov and other officers from the army headquarters halted the flight of men and vehicles and prevented the spread of panic, which was beginning to also affect the 131st Motorized Division of the IX Mechanized Corps.

The Military Council of the Fifth Army immediately took quick and severe measures to reestablish discipline and combat-effectiveness of the affected units. All the roads to the rear were blocked and actively patrolled to prevent desertion. A collection point was set up in the woods north of Tsuman in order to process individuals and small groups which were found wandering around in the rear of the army. After two or three days of reorganization and mental and moral fortification, they were sent back to their units.

In addition to administrative measures, the Military Council of the army, starting on 26th of June and later, issued a series of directives and orders dealing with steps to be taken to increase discipline and morale of the troops. These directives pointed out that the communists and Comsomol members do not take the leading roles in fighting, do not oppose the panic mongers, and often desert themselves. The directives immediately demanded to turn over the deserters, cowards, and panic-mongers to the military tribunals. Communists and Comsomol members were to take a leading role in the struggle and lead by example; there was to be only one slogan for a communist: death or victory. The party bureaus which could not prevent the unauthorized withdrawals were to be disbanded, and the communists who could not reestablish order in their units were to be held accountable.[25]

At the same time, all technical personnel of the whole Volyn region civilian communication apparatus were mobilized. This allowed military communications units to be filled up with highly qualified personnel and equipment. A liaison section headed by Major Shestakov was created at the Fifth Army headquarters. Each division and corps of the Fifth Army was required to send two liaison officers with their own transportation to be part of this section. These liaison officers were to constantly be on the move between the army headquarters and their units in order to provide up-to-date information, not more than two hours old. This was a valuable additional source of communication besides radio and telephone.[26]

Despite taking Lutsk, German command did not actively exploit a continual offensive on this direction. Both panzer divisions of German III Corps received orders in the evening of 25th to shift south. The 14th Panzer Division was to advance on Rovno via Ostrozhets (ten miles southeast of Lutsk), the 13th Panzer Division, via Plosk village, further south. This in effect moved them away from the strategic highway going through Vladimir-Volynskiy to Rovno and then to Zhitomir and Kiev. The stubborn resistance of Soviet forces, especially strong antitank defenses posed by Moskalenko's 1st Antitank Artillery Brigade, forced the Germans to move away from this major road artery and probe forward along secondary roads.[27]

The time lost by the VIII Mechanized Corps was wisely used by Germans, allowing them to pull up at least four infantry divisions on the key Dubno axis. Especially bitter was the fact that the XV Mechanized Corps in the morning of June 25 was moving through the area which it occupied on the

23rd. Unbeknown to Soviet command, on June 26 they would be facing not the porous defenses of panzer divisions, but solid antitank barriers put up by the German infantry divisions. Still, the Soviet counterattack came sooner than expected. Command of Army Group South expected a major Soviet offensive on June 28. Instead, it came on June 26.

The 16th Panzer Division, moving up in the wake of 11th, crossed the border on June 24 near Krystonopol. It had to fight several skirmishes with still-resisting bunkers on the Molotov Line. According to the history of this division, the "border defenses were fiercely defended."[28]

CHAPTER 10

Battle for Dubno, June 26–27

JUNE 26, 1941

AFTER MEETING SPIRITED SOVIET RESISTANCE in the Lutsk area and not being able to develop an attack along the highway onto Rovno, command of the German III Mechanized Corps shifted its 13th Panzer Division south on June 26. Following in the wake of the 11th Panzer Division, the 13th crossed the Ikva River over a bridge near Mlynov and followed the 11th Panzer towards Ostrog. Behind the two panzer divisions came 111th and 299th Infantry Divisions hurrying along on foot into the gap breached by the hard-charging 11th Panzer division. Behind and to the south came the 75th Infantry and 16th Panzer Divisions, anchoring the tenuous supply and communications line of the "Ghost Division" to Berestechko.

Driving determinedly forward, the 11th Panzer Division was not aware of the danger gathering on both of its flanks. Even after suffering severe casualties in fighting up to this point and terrible attrition of combat vehicle due to noncombat losses, the four Soviet mechanized corps moving up to cut off the spearhead of German armored thrust were still very formidable. The clash of armor was promising to be a loud one.

After Lutsk finally fell in the evening of June 25, Germans continued pressing their attack along the highway to Rovno. The 1st Antitank Artillery Brigade, the motorcycle regiment of the XXII Mechanized Corps, and the 131st Motorized Division were barely defending a wide front from Rozhysche to Ostrozhets, ten miles southeast of Lutsk.

XIX Mechanized Corps, Major General Feklenko Commanding

The northern Soviet pincer aimed at Dubno from north and northeast was composed of IX and XIX Mechanized Corps. However, being only vaguely aware of each other's whereabouts, the two corps commanders were not able to meet and work out a coordinated attack plan.

Major General Feklenko had very meager resources to contribute to the offensive, the actual strength of his XIX Mechanized Corps under his direct command being closer to a division size. On paper, the combat-arms portion of XIX Mechanized Corps amounted to five tank, four motorized rifle, four artillery, and one motorcycle regiment. In reality, none of its motorized rifle formations were fully present for action on June 26. Roughly two battalions of infantrymen from the 213th Motorized Rifle Division were loaded up into the few available trucks and brought along with the tank formations. The rest of division trudged forward on foot and were approximately seventy kilometers east of Rovno in the morning of June 26. The bulk of artillery regiments moved with them as well, brought forward mainly by slow tractors and horse teams. Armored vehicles belonging to the 132nd Tank Regiment of the 213th Motorized Rifle Division were split between the two tank divisions.

As mentioned previously, the two tank regiments in each tank division lost so many combat vehicles during the approach phase that they had to be combined into a provisional regiment. Also, advance elements of the 19th Mechanized had been in contact with the enemy since the night of June 24, further adding to the loss of tanks and armored cars. Thus the actual combat strength of the XIX Mechanized Corps which took part in the fighting on June 26 were two tank regiments and an equivalent of a weak rifle regiment, basically an understrength division.

The morning of June 26 found the 40th Tank Division roughly twelve miles northwest of Rovno in the area of Klevan. Its sister division, the 43rd Tank, was near Goscha, ten miles east of Rovno. During the previous night, the motorized rifle regiment of the 43rd Tank Division made contact with a rifle regiment from 228th Rifle Division belonging to the XXXVI Rifle Corps and deployed in the immediate vicinity northeast of Dubno. These two weak regiments formed the advanced Soviet positions.

The 40th Tank Division was to attack Mlynov, capture it, and continue southwest. The 43rd Tank Division was assigned to take Dubno and, after taking it, continue southwest as well, parallel to the 40th Tank.

The attack was supposed to begin at 0900 hours, but not all the units were ready and the start was postponed to 1100 hours and then again to 1400 hours. The Germans did not oblige by waiting for the Soviets and attacked first and steadily pushed the advance elements of the 43rd Tank and 228th Rifle Divisions away from Dubno.

As the main bodies of the 40th and 43rd Tank Divisions advanced, they became intermixed with the units of the 228th Rifle Division. The 40th Tank advanced around and through the right flank of the 228th, and the 43rd Tank took up similar positions on 228th's left.

Opposing the 19th Mechanized Corps on the north side of Dubno were elements of German 11th and 13th Panzer and 111th and 299th Infantry Divisions.

All the available tanks in the 43rd Tank Division were merged into its 86th Tank Regiment. In the morning of June 26 this unit numbered two KV-1 tanks, two T-34s, and seventy-five T-26s. While the Soviet and German numbers were roughly equivalent in this sector, the Germans had distinct advantage of heavy artillery assigned to the 11th Panzer Division from corps assets.

Attacking into the face of heavy artillery and dug-in infantry, commander of the 43rd Tank Division, Colonel I. G. Tsibin, placed his four KV-1 and T-34 tanks in the first echelon, acting as mobile armored screen for his light-skinned T-26s. The see-saw battle lasted all day, with both sides constantly conducting small-unit attacks and counter-attacks. Slowly gaining ground, the 43rd Tank Division reached the Ikva River on the eastern outskirts of Dubno. However, the price it paid was high: Colonel Tsibin's division lost both of its KV-1 tanks and fifteen T-26 tanks, an irretrievable loss of over 22 percent of armored vehicles.

By late afternoon, the Soviet attacks started petering out. German 13th Panzer Division broke through the defensive positions of the 228th Rifle Division and began flanking the 40th Tank Division around the left. The 11th Panzer Division went around the left flank of the 43rd Tank Division south of Dubno, and one of its combat groups raced towards Ostrog and Zdolbunov. A breach began developing between the two tank divisions of the XIX Mechanized Corps.

Fearing his corps being fragmented and surrounded, Major General Feklenko ordered his units to disengage and pull back. The majority of the 228th Rifle Division accompanied Feklenko's corps in retreat.

Ostrog: Task Force Lukin vs. 11th Panzer Division

The German breakthrough to Ostrog was not foreseen by the Soviet command, and this town was lightly held by a small garrison unit, incapable of offering any resistance to the Germans. The way to Shepetovka, an important railroad junction, looked open. Gustav Schrodek, describing the actions of 15th Panzer Regiment of the 11th Panzer Division, writes:

> The regiment's advance resumes already at 0200 hours, and by 0630 hours Mlodowa is taken after a tough fight against enemy infantry and artillery.[1] However, this was achieved at a loss of three of our own panzers.
>
> By 1400 hours the regiment was in a renewed fight with enemy tanks which advanced from northeast—and were stopped again. Part of the regiment, Battle Group Angern, advanced there and in the afternoon already stand five kilometers west of Mizoch, approximately 20 kilometers northwest from Ostrog.[2]

And here the German intelligence failure came into play. Unbeknown to the Germans, the Soviet Sixteenth Army, one of the two armies forming the second strategic echelon, was located near the town of Berdichev. At the start of the war, the Sixteenth Army was just finishing up its move from Siberia. On June 26th, the Sixteenth Army and its sister Nineteenth Army, also newly arrived in Ukraine, received orders to move by train north to Byelorussia to shore up the crumbling Western Front there.

Since the morning of June 26, the units of the Sixteenth Army under Lt. Gen. M. F. Lukin were moving towards their railhead at Shepetovka. Finding out about the German breakthrough at Ostrog and realizing the severity of the situation, Lieutenant General Lukin, on his own initiative, diverted the 109th Motorized Rifle Division of his V Mechanized Corps from the embarkation and personally led it towards Ostrog.

Its 173rd Reconnaissance Battalion arrived in Ostrog just before the Germans. It did not have time to dig in before the German 61st Motorcycle Battalion from the 11th Panzer Division slammed into them. After a sharp fight, the German motorcycle troopers pushed their Soviet counterparts to the northeast of the town, where the Red Army men were able to dig in, partially surrounded.

However, the fighting that raged on the flanks of the 11th Panzer Division created many anxious moments for its men:

Employment of our own Air Force eliminates the activity of the Russian aircraft, which is generally pleasantly noted. Considering the situation which was becoming ever more unclear, it was welcomed to be able to completely turn one's attention on the battlefield alone. The Russians tried to break through everywhere and thereby temporarily created quite critical situations. For a short time the Russians succeeded in closing the route of advance towards Ostrog with a flank attack. . . . By the evening of 26th, however, the situation was again quite secure."[3]

During the night of June 26–27, all the forces that Lieutenant General Lukin could divert from Shepetovka gathered just east of Ostrog. Organized into Task Force Lukin, they were the 109th Motorized Rifle Division composed of 173rd Reconnaissance Battalion, 381st Motorized Rifle Regiment, 2nd Battalion of the 602nd Motorized Rifle Regiment, and the 404th Artillery Regiment, plus several small garrison and rear echelon detachments. The rest of Lukin's army already departed or were in the process of leaving for the Western Front.[4]

IX Mechanized Corps,
Major General K. K. Rokossovskiy Commanding

Realizing that his orders to attack on the 26th would be virtually suicidal, Major General Rokossovskiy was not eager to throw his weak corps into the meat grinder. His motorized rifle division, the 131st, was fighting detached east of Lutsk. The majority of artillery belonging to his 9th Mechanized Corps had not arrived yet, and only his two tank divisions were available for the attack. However, though never blessed with an abundance of tanks, the march towards the sound of the gun further depleted the numbers available to him.

The IX Mechanized Corps started the war with right around three hundred tanks, not a single one of them being new T-34s or KV-1s. In fact, roughly 20 percent of tanks in Rokossovskiy's formation were armed only with machine guns. Approximately a third of his tank strength was contained in the 131st Motorized Rifle Division, which was being steadily ground down east of Lutsk. With large numbers of breakdowns during the march, Rokossovskiy had only small numbers of light T-26s, BT-5s, and BT-7s with which to attack. His 20th Tank Division, numbering around thirty tanks, was basically a reinforced rifle regiment. The 35th Tank Division, with slightly over one hundred tanks, would have to bear the brunt of the offensive.

Even on the day of the offensive, Rokossovskiy did not have contact with neighboring corps, nor coordination from above: "Nobody was tasked with coordinating actions of the three corps. They were committed into combat piecemeal and directly from the march, without any consideration given to condition of the forces which already fought with strong enemy for two days, and without taking into consideration their distance from the area of expected contact with the enemy."[5]

Lack of coordination from the higher echelons could be further demonstrated by the fact that Rokossovskiy thought that the XIX Mechanized Corps would be advancing on his left and the XXII, on his right. He had no idea that XXII Mechanized Corps was so thoroughly disordered that it no longer functioned as a corps.

Not being able to completely ignore his attack orders, Rokossovskiy made a display of being on the offensive, while basically maintaining his positions. In mid-afternoon on June 26, he conducted limited counterattacks. While not achieving territorial gains, Rokossovskiy's attack relieved some pressure from the hard-pressed XIX Mechanized Corps, allowing it to fall back in some semblance of order.

Accepting enormous responsibility, Rokossovskiy decided not to continue attacking. Instead, he assumed a completely defensive posture, shifting his 20th Tank Division to his right flank to further strengthen defense of Lutsk-Rovno highway.

During this day, as already became norm, Rokossovskiy was severely hampered by lack of information, especially from the headquarters of the Fifth Army:

> We were forced to gather information ourselves. Staff officers headed by General Maslov quickly adapted to the seemingly impossible situation in which we found ourselves and were able to provide us with the necessary information. But this was accomplished at a steep price—many staff officers were killed while carrying out their missions.
>
> Judging from disjointed reports, we were somewhat able to piece together what was happening in our direction. We did not know what was happening on the other sectors of the South-Western Front. Apparently, General Potapov was not in a better situation. During the time I commanded the 9th Mechanized Corps, his headquarters were not able to assist us in these matters even once. Besides, communications with him were cut most of the time.[6]

Despite being proud and satisfied with performance of his own corps, Rokossovskiy realized that he was not faced with the main German thrust. He was very frank in his memoirs: "It is difficult to imagine how we would have performed if we would be facing the main German attack."[7]

Attack of the Southern Group: VIII and XV Mechanized Corps

While the threat posed to the German Dubno group of forces by the Soviet southern mechanized group was much greater, it was defeated piecemeal in a similar fashion. Unlike the Soviet northern group of forces, the southern one was facing more German infantry divisions, with their higher antitank defense capabilities. Also, the terrain over which the VIII and XV Mechanized Corps were to advance was more difficult to navigate. Between the starting point of Toporov to Berestechko and Dubno, there were five small rivers, running along the northwest to southeast axis. Although small, these rivers had muddy banks and swampy valleys, some of them over a mile wide. There was a dearth of suitable fords and bridges capable of bearing tanks.

After overcoming natural obstacles, Soviet tankers were faced with bristling antitank defenses of German infantry divisions. To make the matters even worse, German air attacks in this area were especially effective, causing great damage and confusion among Soviet mechanized columns strung out along narrow dirt roads.

The XV Mechanized Corps was slotted to move onto Berestechko, with the VIII Mechanized advancing on Dubno on its right. The left flank of the XV Mechanized and the right flank of the VIII were unsupported.

XV Mechanized Corps, Maj. Gen. I. I. Karpezo Commanding

On June 25, Major General Karpezo did not think that the 10th Tank Division of his corps was in any shape to participate in the offensive on the 26th. Still, working feverishly during the night, the command cadre of this division cobbled its remains into some sort of readiness for the attack.

The corps' motorized rifle division, the 212th, would not be participating in the offensive, protecting Brody in a semicircle extending from northwest to northeast. The 8th Tank Division from the IV Mechanized Corps, assigned to reinforce the XV Mechanized Corps, was still a full day away, around Busk.

Even within this one corps, there was little, if any, cooperation between divisions, and they operated independently. The 10th Tank spent most of the day in local counterattacks. The 37th Tank Division was able to conduct a more telling offensive, but in the end was brought up short.

Both divisions would carry out their counterattacks with their ten KV-1s in front ranks, covering their lightly armored brethren. Still, in a battle between armor and armor-piercing shells, the heavy projectiles of German corps-level artillery, greatly aided by the versatile 88mm air-defense guns used in direct-fire role, carried the day, and the Soviet tankers suffered heavily from punishingly accurate antitank fire.

Russian historian A. V. Isyaev quotes memoirs of former Capt. Z. K. Slyusarenko, then-commander of the 1st Battalion, 19th Tank Regiment of the 10th Tank Division:

> The enemy shells could not penetrate our armor, but damaged treads, knocked off turrets. A KV went up in flames to my left. . . . My heart skipped a beat: "Kovalchuk is burning!" I can not help this crew at all: twelve other vehicles are charging ahead with me. Another KV came to a halt: a shell knocked off its turret. KV tanks were powerful vehicles, but sorely lacking in speed and maneuverability.[8]

In addition to extremely effective German artillery, the XV Mechanized Corps was subjected to heavy German air attacks. The slow-moving Soviet artillery was hit hard on approaches to forward positions. Without their support, the Soviet tank units lacked sufficient firepower to deal with German field artillery.

Dearth of Soviet infantry was also severely felt. Between the two attacking Soviet tank divisions, there were barely four motorized rifle battalions. Attacking without close cooperation from the Soviet armor, the rifle battalions took heavy casualties and could not provide close support for the tankers. Without infantry support, the Soviet tanks could not hold on to their hard-won gains and were forced to pull back at the end of the day.

Around 1800 hours, a particularly punishing air strike was delivered upon the command post of the XV Mechanized Corps. While personnel losses were minor, one of the casualties was the corps commander, Major General Karpezo.

A bizarre episode is connected to his wounding. After debris from the explosions stopped raining, Karpezo's body was discovered amid wreckage of his command post. One of the doctors examined Karpezo and pronounced him dead, and he was promptly buried by headquarters personnel. Several minutes after the commander's body was buried, corps commissar Ivan V. Lutai arrived at the command post.

Hearing upon Karpezo's death and burial, Commissar Lutai, a close friend of Karpezo, flew into rage. Pulling out his pistol and screaming like a mad man, Lutai demanded that Karpezo's body be dug up so he could see for himself that his friend was indeed dead. Cowed staff workers quickly unearthed Karpezo's body. When he was examined again, shocked officers discovered that Karpezo was breathing.

As Karpezo was quickly evacuated to the rear, his deputy, Col. G. I. Yermolayev, took over command of the XV Mechanized Corps. Later Karpezo recovered from his ordeal; however, he was never again sufficiently healthy for a line command. He toiled in obscurity in several rear-echelon postings for the rest of the war, quietly retiring in 1950s. Lutai himself did not survive the war, being killed in a cauldron battle in September 1941 east of Kiev.

With nightfall, attack of the XV Mechanized Corps petered out, and Colonel Yermolayev ordered it to pull back. At the end of the day the XV Mechanized Corps numbered 260 tanks, most of them in the 37th Tank Division. Among them, 44 tanks were the new KV-1 and T-34 models, still a very respectable force. The XV Mechanized Corps started the war with at least 733 tanks. Now, four days later, it was reduced to approximately 35 percent strength.

VIII Mechanized Corps, Lt. Gen. D. I. Ryabyshev Commanding

Because of the limited capabilities of the XV Mechanized Corps, the lion's share of fighting in the southern sector fell to Ryabyshev's VIII Corps. As mentioned previously, this corps was one of the strongest among Soviet mechanized formations. Aggressively led as well, this corps achieved the most success on June 26. Marching and countermarching over the previous several days and covering approximately four hundred miles along poor roads cost the VIII Mechanized Corps dearly. Out of roughly nine hundred tanks in the corps at the beginning of the war (sources vary from 858 to 933), approximately 50 percent were left along the routes of march, broken down, damaged by air attacks, or out of fuel.

These endless marches were especially difficult on the older heavy T-35 tanks. A veritable land dreadnought, it mounted five turrets and was operated by a crew of ten. It was also very finicky and at the end of its useful life. Out of forty-eight T-35s in the corps at the beginning of the war, less than five made it to the area of operations at Dubno.

Starting off from the vicinity of Brody in the morning of June 26, the VIII Mechanized Corps began steadily pushing back German screening forces. It was advancing over similar unfavorable terrain like the one facing the XV Mechanized. After advancing approximately ten miles, Ryabyshev's VIII Mechanized came up against prepared defensive positions of German 57th Infantry Division. This German division, reinforced with its corps' artillery assets, defended the line of Kozyn-Berestechko. The VIII Mechanized Corps spent the rest of the day disputing the line of Plyashevka River and could not advance any further, suffering heavy casualties in the fighting.

Attacking shortly after 0900 hours, the 12th Tank Division of this corps went into the fight without any artillery support. In a particularly brutal air attack, German aircraft destroyed or disabled all the tractors towing the cannons of the division's artillery regiment. Division's chief of staff, Col. N. A. Popov, was killed in a similar attack. The infantry support for the attack came late as well, with Col. A. V. Gerasimov's 7th Motorized Rifle Division going forward around 1300 hours.

We are fortunate that its two senior leaders, Ryabyshev and corps' commissar Popel, left behind their memoirs with very descriptive recounting of the events. A majority of material in the following section describing operations of the VIII Mechanized Corps on June 26 was taken from Ryabyshev's and Popel's memoirs.

Commissar Popel decided to join the attack of corps' spearhead 12th Tank Division under Maj. Gen. T. A. Mishanin. Before climbing into his T-34 tank, he turned to Ryabyshev and shook his friend's hand:

"If anything happens, let my family know."

"Of course. You too."[9]

Popel's tank took place among the ranks of the 24th Tank Regiment under Lt. Col. P. I. Volkov. This regiment was a very powerful formation, its 1st Battalion composed of one company of KV tanks and two companies of T-34s. The second battalion, forming the second echelon behind their heavier brethren, was composed of fast and light BT-7s. East of Volkov's regiment, its sister 23rd Tank Regiment under Major N. S. Galaida took up its attack positions.

The 12th Tank Division was to cross three rivers, Styr, Syten'ka, and Slonovka, capture the village of Leshnov, and advance to Berestechko. If it could carry out this maneuver, German lines of communications between Rovno and Dubno would be cut, and its forward mobile group would be left unsupported.[10]

At the coded command "seven, seven, seven, seven," the 24th Tank Regiment surged from its starting positions in the woods towards the Slonovka River. While command tanks of senior officers like Colonel Volkov and Commissar Popel had radios, the rest of rank-and-file vehicles still relied on signal flags for directions from their commanders: "Binoculars were in Volkov's left hand, signal flags—in his right."[11] As the regiment advanced closer to Leshnov, German interdictory artillery fire began landing among Soviet formations, causing momentary delay and confusion.

Quickly traversing an open field, the 24th Tank Regiment reached the bank of Slonovka River, where it was halted by the impassable terrain. During the previous night, nobody scouted the ground over which the unit was to advance. Now, several leading tanks charged over the muddy bank and became stuck.

Cautiously, Popel ordered his driver to slow down and watched in frustration other floundering tanks:

> First, second, third vehicle plunges into the swamp. The tankers, as often before during maneuvers, were counting on charging right through the narrow river and the swampy river bank. It's possible that they did so impetuously, not able to hold back once their blood was up. But one swamp is different from another. Also, during the night the combat engineers did not scout out the river bank. The companies halted in full view of the enemy anti-tank crews.[12]

Colonel Volkov quickly turned his unit east towards a bridge. Popel notes how after relaying his command over the radio, Volkov stood up in his turret and three times relayed the same command using the signal flags for those tanks without radios. While moving along the river, Volkov's tanks were forced to turn sideways, presenting vulnerable sides to German antitank battery on the other side of the river. One Soviet tank immediately paid the price, knocked out and catching on fire.

However, the bridge was not scouted out either, and now, under accurate German fire, it was the wrong time to discover that the bridge was destroyed. Popel noticed confusion reigning around it. As the German artillery fire concentrated on the bridge and approaches to it, some tanks bunched up in disorder behind Popel, while some began slinking away back towards the tree line where they started from. With difficulty, Volkov and Popel organized a somewhat orderly pull back and began returning ineffective counterbattery fire with their tank cannons.

Major General Mishanin sent in some infantry to repair the bridge. Some of the BT-7 tanks from Colonel Volkov's regiment managed to bring up parts of a disassembled combat bridge, which greatly facilitated repairing the bridge over Slonovka River. Forced to work under fire and taking heavy casualties in the process, Soviet infantrymen managed to repair the rickety bridge well enough to allow one tank across at a time.

One after another, Volkov's tanks went across. In his turn, Popel's tank charged over the shaky bridge, followed in quick succession by several more T-34s. "The Germans zeroed-in on the bridge, and a shell hit a crossing tank head on. The plume of reddish sparks is brighter than the sun. However, the tank, completely unaffected, turns to the right and follows us. Looks like the German antitank guns can not punch through the frontal armor. What is their caliber?"[13]

As more and more tanks crossed over the bridge, Colonel Volkov sent a platoon along the river bank to clear out the German antitank battery there. While this task was being carried out, Volkov began reorganizing his regiment for its main mission—capturing Leshnov village. Slightly shifting its aim, Volkov's 24th Tank Regiment charged at the village from the east. Major Galaida's 23rd Regiment went in from the west.

As the 24th Tank Regiment approached closer to the village, heavier German artillery opened up, immediately knocking out one T-34 tank. At the same time, approximately a battalion-sized force of German Pz III and Pz IV panzers left the woods northeast, attempting to catch the attacking Soviet force in the flank.

A tank-on-tank fight ensued in the tall oat fields. Artillery on both sides joined in the fight. Popel mistakenly stated that a whole howitzer regiment was supporting the attack of the 24th Tank Regiment. This was highly unlikely, since almost all of the 12th Howitzer Regiment, belonging to the 12th Tank Division, was destroyed in an air attack.

Popel again:

Hundreds of black plumes flare up and disappear above the oat field.
Suddenly, my breath caught. Ears felt as if plugged up. This happens

when a plane hits an air pocket. [My] T-34 was lifted up as if on wings and gently lowered to the ground. Once the dust cleared, I saw a smoking hulk in place of neighboring tank. The enemy shell hit its ammunition supply. . . . There is no more field, nor land, forest or sky. Only thunder and fire, smoke and dust. I am trying to figure out whose loses are greater. I try to count knocked out and burning vehicles. I can't, I lose count. Can't see the right flank. Can not tear my eyes from the gun sights."[14]

Outnumbered by Soviet tanks, the Germans pulled back, pursued a short distance by a company of KV tanks. The rest of the 24th Tank Regiment resumed its attack on Leshnov. At the village's edge, German gunners stayed as long as they could at their guns, attempting to stop the attack. The heavy Soviet tanks rolled right over the German cannons. Popel described an incident in which his T-34 tank rammed an antitank cannon: "I notice that one soldier still stayed at his gun, frantically working behind the shield. There is no salvation for him. Instinctively, I close my eyes. The tank tilts sideways and straightened out again. It left behind what a second ago was an antitank gun with its gunner or gun commander."[15]

Soon thereafter, Popel's tank suffered a hit which knocked off a tread. As the rest of the regiment moved forward, Popel's crew had a chance to climb out of the tank and catch their breath:

> Our faces are bloody. When the German shells dented the frontal armor, on the inside, small steel slivers flaked off and imbedded themselves in cheeks and foreheads. We are deaf, poisoned by gun smoke, worn out by turbulence. . . . It seems that if enemy tanks or infantry would suddenly appear from around the corner—we wouldn't be able to move.[16]

As the fight raged on Leshnov's outskirts, Popel and his crew worked frantically to replace two damaged tracks. While they were working, Lieutenant General Ryabyshev's KV-1, with "200" painted on it, pulled up next to them. In another interesting anecdote, Ryabyshev told Popel that his own KV-1 tank had a breakdown: "The brake track failed, and KV spun like a top near the edge of the river."[17]

The fight for Leshnov must have been much fiercer than Popel described in his memoirs. He briefly tells of an encounter with a crew of a T-34 tank that pulled out of fighting and attempted to slink away. Popel returned it back into the fight.

After a bitter fight, the 12th Tank Division took Leshnov, losing at least fifteen tanks near the village and further ten irretrievably stuck in the swampy ground near the river. These loses are even more significant because they were suffered mainly by battalions equipped with the precious new T-34s and KV-1s.

When the VIII Mechanized Corps went into attack, the 12th Tank Division was in the center, the 34th Tank Division on the right, and the 7th Motorized Rifle Division was on the left. Despite being roughly on line with each other, these three divisions operated independently of each other, without coordination or assistance.

While the fight for Leshnov raged on, the 7th Motorized Rifle Division under Colonel A. V. Gerasimov had its own tough fight, attempting to cross the Styr River. Gerasimov's infantrymen went into the offensive without promised contact with the XV Mechanized Corps. After bitter fighting, Gerasimov was able to bring two battalions of riflemen across and hang on to a small beachhead on Styr River. However, this was the extent of its progress in the face of stubborn German resistance.

Advancing to the right, the 34th Tank Division under Colonel I. V. Vasilyev also managed to cross Slonovka River, but was pinned down on the other side by a determined German counterattack.

During this fight, Ryabyshev, instead of directing the battle from his command post, chose to follow the forward echelon. During the fight for Leshnov, Ryabyshev lost contact with his divisions, as clearly stated by Popel: "We did not have a clear picture of the situation, units' locations. It was necessary to immediately return to corps headquarters."[18]

Popel was honest enough with himself about his and Ryabyshev's role in the attack: "I asked Ryabyshev a question that was gnawing at me—were we right in going into the attack? The regiment gained two tanks, but the corps ended up without leadership."[19] Ryabyshev feebly assured him that they were correct, stating that in this fight it was necessary for the common soldiers to see that their commanders were sharing dangers with them. It is apparent that Ryabyshev, like Popel, noticed hesitation and reluctance among his green tank crews.

In late afternoon after Leshnov was firmly secured, Colonel Volkov sent a company of KV tanks to cut the Dubno-Berestechko road. Reaching the road and attacking from ambush, this company caught a small German unit unawares and practically wiped it out.

In the Soviet rear, the town of Brody suffered heavily from German air attacks, and some portions of it were on fire. When Ryabyshev's tank made it to the area where the corps' command post was supposed to be, it wasn't there, delayed in the chaos. Only the chief of communications, Colonel S. N. Kokorin, was in place with a mobile radio station. Soon several more officers dribbled in, Commissar Popel among them. They got together to tally up events of the day.

Despite fighting admirably, the VIII Mechanized Corps did not make significant progress. The 12th Tank Division advanced the farthest, but even that amounted to less than eight miles. For these eight miles, division paid dearly in men and equipment. Its artillery regiment was almost completely destroyed, and division headquarters was hit hard. The 34th Tank Division, while making less progress, also suffered lesser casualties. The 7th Motorized Rifle Division hardly advanced at all.

As their meeting broke up, the poorly camouflaged corps command post was spotted by German aircraft and underwent a heavy attack. Ryabyshev, Popel, Chief of Staff Colonel Tsinchenko, and an enlisted radio operator were inside the radio truck when German bombs began falling on their position. A near hit flung the truck sideways, spilling out the men and destroying precious radio equipment.

Lieutenant Ryabyshev was quickly back on his feet, attempting to restore order. Popel, suffering from a minor scalp wound and a light concussion, was able to move around in a little while. Colonel Tsinchenko received a more serious head wound and severe concussion, but refused to go to a hospital. The young radioman was killed.

As Popel, leaning on a makeshift cane fashioned from a tree branch, hobbled around the command post, he was presented with a nightmarish view:

> Fifteen meters away the overturned frame of the radio truck was still smoldering. The woods were on fire. The flame ran along the bronze bark of the elms. Up, down, along the branches to the neighboring trees. The burning trees were falling, setting on fire trucks, tents, motorcycles. . . . Bodies of dead and wounded were at every step. There weren't enough medical personnel. Healthy and lightly wounded men were helping their comrades.[20]

After a while, the remaining men resumed operations:

> The headquarters were slowly returning to normal after the attack. I did not yet know how misleading the first impression was after an air attack. It seemed as if everything was destroyed, ground into dirt. But an

hour goes by and picture changes. The dead are removed, wounded are evacuated, and the survivors pick up their interrupted tasks.[21]

Scattered reports continued coming in. Positions of the 12th Tank Divisions were still undergoing heavy air attacks, and the two beachheads established by the 7th Motorized Rifle Divisions were being counterattacked. Communications were finally reestablished with command of South-Western Front's Air Force, but there were no aircraft available to assist the VIII Mechanized Corps.

During the fight for Leshnov communications with Col. I. V. Vasilyev's 34th Tank Division were lost. There were reports that there was still fighting on his flank of corps' deployment, but nothing clear. Lieutenant General Ryabyshev tasked Popel with visiting the 7th Motorized Rifle Division, while he himself set off to Colonel Vasilyev's 34th Tank Division.

Here, again, senior commanders set off in lone tanks to gather information by themselves. The VIII Mechanized Corps would have been much better served had General Ryabyshev stayed at his command post and directed his corps from there, instead of acting like a junior officer and motoring off in search of information.

Following the wake of battle debris, knocked-out tanks, corpses, ironed flat by heavy tank treads, destroyed cannons, Ryabyshev located Colonel Vasilyev in the Khotin village. The small village was a collection of demolished houses and smoking ruins, a sad testimonial of a bitter fight.

While happy with Vasilyev's capturing the village, Ryabyshev, nevertheless, chastised him for not sending situation reports on schedule. After briefing Vasilyev and his command staff about corps' overall situation, Ryabyshev moved off to his own command post at Brody.

> The night caught us on the Brody-Dubno highway. [My] tank turned southwest towards Brody. To the left and right of the road the haystacks, individual houses were burning. . . . Everywhere in our rear there was heavy rifle and submachine-gun fire. Bullets whistled in all directions. It was difficult to figure out who is shooting at whom. . . . German bombers were droning overhead nonstop. They flew east in wave after wave to bomb our peaceful cities and villages.[22]

Following a similar path of destruction, Commissar Popel arrived at positions of 7th Motorized Rifle Division in the middle of a fight. The 27th Motorized Rifle Regiment under Col. Ivan N. Pleshakov was heavily engaged in holding the two beachheads on the western side of the Styr River. There were only several light regimental guns with Pleshakov, and several light BT tanks were attempting to support his regiment with gunfire from the east bank: "The woods butted up against Styr. Light tanks would dart to the edge of the river, quickly fire off several rounds from their 45mm cannons towards the west, and would again disappear among the thickets. Not a significant aid to the infantry."[23]

Popel did not find division's commander Colonel Gerasimov at his command post. Instead, Popel was informed that Gerasimov was in the beachhead with his forward regiment. Again, an example of another senior commander going forward instead of directing the whole unit. Dodging shell and mortar explosions, Popel ran on foot across the flimsy combat bridge onto the beachhead.

The narrow territory of the beachhead was blanketed by German artillery and mortars: "Dead were everywhere. Coming here, we stumbled many times over their bodies. There were no shelters for the wounded, and it was possible to evacuate only few of them."[24]

While Popel was visiting colonels Gerasimov and Pleshakov, the Germans crossed the Styr River approximately two miles south of the Soviet beachhead and attacked rear echelons of Pleshakov's 27th Motorized Rifle Regiment. Division's commissar, Y. A. Lisichkin, diverted a battalion of BT tanks from division's 405th Tank Regiment to restore the situation in the rear. Upon hearing of this threat, Colonel Gerasimov returned to the east bank, while Popel decided to remain in the beachhead a little longer.

Soon, the situation on the eastern bank was restored. Fortunately for the Soviet side, the German probe was more of a feint than a full-scale attack. It hit the area of regimental headquarters and few rear echelon detachments. After the initial shock, survivors of the headquarters element put up a determined fight that held off the German attack. After the battalion of BT tanks sent by Commissar Lishichkin arrived to restore situation, the Germans pulled back across the river.

Headquarters, South-Western Front, Tarnopol

Since the early morning of June 26, situation reports were trickling into the headquarters of the South-Western Front in Tarnopol. Slowly, ever so slowly, the Soviet units were taking up positions in preparation for the offensive. A major concern was whether the mechanized corps that had already become engaged with the Germans could free up enough strength to conduct a concentrated offensive.

All mechanized corps commanders were requesting air support, especially by fighter aircraft. But by this fifth day of the war, the Soviet fighter formations were so severely depleted that there were almost no fighters to go around. Still, some missions were flown by the Soviet bomber aviation into the areas now in German rear. Fifty-four Soviet bombers struck German concentrations near Rava-Russakaya, sixty more in the area of Lutsk, and further sixty-five at Sokal. However, these strikes were conducted at a steep cost; the slow bombers conducted their bombing runs at low altitudes and suffered heavily from lack of fighter cover and accurate German antiaircraft fire.

Also on the 26th, commander of the Air Forces of the South-Western Front, E. S. Ptukhin, and his chief of staff, Major General Laskin, were recalled to Moscow. Within the next several months, both of them, along with a number of their counterparts from other fronts, were shot for their failures, real or imagined, during the first days of war.

Ptukhin was replaced by Lt. Gen. F. A. Astakhov, who used to be chief of Air Forces of Kiev Special Military District until his transfer in the spring of 1941. Already knowing majority of his senior subordinates, he quickly went to work. One of the top priorities assigned to him by Kirponos was rebuilding aerial reconnaissance. Soon, information began coming in.[25] Based on information delivered by Astakhov, in the evening of June 26 Colonel Bagramyan was able to make the conclusion that the rumors about German armor coming from Brest direction were just that, rumors.

Despite efforts by the VIII and XV Mechanized Corps, Colonel General Kirponos was not generous in describing their actions in a situation report issued by his headquarters at 2000 hours:

> The 8th Mechanized Corps at 0900 hours on 06/26/41 indecisively attacked the enemy mechanized formations from the vicinity of Brody in the direction of Berestechko, and not having sufficient support from aviation and his neighbor on the left, the 15th Mechanized Corps was halted by the enemy in the area of its jump-off positions.
>
> The 15th Mechanized Corps, acting just as indecisively, did not carry out attack orders. By 0900 hours on 06/26/41 (beginning of the offensive by the mechanized corps), it was not concentrated in the staging areas.[26]

Activities of the 36th Rifle Corps also received an unflattering review: "The 36th Rifle Corps reached the defensive line of Targovitsa-Dubno-Kremenets. Due to poor organization, poor cooperation, and inadequate supply with artillery ammunition, the units demonstrated lowered combat capability while fighting the enemy in the vicinity of Dubno."[27]

During a command meeting that evening, Purkayev expressed thoughts that the reserve XXXI, XXXVI, and XXXVII Rifle Corps needed to set up a defensive line along rivers Stokhod and Styr and towns of Dubno, Kremenets, and Zolochev. The remains of the mechanized corps would be pulled back behind them for refit and reorganization. Then, another offensive could be organized with joint cooperation of mechanized and rifle formations.

Kirponos was in overall agreement with him; temporary defensive stance was completely necessary. At the same time, he issued orders to begin reactivating the old, mothballed fortified regions of Kiev, Shepetovka, Izyaslav, Staroconstantinov, and Ostropol and form machine-gun battalions to garrison them.[28]

Because of the breakthrough by the 11th Panzer Division towards Ostrog, Kirponos was concerned with German encirclement of the right flank of his Sixth Army. Therefore, at 2100 hours he ordered Lt. Gen. I. N. Muzychenko, commanding the Sixth Army, to begin pulling back to new defensive positions and anchored his right flank on Kremenets. At the same time, the XXXVII Rifle Corps was transferred under Muzychenko's command. The Twelfth Army under Maj. Gen. P. G. Ponedelin was to pull back its right flank as well in order to maintain cohesive lines with the Sixth Army.

Colonel Bagramyan barely had time to send plans for disengaging the mechanized corps to Moscow for approval, when he received a prompt reply: "Immediately inform commander [Kirponos] that Stavka forbids the retreat and demands continuation of counteroffensive." Kirponos rushed to the teletype room and contacted Stavka representatives in a futile attempt to get approval for his plans. He was refused and, dejectedly, instructed Bagramyan and Purkayev to inform the mechanized corps to continue the offensive on the 27th of June.

Summarizing the situation for day, Halder wrote:

> Army Group South is advancing slowly, unfortunately with considerable losses. The enemy on this front has energetic leadership. He is continuously throwing new forces against the tank wedge, attacking frontally, as before, and now also the northern flank, and, on the railroad to Kovel,

apparently also the northern flank. The latter attack will hardly develop to anything serious, but the southern flank at present is still vulnerable because we do not have sufficient forces available to give adequate infantry protection (the conveyor-belt system would be necessary here), and also because Armored Corps von Wietersheim (XIV Motorized Corps), which is still far in the rear, cannot get to the front at the moment because the bad roads are crowded with vital supply traffic. It will be the overriding task of OKH to maintain a steady flow of reinforcements behind Army Group South.[29]

JUNE 27, 1941

Morning of June 27 found the lines of the Soviet South-Western Front broken into two distinct fragments. The southern portion, composed of Sixth, Twelfth, and Twenty-Sixth armies, was firmly holding the Lvov salient and the Hungarian border. While the Sixth and Twenty-Sixth armies were heavily engaged, the situation along the front of the Twelfth Army was relatively calm, punctuated by minor skirmishes with Hungarian troops along the Carpathian Mountains. Of these three armies, the Sixth Army was the hardest-pressed, especially on its right flank, forcing it to hinge the right flank back and now face north.

The Soviet Fifth Army was now almost completely separated from the rest of the South-Western Front. The German spearhead, composed of the von Kleist's Panzer Group 1, was forcing the flanks of Fifth and Sixth armies farther and farther apart. The *schwerepunkt* of the German attack now shifted towards Ostrog with only Task Force Lukin preventing a German break-through deep into operational maneuver space. In the area stretching from Rozhysche to Lutsk-Rovno highway, the shattered remains of the XXXVII Rifle and XXII Mechanized Corps and 1st Antitank Artillery Brigade were attempting to stem the German advance along the strategic highway.

The XV Rifle Corps with attached units, being the farthest forward, was preparing to begin falling back to come on line with the rest of the Fifth Army along the Goryn River. To bolster the chances of success of the mechanized corps' attack, General Potapov detached the still-combat-capable 41st Tank Division, minus its motorized rifle regiment, away from the XV Rifle Corps and shifted it south to reinforce the IX and XIX Mechanized Corps.

Chief of staff of the 41st Tank Division, Col. K. A. Malygin, described condition of his unit in the following manner:

We had roughly 150 tanks, less than 100 dismounted tank crewmen, 24 howitzers; the motorized rifle regiment was left subordinated to the commander of the XV Rifle Corps. We did not have mortars or anti-tank cannon; our antiair defenses consisted of a lone air defense battery and four antiair machine gun systems. Obviously, it was extremely difficult to accomplish our mission in this situation. We could only temporarily halt enemy advance. German aviation bombed us nonstop until sunset. Even though casualties were minor, preparations for the counteroffensive were carried out in a difficult situation.[30]

Following Stavka's instructions, Kirponos again ordered the VIII Mechanized Corps to attack Dubno from the south, the XV, Berestechko, and the IX and XIX were to operate against Mlynov and Dubno from the northeast and east. However, the IX and XIX Mechanized Corps were in no shape to advance, barely hanging on to Rovno under intense pressure from Germans divisions advancing along the Lutsk-Rovno highway.

General Kirponos became concerned that the Germans would turn their armored formations south, into the rear of Sixth and Twenty-Sixth Armies, in order to cut them off from the fortified districts along the old border. That was why he was deploying his reserve infantry corps and parts of three antitank brigades in the cutoff positions facing north. However, as I have already mentioned, the German command planned to carry out their southerly offensive later and further east—after breaching the old Soviet defensive line on the old border in the areas of Novograd-Volynskiy and Staroconstantinov.

IX Mechanized Corps, Maj. Gen. K. K. Rokossovskiy Commanding

While the XIX Mechanized Corps was falling back under intense German pressure, the IX Mechanized Corps made one last convulsive attempt to attack on Mlynuv. Its 35th Tank Division under Col. N. A. Novikov advanced to within ten miles north of Mlynov by 1300 hours. It was met by the German 299th Infantry Division and spent all day locked in combat with it. The 20th Tank Division under Col. M. E. Katukov, advancing on the left flank of the 35th Tank division, was engaged by German 299th and 13th Panzer Divisions. A spirited fight lasted most of the day. In the afternoon, the Germans discovered the unprotected flanks of the 20th Tank Division and gaps between its units and began to flank this division, threatening to take it from the rear and encircle it.

After holding on most of the day and buying the XIX Mechanized Corps as much breathing room as he could, Rokossovskiy ordered his corps to disengage and fall back. Attempting to preserve as many of his armored vehicles as possible, General Rokossovskiy's corps pulled back to Rovno, bolstering beleaguered defenses of the city.

Isayev quoted Rokossovskiy's reasoning: "I think, in this case it was more prudent to take personal responsibility and give the troops a mission that was based on existing situation before [we] received the directive from General Staff."

XIX Mechanized Corps, Maj. Gen. N. V. Feklenko Commanding

Despite demands by the commander of the South-Western Front, the XIX Mechanized Corps was in absolutely no shape to conduct offensive actions on June 27. In fact, it was steadily being pushed east by elements from German 13th Panzer and 299th Infantry divisions. General Feklenko's corps was being slowly squeezed into diminishing positions south and southeast of Rovno, desperately attempting to prevent or minimize German crossing of Goryn River.

After the Germans breached the defensive positions of the 228th Rifle Division approximately five miles south of Rovno, the Soviet forces defending the city were in real danger of finding themselves on the wrong side of the river. In late evening, one particularly fierce German probe reached the southern outskirts of the city before being beaten back by a tank counterattack. Shortly thereafter, and with heavy heart, I. I. Feklenko ordered his corps to pull back across the Goryn River, less than fifteen miles east of Rovno, exposing the southern approaches to the city.

XV Mechanized Corps, Col. G. I. Yermolayev Commanding

After receiving Kirponos' original orders about the pullback behind defensive lines of the 37th Rifle Corps, Colonel Yermolayev ordered his 10th and 37th tank divisions to disengage. His 212th Motorized Rifle Division remained in place, covering the withdrawal of tank formations. However, it paid dearly for the rear-guard action, struck again and again by punishing German air attacks.

At around 1000 hours a liaison officer from the headquarters of the South-Western Front arrived at Yermolayev's command post. He informed Yermolayev that pullback orders were cancelled and he was to turn around his tank divisions once again and attack toward Berestechko. It took over two hours to relay the new orders to commanders of the 10th and 37th Tank Divisions and turn their units around. Exhausted by marching and countermarching, the tank divisions could not attack during June 27.

Task Force Lukin, Ostrog

General Lukin had not been idle the previous night, moving whatever forces he had available to engage the Germans at Ostrog. In addition to the 173rd Reconnaissance Battalion, which already engaged the Germans the previous night, Lukin was able to concentrate at Ostrog the following forces from the 109th Motorized Rifle Division: the 381st Motorized Rifle Regiment (three battalions) under Lt. Col. A. I. Podoprigora; 2nd Battalion from the 602nd Motorized Rifle Regiment; 229th Engineer Battalion; six tanks from the 16th Tank Regiment; and the 404th Artillery Regiment; however this unit was still en route and not available for operations in the morning. The rest of the division, along with the rest of the Sixteenth Army, had already departed for Byelorussia.

Leaving one rifle battalion in reserve on the east bank of Viliya River, the other three battalions, without artillery support, advanced on Ostrog across the one available bridge. However, the small bridge was not able to accommodate timely advance of the three battalions, and some of the men had to commandeer whatever boats were available or swim across the narrow river.

The 2nd Battalion of the 602nd Motorized Rifle Regiment under Captain Morozov met with initial progress and soon was disputing the south edge of town near a Catholic monastery. The two battalions from the 381st Regiment had tougher going against Germans entrenched in basements and upper floors of buildings. Only after the regimental artillery battery, brought up into direct-fire mode, suppressed some of the more stubborn German positions were the battalions able to advance.

The 173rd Reconnaissance Battalion, barely hanging onto the north-eastern edge of town, was under heavy German pressure. After its commander Major Yulborisov was killed, the 3rd Battalion from the 381st Regiment was sent to reinforce it.

While visiting Lieutenant Colonel Podoprigora's command post, roughly two miles east of Ostrog, commander of the 109th Motorized Rifle Division, Col. N. P. Krasnoretskiy, was struck down by a shell fragment. His deputy, Col.

N. I. Sidorenko, took over. The seriously wounded Colonel Krasnoretskiy was evacuated to the rear, where he partially recovered and returned to duty, only to fall in battle near Moscow in October the same year.

Since the early morning, the German forces at Ostrog numbered one infantry regiment and some reconnaissance elements from 11th Panzer Division. More help was on the way, namely the 15th Panzer Regiment of that division, which spent the night in Mizoch, approximately twenty-five miles west of Ostrog. Gustav Schrodek, after dropping off his damaged tank at the repair shop, joined a reconnaissance platoon, tasked with scouting the route of advance for the regiment.

Traveling in darkness over roads not indicated on the map, the platoon cautiously probed its way forwards, constantly on alert for Soviet opposition: "Contact with enemy could happen at any instant, so keep machine-guns clear."[31]

Sometimes losing their way, they drove on to the sound of the guns:

> Far away from us on the left, we observed night combat and saw flashes of artillery and tracers. We became more careful, halting from time to time and listening with our engines off. . . . After a long travel, we arrived at dawn and began to discern some buildings ahead of us. . . . Suddenly, a rifle shot rang out. We immediately stopped and positioned machine guns. . . .
>
> In the meantime, Lt. Karge shot towards the houses with his machine gun. It came to life over there. Rifle and machine-gun shots whipped through the area and came perilously close over our heads. We also returned fire immediately. There was a flash over by the houses, and immediately thereafter it hit close to us. Afterwards all hell broke loose. Shells exploded all around us. I believed that several cannons were zeroed in on us. "Mount up and withdraw!" ordered Lt. Karge. The drivers immediately jumped to their vehicles and started them, while the other men grabbed their weapons and began jumping aboard. A scout car and two motorcycles were unfortunately left behind. Their drivers and riders were picked up by other vehicles. More steel greetings followed us from over there, but caused no more damage, with company putting a good distance between us.[32]

After being appraised by the scout detachment of contact with the Soviets, the 15th Panzer Regiment entered the fight in earnest, vigorously attacking the Red Army defensive positions north of Ostrog. Arrival of the panzers permanently tilted the fight in German favor.

Colonel N. I. Sidorenko, replacing the fallen Krasnoretskiy, cobbled together a stop-gap force of seventeen BT-7s, fifteen armored cars, and several companies from rear-echelon units and sent them in to support the crumbling center. It was too late, and the 381st Motorized Rifle Regiment began falling back in disorder. The retreat over narrow bridge was verging on panic, with German mortar and artillery shells falling among the withdrawing men. Some men drowned, falling off the bridge or unable to swim the river. Casualties were heavy, including 1st Battalion's commander Senior Lieutenant Hayrutdinov.

The remnants of the 173rd Reconnaissance Battalion and the 2nd Battalion of the 381st Motorized Rifle Regiment were not able to disengage and became trapped in town.

In the afternoon, retreating Soviet units rallied in the woods near Vilbovnoye village on the east bank of Viliya River. In the late evening, the 404th Artillery Regiment and the 229th Engineer Battalion finally arrived in the area. However, the engineer battalion, having already sent off its heavy equipment and part of personnel to Byelorussia, numbered roughly two-companies–worth of men. Colonel Sidorenko posted them several miles north of Vilbovnoye, guarding a nearby railroad bridge at Mogilyany across Goryn River and covering division's right flank.

Giving his men a chance for brief rest, Colonel Sidorenko made a second attempt at Ostrog in the afternoon. Leaving one rifle battalion in reserve, the remaining two battalions, this time supported by fire of the 404th Artillery Regiment, threw themselves at the hard-fought-for town, attempting to reach the survivors of the other two battalions trapped in Ostrog. Despite friendly artillery support, the two Soviet infantry battalions ran into serious German opposition and could not make progress. With nightfall, they fell back across the river once more, in the relative safety of the woods around Vilbovnoye.

The fight for Ostrog was a costly one for the Germans as well. By the end of the day, the 1st Battalion of the 15th Panzer Regiment numbered only twelve operational tanks.

VIII Mechanized Corps, Lt. Gen. D. I. Ryabyshev Commanding

Shortly after midnight, after visiting Colonel Gerasimov's 7th Motorized Rifle Division, Commissar Popel arrived at the 34th Tank Division. He barely missed Ryabyshev, who himself departed for Gerasimov's division less than an hour earlier. While Popel was familiarizing himself with the situation of Vasiliev's division, chief of counter-intelligence of the VIII Mechanized Corps, Commissar M. A. Oksen, found him there. Oksen had disturbing news: several Soviet soldiers, apparently deserters from a different corps, were picked up in the VIII Mechanized Corps' rear. According to these men, rumors were spreading that 12th Tank Division was retreating, with two Soviet generals surrendering to Germans. One of the men swore that he actually saw large bodies of Soviet soldiers retreating through the woods.

Unable to reach neither General Mishanin's 12th Tank Division nor the headquarters of the VIII Mechanized Corps by radio, Popel raced off there in his lone T-34. As he was approaching the location of the corps command post in the woods outside Brody, Popel was surprised to see intense air attacks to which German aviation was subjecting this small town. As far as he knew, there wasn't much of military value located in the town.[33]

Another unpleasant surprise awaited him at the command post—it was deserted. Minutes later, a motorcycle platoon pulled into the command post's perimeter. Its commander, a junior lieutenant, reported that he was sent to Colonel Gerasimov's 7th Motorized Rifle Division, but could not get through the burning woods along Styr River and had to turn back. The young lieutenant was also surprised seeing the vacated corps command post, informing Popel that the command post was occupied less than two hours earlier.

A staff car pulled in. Major Petrenko, Oksen's deputy, informed Popel that Mishanin's tank division did indeed abandoned its positions. On the way to the corps command post, Petrenko spoke with several retreating soldiers who insisted that division received orders to pull back. While the bulk of the 12th Tank Division was pulling back to Brody in disorder, it left the flank of Colonel Gerasimov's division exposed. Now Popel understood why German aviation was bombing Brody so heavily.

Stragglers began gathering at the corps command post:

> Approximately an hour went by, and roughly one hundred men belonging to corps rear elements and battalions and regiments from Mishanin's division gathered in the tree line. In the night's disorder, men would lose their way, wander around the woods and, glad to have stumbled upon us, remained at the former command post.[34]

They were quickly put to work digging in and improving existing defenses.

Leaving Major Petrenko in charge of the command post, Popel again set off in his T-34 towards the highway in hope of getting some news. The road cross-country in heavy rain was difficult. The great forest fires raging throughout the day were slowly suppressed by the torrents of water. Visibility dropped to almost nothing, and Popel was forced to open the cupola hatch so that he could guide his driver. The insides of the tank immediately became drenched, adding to misery of tired men.

To his great relief, Popel found Lieutenant Colonel Volkov, commander of the 24th Tank Regiment, on the road. "Pale, dirty, with dried blood on his cheek, in ripped jumpsuit," Volkov informed Popel that he was the rear-guard of the 12th Tank Division:

> Volkov briefly, tiredly answered my questions, rubbing his wide, balding forehead.
>
> "At two o'clock we received orders from division commander to immediately begin retreat to Brody-Pochayev-Podkamen. We are to concentrate at Podkamen by daybreak."
>
> "Who delivered the orders?"
>
> "Chief of Staff Popov, by radio. I heard it myself."
>
> "Did you see General Mishanin?"
>
> "No."
>
> "General Ryabyshev?"
>
> "No."
>
> "Where are the divisional headquarters?"
>
> "I don't know."
>
> "Corps headquarters?"
>
> "I don't know. I don't have communications with anybody."[35]

Lieutenant Colonel Volkov, fighting so bravely the previous day, was visibly discouraged by this retreat, lamenting the losses suffered by his regiment in now-useless attack. Both Popel and Volkov were in agreement that the 12th Tank's pullback exposed the flanks of the other two divisions. On his own risk, Popel halted Volkov's retreat, ordering him to hold the road at all costs. Volkov happily began gathering his regiment and stragglers from other units and taking up defenses across the road. Popel himself set off for Brody.

With the sky lightening and the rain letting up, Popel's tank entered a small town, which presented a nightmarish scene:

The rain . . . extinguished the fires. Only here and there, hissing pieces of logs and wooden boards were burning out. The streets were impassable. Bomb craters, bricks, masonry, and corpses. Corpses—in the street, on sidewalks. . . . When [tank halted], we climbed outside and discovered that we [were] in a room. Three walls were knocked down; only the fourth remained.[36]

The grisly scenery continues: "A [car halted] around the corner. Two steps away from it, a body of an officer, with a bloody wound in the back of his head. A dead hand is clutching a field bag. I roll over the corpse. [It is] Colonel Popov, division's chief of staff. I take his bag, remove from his pocket documents, unsent letter, two photos."[37]

It goes on:

Slowly, halting at every step, we drive along the dead town . . . across a church—KV. This is the first tank that we found in Brody. Whose vehicle is it? . . . The tank tucked in next to half-collapsed wall of a two-story building. Bricks and pieces of masonry are on the armor. The forward hatch is open, and I peek in.

General Mishanin is in the driver's seat. His head, with thin, gray hair, rolls lifelessly, arms lowered along his body. The uniform blouse and under-shirt are torn from collar to belt. [His] chest is covered in blood and bruises. The right sleeve is singed. Now I also noticed that his hair is singed as well.

"Comrade General . . . Timofey Andreyvich!"

No signs of life. I climb into the hatch and shake Mishanin's shoulder. An incoherent moan: "M-m-a-a-a . . . ." [His] lowered head does not move. Another moan and not a sound more."[38]

To Popel's surprise and joy, another man climbs out of Mishanin's tank: "It's Mishanin's adjutant. I only briefly saw this pink-cheeked young lad before. He is pink-cheeked no longer, and his age is undeterminable—unshaven, dark, grimy."[39]

Speaking loudly due to a concussion, Mishanin's adjutant told Popel a sad tale. While directing movements of his division, Mishanin was half-buried by a collapsing wall. His adjutant, driver, and radio-operator dug the general out and placed him inside the tank. When the young lieutenant climbed in with Mishanin, the other two men stayed outside. A near bomb miss mangled the two exposed crewmen while bouncing the adjutant inside the tank.

Leaving the young man with the still-unconscious Mishanin, Popel hurried south through the town, attempting to catch up to the other two of Mishanin's regiments and turn them around.

Popel found Lieutenant General Ryabyshev on a road south of Brody. The corps commander, who looked liked he aged about ten years, brought his commissar up to date. Shortly before 0300 hours, a liaison officer from headquarters of the South-Western Front arrived at Ryabyshev's command post with the pullback orders.

As we already know, the VIII Mechanized Corps was to retreat behind the XXXVI Rifle Corps, which was in defensive positions along the line of Kremenets-Podkamen. Ryabyshev wrote in his memoirs that this officer, Gen. V. P. Panyukhov, did not inform him about the reasoning behind the order, merely stating that the VIII Mechanized was to be in reserve of the South-Western Front. Panyukhov did not have any information about progress of his neighboring XV Mechanized Corps, nor about the IX and XIX Corps.

Ryabyshev immediately sent out his own liaison officers to his divisions. His main concern was to reach his units before they continued their offensive. He did not have functioning radio communications with his divisions, and everything depended on how fast his liaison officers would get the word out.

As already shown, the 12th Tank Division received their instructions in time and began pulling back, albeit under heavy air attacks. Ryabyshev was shocked when Popel informed him that the 7th Motorized Rifle and 34th Tank Divisions did not get the word about the pullback and remained in place.

The tremendous efforts which Ryabyshev's divisions had to expend in order to pull back were in vain. Shortly before 0700 hours, another liaison officer from the South-Western Front headquarters arrived at their impromptu command post at the side of the road with another set of conflicting instructions. The VIII Mechanized Corps was to renew the offensive, push Germans out of Dubno, and defend the city until relieved!

Incredulously, Ryabyshev and Popel attempted to question this officer, Col. A. N. Mikhailov, who apparently did not have much information to share. Shrugging off questions by the two men, Mikhailov quickly beat a retreat and raced off to find the XV Mechanized Corps, evidently with the same instructions.

These two conflicting sets of orders received by the VIII Mechanized Corps, even though puzzling, could be explained by the fact that command of the South-Western Front still operated in the environment of limited and late information. Knowing that the attack of the northern pincer, by the IX and XIX Mechanized Corps, was defeated, Kirponos and his command group possibly assumed that the southern pincer, the VIII and XV Mechanized Corps, were defeated as well and ordered them to pull back. Then, finding out that the VIII Mechanized Corps actually made good progress, ordered the two southern corps to turn around and continue the offensive. Off course, this is only a possible explanation, since Colonel General Kirponos' reasoning died with him in September of 1941.

Ryabyshev and his staff began making preparation for the renewed attack lacking any concrete information about the overall situation:

> Who were our neighbors on right and left, what will be their course of action—was unknown to me. In this case, it would be difficult for me, as the corps commander, and my staff, to make appropriate decision. We needed to know where the enemy was, what was he doing, what are his intentions and numbers. But we did not have that information. This was characteristic of the first days of war. Orders coming from Front's headquarters, due to lack of needed information, not always reflected the current situation, which due to the fluid character of combat actions was changing hourly.[40]

Taking into consideration distance to their objective and condition of his corps, Ryabyshev knew that he would not be able to start his mission at least until 0200 hours on June 28.

Around 0900 hours on 27th, Ryabyshev gave orders to commander of 6th Motorcycle Regiment, Col. T. I. Tributskiy, to scout out enemy dispositions. The divisions were to concentrate at their staging areas by 0200 on June 28. They were to be deployed in two echelons: the two tank divisions in the first and the motorized rifle division in the second. He assigned the 12th Tank Division the main task of taking Dubno by attacking along the Brody-Dubno highway. The 34th Tank Division was to secure the left flank of the 12th. The 7th Motorized Rifle Division was to follow up and exploit the 12th Tank Division's expected progress.[41]

As General Ryabyshev was poring over maps and situation reports, his adjutant announced that visitors from the South-Western Front headquarters were arriving. He remembered an uncomfortable, to say the least, scene that unfolded:

> I stepped out of the tent and saw several cars. The first one already stopped. The Member of the Military Council of the South-Western

Front, Corps Commissar N. N. Vashugin, was inside. Adjusting [my] cap, I hurried up to him with a report. Vashugin's tired face was unfriendly:

"Why did you not carry out orders about advancing on Dubno?" interrupting me, [Vashugin] curtly asked.

I tried again to make my report.

"Quiet! This is treason!"

"Comrade Corps Commissar," interrupted Brigade Commissar N. K. Popel, standing next to me. His voice was calm and decisive. "You can demand that the order be carried out. But you need to hear us out, too."

[Vashugin] glared angrily at Popel. Then, glancing at a wristwatch, in calm tones ordered [us] to report the situation and decision to continue fighting.[42]

When Ryabyshev reported his situation, stating that his corps would not be able to resume the offensive until the next morning, Vashugin blew up.

"What?!" exclaimed [Vashugin]. "Make an immediate decision— and forward!"

"With what, forward?" I asked. But he did not hear my question.

"I am ordering you to immediately begin the offensive!" Vashugin demanded again.

"I consider it a crime before Motherland to commit [my] forces into combat piecemeal. This means useless suicide. At most, some partial units could not attack today until after 1400 hours."

"Good," agreed [Vashugin]. "I can accept the last suggestion. Make it happen!"[43]

In his descriptions of the same encounter, Commissar Popel is a lot less charitable towards Vashugin than Ryabyshev was. Here's Popel's depiction:

[Vashugin] walked directly at Ryabyshev, trampling bushes with his highly polished boots. When he got close, looking up at [Ryabyshev], in a voice tense with fury, he asked:

"How much did you sell yourself for, Judas?"

Ryabyshev was standing at the position of attention in front of [Vashugin], confused, not knowing what to say; we were all were looking at [Vashugin] in confusion. Ryabyshev spoke up first:

"Comrade Corps Commissar, if you would hear me out . . . "

"You will be heard by military tribunal, traitor. Right here, under this fir, we'll hear you out, and right here we'll shoot you."[44]

Vashugin's threat was not an idle one. Among the entourage accompanying Vashugin, Popel recognized the prosecutor and the chief of military tribunal of the South-Western Front. Vashugin even brought along a platoon of soldiers. Knowing that his fate was tied to Ryabyshev's, Popel made an attempt to save both of their lives:

> I could not contain myself any longer and took a step forward:
>
> "You can accuse us all you want. However, you have to hear us out."
>
> Now the torrent of curses fell upon me. Everybody knew that [Vashugin] hated being interrupted. But I had nothing to lose. I used his own tactic. This was not an intentional action; the fury guided me:
>
> "It is still to be determined, what was the reasoning of those who ordered us to cede to the enemy territory which we took in combat."
>
> [Vashugin] halted. His voice has a barely perceptible confusion:
>
> "Who ordered you to cede territory? What are you babbling about? General Ryabyshev, report!" Ryabyshev made his report while [Vashugin] paced in front of him. . . . [Vashugin] understood that he was not on solid ground, but was not giving up. Consulting his watch, he ordered Ryabyshev: "You have twenty minutes to report your decision."[45]

It is interesting that while describing this encounter in his memoirs, Popel never called Vashugin by his name. He always referred to Vashugin by his rank of "Corps Commissar" or duty position "Member of Military Council."

While Ryabyshev and his staff officers gathered to quickly hash out possible course of action, Popel noted how Ryabyshev's "hands were shaking and eyes were moist."[46] One can appreciate the courage that Ryabyshev summoned several minutes later to give Vashugin bad news: "[VIII Mechanized] Corps could be ready for action only by tomorrow morning."[47]

Barely containing his anger, Commissar Vashugin ordered Lieutenant General Ryabyshev to immediately renew his offensive. He gave Ryabyshev two choices: begin offensive now or be relieved of duty and court-martialed. With members of military tribunal and a platoon of enforcers present at their command post, neither Ryabyshev nor Popel had any illusion as to what would happen if Ryabyshev were to continue insisting on inability to advance. With their own side more fearsome than the enemy, Ryabyshev and Popel made "suicidal decision—commit the corps into combat piecemeal."[48]

After another brief conference, the following decision was made. A mobile group under command of Popel would be formed from Colonel Vasilyev's 34th Tank Division, Lieutenant Colonel Volkov's 24th Tank Regiment, and 2nd Motorcycle Regiment. This task force would advance immediately, followed the next day by the rest of the VIII Mechanized Corps. As a send-off encouragement, Vashugin told Popel: "If you take Dubno by evening, you'll get a medal. If you don't, you'll be expelled from the [Communist] Party and shot."[49]

After thoroughly demoralizing everyone present, Vashugin finally departed, allowing Ryabyshev and his staff to breathe easier and get to work. At the same time, Ryabyshev ordered his combat engineers to begin setting up a new command post just south of Sitno. The headquarters of the VIII Corps stayed put, awaiting arrival of the rest of the 12th Tank Division and the 7th Motorized Rifle Division.

Not long after Vashugin's departure, another representative from the headquarters of the South-Western Front arrived at Ryabyshev's command post. This was Maj. Gen. R. N. Morgunov, chief of Armored Forces of the South-Western Front. He informed Ryabyshev that he [Morgunov] was in charge of coordinating actions of VIII and XV Mechanized Corps in destroying the enemy group of forces around Dubno. More information delivered by Morgunov surprised Ryabyshev:

> I found out that Major-General K.K. Rokossovskiy's 9th Mechanized Corps [would] be attacking the enemy from Klevan area and Major-General N. V. Feklenko's 19th Mechanized Corps—from the vicinity of Rovno towards Dubno. This information was not only news to me, but also unexpected. . . . [Morgunov] set off for the 15th Mechanized Corps. We were not to meet again. He did not relay any instructions for us.[50]

It would not be hard to imagine Ryabyshev's thinking. His corps fought bravely on the 26th, sustaining heavy losses in the progress. What fury he must have felt being lambasted by that party hack Vashugin! What frustration he must have felt finding out that significant results could have been gained if his efforts were coordinated with the northern pincer of the offensive!

Commissar Popel found Colonel Vasilyev's 34th Tank Division in its old positions. Receiving neither the initial orders to withdraw and nor their reversal, Vasilyev was blissfully unaware about the night's travails. After Popel brought him up to date, they worked out their plan of action for the day. The attack would be led off by the Major Trubitskiy's 2nd Motorcycle Regiment and Lieutenant Colonel Volkov's 24th Tank Regiment, advancing along the highway and the railroad. Vasilyev further detached two units from his own 34th Tank Division to go round the woods southwest and west of Dubno to attempt to further expand the attack frontage.

The attack began shortly after 1400 hours. Initially it met with success. A small German detachment in Granovka village was brushed aside, and the Soviet tanks and motorcycle troops reached the highway. Some rear echelon units of German 11th Panzer Division were caught in a surprise attack and almost wiped out. In some cases, the Soviet motorcyclists raced along the German truck columns and hosed them down with their machine guns. Several Soviet tanks rammed German trucks, turning the enemy vehicles into bloody wrecks.

A small German artillery detachment opened fire upon the attacking Soviets from the outskirts of Verba village, but Popel and Vasilyev continued pushing their men and machines forward. Racing past Verba, Lieutenant Colonel Volkov's T-34 was knocked out, and he, wounded in arm, climbed into another tank, this one without a radio.

A spirited fight developed around Tarakanov village, roughly six miles southwest of Dubno. When Lieutenant Colonel Bolokhvitin's 67th Tank Regiment struck the village from the west, the pendulum of the fight swung in Soviet favor. The struggle was costly, with Bolokhvitin's own tank being one of the lifeless burned-out hulks left in the oat fields.

Aftermath of the fight for Tarakanov was brutal:

> Dead bodies are everywhere—in the street, in the smoking wrecks of cars, motorcycles' sidecars. Pieces of bodies in shreds of gray-green uniforms are even in the trees. . . . It's terrible to look at our tanks now. It is difficult to believe that their initial paint scheme is green, and not reddish-brownish, which even the light rain cannot wash off."[51]

Maj. A. P. Sytnik, who replaced Lieutenant Colonel Bolokhvitin at the helm of the 67th Tank Regiment, reported to Popel that Germans fought very stubbornly, refusing to surrender.

That night Popel's task force could not move any farther than Tarakanov and took up defensive positions around the village. The soldiers from the units that fought that day were so exhausted that Popel released them to rest, while utilizing the men from support units to work on creating defensive positions.

By late evening, the situation southwest of Dubno resembled a layered cake. Rear echelons of German 11th Panzer Division, leading elements of 16th Panzer Division, rear elements of Vasilyev's 34th Tank Division, and approaching small units of the VIII Mechanized Corps became intermixed in the dark.

Despite its best efforts, the main body of the 7th Motorized Rifle Division could not link up with Popel's force. Two battalions from this rifle division's 27th Motorized Rifle Regiment that did reach him became cut off with Popel.

While the 34th Tank Division fought southwest of Dubno and the 7th Motorized Rifle Division raced to reinforce it, their sister 12th Tank Division remained behind the lines of the XXXVI Rifle Corps, not receiving notification for renewal of the offensive. Even if it would have, the 12th Tank could not move. Its tanks and other vehicles were nearly out of fuel, and division's commander Colonel Mishanin was urgently requesting that fuel tankers be sent to him.

By the early morning of June 28, Lieutenant General Ryabyshev's corps was effectively cut into three parts. The 34th Tank Division was cut off immediately southwest of Dubno, the 7th Motorized Rifle Division was strung out along the Dubno-Brody highway, and the 12th Tank Division bivouacked near the town of Kremenets.

South-Western Front,
Colonel General Kirponos Commanding

At the headquarters of the South-Western Front, senior officers were desperately scrambling for any forces that they could place in the way of the advancing German 11th Panzer Division at Ostrog. There were no direct communications with General Lukin, who was commanding the fight at Ostrog from Shepetovka, so Colonel Bagramyan's deputies reached him by routing the calls through Front's headquarters in Kiev and by going through the military commandant of Shepetovka railroad station. This link, however, was intermittent and unreliable.

While Bagramyan was establishing communications with Lukin, Nikita Khruschev, the future Soviet premier, who was now more or less permanently at Kirponos' headquarters, got on the phone with Moscow to request permission to temporarily delay full departure of Lukin's Sixteenth Army until this situation was dealt with. He was unsuccessful.

Being stymied in their efforts to refit and reorganize their mechanized corps behind the infantry screen, Kirponos and his staff continued working on the renewed counterattack plans. The overall objective for all the four mechanized corps was to link up around Dubno and cut off and encircle the German armored spearhead. Staff officers were sent out to hand-deliver orders to the involved formations. Ominously, Front's commissar Vashugin decided to follow them to familiarize himself with the situation up front. We already know the results of his encouragements from Ryabyshev's and Popel's descriptions of his visit.

Despite this being the fourth day of war, communications were still spotty. Bagramyan described the situation of controlling large numbers of troops in an information vacuum:

> The hours of painful waiting dragged on. It seemed that the headquarters of the Fifth Army disappeared: not a single report. Headquarters of various mechanized corps were silent as well. How are they doing? Did they begin the offensive? I could not answer any of these questions posed by Chief of Staff of the Front. I sent out the most capable officers from the Operations Section. So far none of them came back yet. . . . Only General Astakhov was providing us with some information: his pilots can see where the fighting is the heaviest. However, they are having difficulty making sense of the situation from high altitude: there are no clearly defined front lines, instead some sort of a "layered cake" developed: ours and enemy units are intermingled. It goes without saying how difficult it is to direct troops dispersed over a huge territory.[52]

It is interesting to note that in the previous passage Bagramyan described the Soviet reconnaissance flights as being conducted at high altitude. This is a good illustration of German complete dominance of the air space above the battlefield, testament to effective German air defense and tactical fighter operations.

Only after the officers sent to the VIII and XV Mechanized Corps returned in the afternoon, the situation cleared up somewhat. They universally described difficulties imposed on the mechanized formations by the conflicted orders:

> During the night, after receiving orders about pulling back, some divisions already left positions and, under cover of rear guards, began moving east. Then orders came in about returning and continuing the offensive in the same direction. Ryabyshev and Yermolayev barely had time to halt the retreating units, when new instructions came in: change direction of the attack.[53]

There was still no news from the northern wing of the attack:

> Situation on the right flank continued to be unclear. We did not know
> results of Rokossovskiy and Feklenko corps' attacks. Communications
> with Ryabyshev was intermittent, and we did not know if he took Dubno.
> [Lukin] also did not inform us if he was able to create a strong barrier to
> halt the enemy racing to take Ostrog.

In his memoirs, Bagramyan mentioned the previously described incident
which occurred at Lieutenant General Ryabyshev's headquarters. Bagramyan's
knowledge of the event was secondhand, possibly relayed to him by his liaison
officer to the VIII Mechanized Corps: "Hot-tempered, energetic, [Vashugin]
angrily berated [Ryabyshev] for delaying, and insisted that a mobile group be
formed immediately."[54]

No known memoirs exist about what transpired at the headquarters
of the XV Mechanized Corps; however, Bagramyan writes: "[Vashugin's]
insistency was in vain. [XV Mechanized] Corps was heavily pinned down
by constant enemy attacks and could not advance. Upset, Vashugin returned
to Tarnopol."[55] Knowing the extent of his rage displayed at Ryabyshev headquarters, where he at least obtained a small measure of compliance, it is
easy to imagine the torrent of abuse and accusations that Vashugin must
have heaped upon Colonel Yermolayev and the staff of XV Mechanized
Corps's headquarters.

After Zhukov departed Tarnopol for Moscow in the evening of June 26,
Kirponos allowed himself to be swayed by Purkayev's defensive strategy. A
major factor in Kirponos' decision-making was an incorrect belief that the
German mobile group of forces would turn south from Dubno and Berestechko, with the goal of cutting off the Soviet armies in the Lvov pocket. This
defensive posture is illustrated in the intelligence report issued by Kirponos'
staff at 2200 hrs the previous evening:

> Radekhov-Brody direction. The enemy, deploying their . . . moto-
> mechanized group of forces in the area of Berestechko and the forward
> units in Dubno, Verba, Radzivilov, was attempting to widen the break-
> through in the direction of Brody-Tarnopol, but encountering fierce resis-
> tance of out units, was not successful.[56]

Another intelligence report, issued twelve hours later, recognized that German infantry divisions were being deployed in a defensive posture on the flanks of their mobile mechanized group.

Therefore, Kirponos was concentrating the XXVII Rifle Corps along the Zdolbunov-Kremenets line. Farther south, another rifle division, the 199th, belonging to the XLIX Rifle Corps, reinforced by three partially mobilized antitank brigades and the XXIV Mechanized Corps, was forming the second line of defense.

By the end of the day, the three Soviet armies holding the Lvov pocket, the Sixth, Twelfth, and Twenty-Sixth, remained mainly in their old positions. Only the Sixth, having to deal with a gapingly exposed right flank, gave up any territory of note to the Germans.

CHAPTER 11

Continue Mission, June 28

South-Western Front,
Colonel General Kirponos Commanding

THE MORNING OF JUNE 28 found General Purkayev and Colonel Bagramyan scrambling for information about Potapov's Fifth Army. Still out of communication with the Fifth Army, Colonel Bagramyan sent his deputy, Lt. Col. N. D. Zakhvatayev, to Potapov in order to get the most up-to-date information and evaluate the situation.

While the Sixth and Twenty-Sixth armies were still holding their own in Lvov pocket, a new player entered the scene against the Twelfth Army. Shortly before midnight, Hungarian troops crossed the Soviet border and were slowly moving forward under cover of intensive artillery barrages.

The situation at Ostrog was still unclear, and Kirponos positioned some of his reserves facing north approximately forty miles south of Ostrog. These reserves consisted of the XXIV Mechanized Corps, the 199th Rifle Division, three more-or-less mobilized antitank artillery brigades, and the 14th Cavalry Division. They were to intercept the possible German swing south from Ostrog. As usual, Purkayev disagreed with Kirponos, believing that the Germans would press on to Kiev as fast as possible. However, he was overruled by Kirponos, inadvertently reinforced in his belief by Zhukov, who acknowledged the possibility of German enveloping maneuver south of Ostrog.

The XXIV Mechanized Corps was the weakest and the least combat-capable mechanized corps available to commander of the South-Western Front. Approximately three quarters of its enlisted personnel were brand-new recruits, large portion of whom have not yet completed their basic training. At the start of the war, the XXIV Mechanized Corps had roughly 220 tanks, all of which were the older models. Over forty of them, or almost 20 percent, were the old two-turreted T-26s.

This corps, having virtually no wheeled transport, had been moving up on foot since June 24 towards Kremenets, a distance of almost seventy miles from their garrisons around Proskurov. The later stages of its road march was conducted under heavy pressure from German aviation.

While XXIV Mechanized Corps was still a day away, its commander, Maj. Gen. V. I. Chistyakov, an old friend of Bagramyan's, stopped by to chat with his friend. Chistyakov was less than enthusiastic about his corps' combat worthiness: "Our corps is far from what I would like to see. We just began its formation. We have not yet received new tanks, there aren't any trucks. . . . Therefore, my friend, if you hear that we don't fight the best, don't judge us too harshly. You need to know that we'll do all that we can."[1]

Towards the end of the day, staff of the South-Western Front received news of Ryabyshev's VIII Mechanized Corps reaching the immediate vicinity of Dubno. Rejuvenated by these encouraging news, Kirponos ordered counterattacks to continue on June 29. Not knowing the true situation of the IX and XIX Mechanized Corps, he sent them instructions to push again towards Dubno to link up with the VIII and XV Mechanized Corps advancing from the southwest. The two southern mechanized corps were to be supported by the XXXVI and XXXVII Rifle Corps as well as the 14th Cavalry Division belonging to the V Cavalry Corps. Task Force Lukin was to plug up the eastern direction.

Overall, the situation around Rovno was still sketchy. The IX and XIX Mechanized Corps, after suffering severe casualties during the two previous days, were not in any condition to renew the offensive. The good news from the VIII Mechanized Corps quickly soured once Kirponos' staff found out that Popel's group was bottled up near Dubno.

Bagramyan later wrote that it seemed that the Soviet High Command in Moscow began doubting South-Western Front's ability to halt the German panzer thrust:

> Apparently Stavka no longer counted on us to destroy the main thrust
> of Army Group South and fight through to the border. This was witnessed
> by a telegram demanding to inform commanders of 87th and 124th Rifle

divisions, which were supposed to be still fighting surrounded near the border, of an order: "Abandon equipment after burying it; and with light weapons fight through the woods towards Kovel."[2]

Looking at the orders for the two surrounded divisions, the Stavka did not hope that they could rejoin the Fifth Army. It was trying to save any survivors by directing them north to Kovel, away from main fighting. Of course, neither Stavka nor Kirponos' staff knew that 124th Rifle Division no longer existed and that the handful of survivors from the 87th Rifle Division was already heading east. Miraculously, approximately one thousand men from this division were able to rejoin the Fifth Army in July.

At the same time as the Soviet High Command was attempting to direct the survivors of the two surrounded division to Kovel, the Soviet XV Rifle Corps was falling back from it in good order. This corps, commanded by Maj. Gen. I. I. Fedyuninskiy, managed to disengage from the forward German units and was crossing to the eastern bank of Stokhod River. His 45th and 62nd Rifle Divisions, while suffering heavy casualties during the past several days, still remained combat capable. The 16th Rifle Regiment, the only unit from the surrounded 87th Rifle Division to break out, consti-tuted the corps reserve.[3]

Once behind Stokhod River, the XV Rifle Corps had a chance to catch its breath, while Fedyuninskiy and his staff had an opportunity to review the events of the past week and sum up the lessons learned. In his memoirs, Fedyuninskiy was critical of the overall Soviet performance:

> Enemy aviation and commando groups put communication centers and lines out of action. There weren't enough radios in [various] head-quarters; and, besides, we were not accustomed to using them. Mobile means of communications suffered severe casualties and, in a fluid, rapidly changing environment, turned out to be of little use. All of this led to orders and directives reaching the [addressees] late or not at all. This was the cause of the piecemeal nature of our counteroffensive, disruption in cooperation between branches of service.
>
> Particularly poorly carried out was cooperation between infantry and tanks. This was especially apparent on June 24th, when we undertook a counterattack in the Lyuboml area. Commander of the 41st Tank Division, Colonel Popov, displayed indecisiveness. He was mainly "worried" about

preserving equipment and not about the most effective ways to utilize it in the developing situation.

We poorly conducted reconnaissance of the enemy, especially at night.

Communication with neighbors was often lacking, especially when often nobody would even try to establish it. The enemy, taking advantage of this, would infiltrate into our rear and attack units' headquarters.

Despite enemy air superiority, camouflage measures during road marches were poorly carried out. Often troops, vehicles, artillery pieces, field kitchens would converge on narrow roads. The fascist aircraft conducted quite painful strikes on such bottlenecks.

It is necessary to also note that [our forces] initially did not sufficiently appreciate significance of engineering work. There were instances when soldiers did not dig foxholes due to low expectations of individual commanders, often due to lack of entrenching tools. Situation with entrenching tools was so bad that in some units soldiers used helmets instead of shovels.[4]

Throughout all of June 28 there was only one radiogram from the Fifth Army. Even this one message that got through did not carry any useful information, just a routine notification of changing location of its headquarters.

Bad news continued raining down. Two senior officers from 12th Tank Division, Regimental Commissar V. V. Vilkov and Col. E. D. Nesterov, reported that a significant part of Lieutenant General Ryabyshev's VIII Mechanized Corps was fighting surrounded just south of Dubno. While these two men were making their report:

Vashugin walked in during the conversation. We noticed how he turned pale, but nobody attached any significance to it. We thought: the man simply feels bad for the setback, *for which he was partially responsible* [emphasis added]. Nobody could have guessed what kind of blow this represented to him. Not waiting for the end of the conversation, Vashugin left.[5]

Despite the obvious inability of his Front to continue the offensive, Kirponos nonetheless ordered to proceed. Hopes now were pinned on Potapov's Fifth Army, plus the XXXVI Rifle Corps and Task Force Lukin, with whatever aviation assets could be scraped up. Below are the excerpts from order disseminated on June 28, 1941:

—The 5th Army, minus XXXVI Rifle Corps, capitalizing upon success of the VIII Mechanized Corps, go onto offensive and reach with its left flank the Styr River, securing river crossings near Lutsk.

—The XXXVI Rifle Corps at 1200 hrs on 06/28/41 go onto offensive with immediate objective, capitalizing upon success of the VIII Mechanized Corps, reach the line of Mlynov-Bakuyma-Kozin.

—The V Cavalry Corps (headquarters and the 14th Cavalry Division), going onto offensive at 1200 hours, by the end of the day reach the area of Teslukhov-Khotyn-Kozin.

—The XXXVII Rifle Corps (141st and 139th Rifle divisions) advance at 0800 hours and by the end of 06/28/41 reach the line of Boldury-Stanislavchik-Polonichna.

—The XV Mechanized Corps to continue with already-defined mission. By the end of the day to be in vicinity of Berestechko. To be ready to repel possible enemy mechanized attacks from north and northwest and support the VIII Mechanized Corps in destroying enemy groups of forces which broke through beyond Ikva River.[6]

Simultaneous with the above-mentioned formations, the VIII Mechanized Corps was diverted from its push on the city and sent east: "The VIII Mechanized Corps, after securing the line of Ikva River behind it, attack the enemy moto-mechanized units operating east of Ikva River in the direction of Ostrog. After destroying the enemy, rally by the end of the day in the areas of Zdolbunov, Mizoch, Ozhenin."[7]

However, all the planning was conducted in the most generous outline, often not even being aware of location of formations that were to participate in the offensive. Their situation report released around 0800 hours on June 28 reflected the dearth of concrete information: "Situation of the Fifth Army is being clarified." "There is no information about situation of VIII and XV Mechanized Corps."[8]

After Kirponos, Purkayev, and Bagramyan arrived at this decision, Kirponos delegated Bagramyan to inform Vashugin and Khrushchev about it. In doing so, Bagramyan found out shocking news:

After picking up the working copy of a map and my notes, I went to see N. S. Khrushchev. He was unusually sad. [He] listened to my report and without hesitation approved the planned efforts. Finding out that I was going to see Vashugin next, Nikita Sergeyeevich [Khrushchev] bitterly said: "Don't go. No need to report to him any longer. For [Vashugin] the war is over." Vashugin shot himself. He was an honest, uncompromising, energetic human being, but too excitable and easily hurt. The burden of disaster broke him.[9]

It was probably not too difficult for Bagramyan, writing his memoirs years later, cushioned by passing years, to give a less scolding description of Vashugin. In reality, it was quite possible that the staff officers at Kirponos' headquarters suddenly were able to breathe easier without Vashugin's menacing presence. Vashugin quite clearly realized that he was directly responsible for putting Ryabyshev's VIII Mechanized Corps out of action and trapping a large portion of it with Popel near Dubno. He did one decent thing and shot himself.

Around 2200 hours, first Bagramyan and then Kirponos were called to the telegraph machine on direct line to Moscow. The upper echelon continuously demanded news:

> One after another requests for information . . . . We could feel that Stavka was worried about the situation of our Front. . . . For several minutes the telegraph was clicking off the questions: "What is going on at Dubno, Lutsk, Rovno? How far did enemy tanks penetrate those regions? Where is Potapov? Where is his 15th Rifle Corps? What are results of the counteroffensive by 8th and 15th Mechanized Corps?"[10] There wasn't much that Bagramyan or Zhukov could report about Potapov's 5th Army: "Since 2400 hours on 06/27/41 command group and headquarters of [5th] Army lost communications with [their] units, subjected to strong enemy mechanized attacks. 15th Rifle Corps—situation not clarified; 27th Rifle Corps—situation not clarified; 22nd Mechanized Corps—situation not clarified."[11]

Fortunately, the pullback of the three Soviet armies defending the Lvov salient and Hungarian border was proceeding in relatively orderly manner. In conclusion, Kirponos reported: "Overall, the South-Western Front feels itself to be sufficiently capable to continue further struggle. The enemy mechanized group of forces operating in the area of Ostrog presents the biggest threat to the South-Western Front. The unclear situation on the right flank deepens the overall unfavorable position of the Front's right wing."[12]

Zhukov continued pressing Kirponos about not letting up his offensive, once advising him to "use all of Lukin's mechanized forces" in the counter-attack against the German forces. Kirponos had to explain to Zhukov that both tank divisions of Lukin's V Mechanized Corps already departed for the Western Front. The only tank force available to Lukin was a tank regiment belonging to the 109th Motorized Rifle Division.[13] However, Kirponos himself did not know that this tank "regiment" was in reality about a score of light tanks, mainly belonging to Lukin's reconnaissance battalion.

After midnight of June 28–29, Bagramyan's deputy, Lieutenant Colonel Zakhvatayev, returned from his information-gathering trip to Potapov's Fifth Army. It was a dangerous and arduous endeavor. Between Kirponos' head-quarters in Tarnopol and Potapov's headquarters northeast of Rovno, a great number of Soviet and German units were fighting in close quarters, often inter-mixed. On the return leg of his trip, Zakhvatayev's plane was damaged by flak and forced to land. Luckily, Zakhvatayev was uninjured and, commandeering a truck, returned to Tarnopol, making a wide loop east through Shepetovka.[14]

The news delivered by Zakhvatayev wasn't encouraging. The XV Rifle and remains of the XXII Mechanized Corps abandoned Kovel and were moving east across Stokhod River. The XXXI Rifle and IX Mechanized Corps plus the 135th Rifle Division from the XXVII Rifle Corps were defending approaches to Rovno, while the XIX Mechanized Corps was already pushed back to the very suburbs of Rovno.[15]

Kirponos and his senior officers did not know that Zakhvatayev's report was already outdated. By this time fighting mostly died down on June 28, the Soviet forces abandoned Rovno and fell back almost fifteen miles to the east bank of Goryn River. This river became a rough temporary demarcation line between Soviet and German forces.

Potapov's Fifth Army was still pulling into the river bend north of Rovno along the Stokhod River. The XXII and IX Mechanized and XXXI Rifle Corps, along with the 1st Antitank Artillery Brigade, held the river line down to the Rovno-Novograd-Volynskiy highway. The XIX Mechanized and XXXVI Rifle Corps extended south almost to Ostrog. From there, full of gaping holes were the lines of The VIII and XV Mechanized and XXXVII Rifle Corps to Brody.

However, with the XXXI, XXXVI, and XXXVII Rifle Corps coming up on line, the area between Goryn River east to the Stalin line was stripped of Soviet reserves. In the case that Germans broke through at Ostrog and raced on to the plum prize of Kiev, the Nineveeth Army under Gen. I. S. Konev was ordered north into the Kiev Fortified District.

Mechanized Corps,
Maj. Gen. K. K. Rokossovskiy Commanding

After abandoning its attack on Dubno the previous day, Major General Rokossovskiy's IX Mechanized Corps was stubbornly defending the Lutsk-Rovno highway in the area of Klevan against the determined efforts by German 14th Panzer and 25th Motorized Infantry Divisions. The terrain in this location favored defense:

> In those wooded, swampy areas the Germans moved only along major roads. After using Novikov's division to cover our lines on Lutsk-Rovno highway, we shifted the 20th Tank Division, including its artillery regiment armed with new 85mm cannons, here from the left flank. . . . Canons were emplaced in roadside ditches, on hillocks along the highway, and some—directly on the road in order to be able to conduct direct fire.[16]

Not only was Rokossovskiy able to set up effective antitank defenses, General Novikov's 35th Tank Division and the 41st Tank Division even conducted local counterattacks, resulting in capturing some vital high ground.

Moving off before midnight, by early morning of June 28, the 41st Tank Division gained some ground, capturing a small village called Petushki. This division, numbering around 150 tanks, ran into hail of enemy fire. The village was taken at a heavy price:

> The battlefield resembled hell. The smoke of burning tanks, ours and German, was stifling; flakes of ash floated through the air. Screeching, thuds, howling, shots [smothering] the voiced commands, tankers' faces turned black. People jumped out from burning and knocked out tanks and fell, cut down by rifle and machine-gun fire, fragments of shells and mortars.[17]

All efforts of the 41st Tank Division were in vain. Daylight brought increased German pressure, and the Soviet division was forced to give up the bloody ground. Germans immediately noticed the pullback and went after the 41st Tank Division with a vengeance. Division's pitiful air defenses, represented by one battery and four antiaircraft machine guns, were quickly bombed out of existence.

A small Soviet rear guard made up of a company of flame-throwing OT-26 tanks with several heavy KV-2s temporarily slowed down the Germans. In this tough fight, the Soviet rear guard was completely destroyed.

After returning to the starting positions, division's chief of staff, Lieutenant-Colonel Malygin, walked up to the last surviving KV-2 tank: "The tank resembled a wounded animal. The turret was gouged, the howitzer's frontal plate had armor-piercing rounds stuck in them, the engine barely worked."[18]

By the time 41st Tank Division finished falling back east of Rovno on June 29, it was a division in the name only:

> Only the artillery regiment remained intact. The air defense battery had only two cannons. Tank regiments numbered around 20 T-26s each, number of dismounted tank crewmen increased to 500. Forming them into companies, we included in them crewmen from destroyed air defense weapons. These companies were armed with machine guns [removed from disabled tanks], mainly without bipods, revolvers, and rifles. The heavy tank battalion existed only on paper, consisting of one mangled KV-2, one mobile repair truck, and [several] fuel trucks.[19]

XIX Mechanized Corps, Major General Feklenko Commanding

During the previous day, the task of defending Rovno against German 13th Panzer and 299th Infantry Divisions fell upon Feklenko's severely weakened XIX Mechanized Corps. Stretched to the breaking point, Feklenko's corps was unable to contain German probes everywhere, and by afternoon on June 28, Germans began working through the gaps between him and Rokossovskiy's corps northwest of town.

The final blow was the appearance of advance elements from 11th Panzer Division, which found their way across Goryn River in the evening. German troops now stood twenty miles southeast *behind* Feklenko's units. Even though the 11th Panzer Division was not directly operating against the XIX Mechanized Corps, this created a threat to the XIX Mechanized Corps of being taken around the southern flank and being cut off from its own Goryn River crossings. Reluctantly, in the evening of June 28 Major General Feklenko was forced to abandon Rovno and began pulling back behind Goryn River. By the morning of the 29th, the 40th Tank Division took up positions in the area of Tuchin-Goscha, and the 43rd Tank Division, in the area of Goscha-Velbovo.[20]

Task Force Lukin,
Lieutenant General Lukin Commanding

During June 28, the two Soviet battalions belonging to the 109th Motorized Rifle Division continued fighting surrounded in Ostrog. On the other side of Goryn River, Lieutenant General Lukin was frantically gathering any warm bodies he could find and throwing them against Ostrog: stragglers, retreating units, small garrison detachments, newly mobilized and untrained recruits, anything. The 404th Artillery Regiment, making up for its late arrival the day before, was subjecting the bridgehead of the 11th Panzer Division to significant and effective fire: "In the Ostrog bridgehead, there were constant and strong enemy attacks with artillery support."[21]

During the day, the 213th Motorized Rifle Division, separated from Feklenko's XIX Mechanized Corps, retreated towards Ostrog and linked up with Lukin's group. However, it needed most of June 28 to reorganize.

Unbeknown to Lukin, German reconnaissance troops discovered an undefended gap between his task force and the right flank of the XXXVI Rifle Corps, which was resting on the Ikva River. During the night of June 28–29, the German units began shifting south of the town, ready to exploit the gap in the morning.

XV Mechanized Corps,
Colonel G. I. Yermolayev Commanding

Throughout June 28, the XV Mechanized Corps continued its push to Berestechko. After reaching vicinity of this small town by the end of the day, Yermolayev's corps was to prepare for possible enemy counterattacks and offer whatever help possible to the VIII Mechanized Corps.

During the previous several days, the Germans set up formidable antitank defenses along rivers Styr and Ostruvka, along with strong points in the villages of Okhladov, Kholyuev, and town of Radekhov.

Attack of the 10th Tank Division faltered at the Severuvka River, on the way to Lopatin. Germans set up strong antitank defenses on the north bank of the river, and the Soviet division could not cross the river over only one available ford in the face of withering artillery fire. Colonel Yermolayev, seeing this situation with his own eyes, sent a liaison officer to the 8th Tank Division, ordering it to support the 10th Tank Division from the west in its drive on Lopatin. However, while these orders were being delivered, the Germans were pressing the 10th Tank Division hard and were beginning to encircle it.

At 1400 hours, the 37th Tank Division under Colonel F. G. Anikushkin launched its attack towards Berestechko. Advance of its 74th Tank Regiment started off well, and it was able to cross over to the north bank of Styr River in the vicinity of Stanislavchik village. On the other hand, its sister 73rd Tank Regiment could not cross the river in its assigned area near Bordulyaki village and around 1830 hours began crossing at Stanislavchik, following the rear elements of the 74th Regiment.

Thus, instead of advancing over a broad front, both regiments became stacked up one behind the other. While maneuvering to expand the attack frontage, the 73rd Tank Regiment found itself in a swampy area along the small Ostruvka River, a tributary of Styr. One of the battalions from the 74th Tank Regiment followed the 73rd and also foundered in the marshy terrain.

These units were in completely exposed positions when German antitank artillery began firing practically point blank upon them from surrounding woods. Their situation worsened when German heavy artillery from Lopatin added its weight to the fray. As the losses mounted, the Soviet tankers were forced to give up the offensive. What's worse, German artillery fire destroyed the two bridges across the Ostruvka River, trapping the 73rd Tank Regiment and the 3rd Battalion from the 74th Regiment on the wrong side of the river.

The 37th Motorized Rifle Regiment, following in their wake, crossed the Styr River in vicinity of Bordulyaki-Stanislavchik. However, poorly supported by Soviet artillery, it suffered casualties around 60 percent. Both commander of the regiment Major Shlykov and his deputy Major Shwartz were killed. "Positions occupied by 37th Motorized Rifle Regiment along the southern bank of Styr River in area of Bordulyaki-Stanislavchik are littered with dead and wounded. The 37th Motorized Rifle Regiment is severely demoralized."[22]

In his report on the events of the day, Colonel F. G. Anikushkin, commander of the 37th Tank Division, wrote:

I ordered Captain Kartsev, temporary in command of the 37th Motorized Rifle Regiment, to evacuate all the wounded during the night and offer them necessary help, to pick up the dead and bury them in the area of Zbroye, take detailed head count of the regiment, collect all weapons and ammunition, reorganize the regiment, and hold river crossings at Bordulyaki and Stanislavchik, not allowing the enemy to cross to the southern bank of Styr River.[23]

Summarizing the events of the day, Colonel Anikushkin requested one pontoon-bridging battalion to assist him in river crossings, over-optimistically stating that while the 37th Motorized Rifle Regiment was no longer combat capable, the division overall could still carry on its mission. He sent up a word of caution: "The combat materiel, due to its incorrect employment from 22nd to 28th of June, 1941, is beginning to fail in large numbers due to its technical condition and requires evaluation."[24]

By nightfall, positions of the 10th Tank Division, raked by enemy fire from three directions, became untenable, and Colonel Yermolayev shifted it east to link up with the 37th Tank Division. Both divisions became bogged down between the two rivers, Ostruvka and Styr. Around midnight, Colonel Yermolayev permitted them to return to their starting positions.

The 8th Tank Division, fighting on the left flank of the XV Mechanized Corps, was not able to take Okhladov village, suffering heavily from concentrated German artillery fire. Despite not being able to make any headway in its own sector, this division allowed the 10th and 37th Tank Divisions to pull back to their original morning positions on the Radostavka River.

The 212th Motorized Rifle Division of the XV Mechanized Corps not only was not able to attack, it was even pushed back by Germans.

Task Force Popel, Southwest of Dubno

Daybreak of June 28 found Commissar Nikolai Popel's task force spread out from Ptycha village on the Brody-Dubno highway to the Dubno suburbs, a distance of approximately ten miles. Popel spent a restless night preparing his unit for inevitable counterattacks. While he seemed quite sure in his memoirs about occupying Dubno, most likely Popel's force was in possession of some outlying suburb of the town, possibly the Maliye Sady township, roughly three miles from Dubno. The city itself was solidly under German control.

During the previous day's fighting, his forces severely depleted their ammunition and fuel stocks. Some of the men defending positions around Ptycha village were down to ten to fifteen rounds per rifle. The tank crewmen from disabled vehicles were almost completely unarmed. Some of the Soviet riflemen gave up their bayonets so that tankers would have at least a modicum of weapons. A makeshift Dubno militia company formed from the town's Communist Party and civil officials was likewise poorly armed.

The area south and southwest of Dubno became a quagmire of small groups of men from various formations blundering from one confused fight to another. In the early morning, commander of the 27th Rifle Regiment, Col. Ivan N. Pleshakov, stumbled in, accompanied by an aide and a commissar from a cavalry battalion from 14th Cavalry Division. This unidentified commissar informed Popel that during the night, a column of trucks bearing ammunition, fuel, and lubricants attempted to get to Dubno from Kremenets. It was turned back by some well-meaning cavalry officer, who did not know that Popel was near Dubno.

Despite Popel's fears, no serious efforts were undertaken against his force by Germans throughout the day. The Soviet attack was more effective than they realized. According to Gustav Schrodek: "Situation at Dubno became critical in the evening of June 28. Utilizing the available forces, including drivers and clerks, Russian attacks were repelled on the outskirts of town. . . . Until the situation in the rear was resolved, naturally, there was no thought of further advance by 11th Panzer Division."[25]

VIII Mechanized Corps, Lt. Gen. D. I. Ryabyshev Commanding

In the early morning of June 28, the 7th Motorized Rifle Division under Colonel A. V. Gerasimov again tried to break through the German defenses along Plyashevka River, but was unsuccessful. By noon, Mishanin's 12th Tank Division joined the 7th, but all attempts to link up with Popel's group failed.

Around 1300 hours, the 7th Motorized Rifle Division, under Ryabyshev's direct control, now only six miles from Popel, reached Plyashevka River. However, they could go no farther. German antitank defenses stopped the depleted Soviet units cold, and in some places they undertook successful local counterattacks.

German historian Werthen described an episode of this battle from the viewpoint of the 16th Panzer Division:

The main body of the enemy continued moving towards Kozin, later turning east. Only the 2nd Bn from 64th Motorized Infantry Regiment, reinforced by 11th Company of the same regiment; one company from 16th Antitank Battalion; and one battery of 88mm gun were destroying the enemy in the woods north and south of Tarnovka. The infantry companies took up initial positions on the edge of Tarnovka. 8th Company of 64th Motorized Infantry Regiment under *Oberlietenant* Muus attacked towards Ivani-Pusto village, with the objective to catch the enemy in a "vise" from the east. The soldiers from this company had a tough time fighting against a heavy Russian tank. These tanks constantly moved from one firing position to another, suppressing infantry and postponing the capture of the village. Still, approximately a battalion of Russian forces were caught in a "vise" and thrown back. However, they soon counterattacked with tanks, and the 64th was forced to return to initial position. Tarnovka was shaking from explosions of anti-tank grenades, homes were burning, all possible weapons were turned to destroying the tanks. The wind was spreading smoke and soot. One heavy infantry gun managed to knock out two medium tanks. The 5cm anti-tank guns were useless even at distance of 400 meters. More and more steel columns were entering Tarnovka, but soldiers of 16th Panzer Division held on tenaciously. One 88mm anti-tank gun in half an hour destroyed four tanks. When the attack was repelled, dead and wounded picked up, and smoke cleared, we could count 22 knocked-out tanks on the battlefield.[26]

Ryabyshev's scouts reported the arrival of additional German units. Besides the 16th Motorized and 16th Panzer Divisions, the 75th and 111th Infantry divisions were now committed in the area of operations of Soviet VIII and XV Mechanized corps.

Germans began pressing their attacks harder, and the two weak Soviet divisions of the VIII Mechanized Corp were forced to go on the defensive. While German artillery pounded the forward Soviet positions and panzers and infantry pressed frontally, the German aviation was working over Soviet rear echelons. Taking advantage of the absence of virtually any interference from the Soviet air forces, the German aircraft pounded Soviet positions. Ryabyshev wrote:

> Often up to ten vultures, formed up in a closed circle, would dive on our positions, dropping bombs and strafing troops with machine guns.

Our aviation still did not make its appearance, while we had very little of air defense artillery. It could not cover all of corps' positions. The Fascist fliers knew that and with almost complete impunity bombed our rear echelons, destroying ammunition trucks and fuel tankers.[27]

The 12th Artillery Regiment received the full brunt of German un-tender mercies. Regiment's commander, Maj. I. I. Tseshkovskiy, and his deputy, Captain N. F. Ozirniy, were both wounded. Losses of command personnel were such that a Senior Lieutenant Klinka took over command of one of the battalions. Still, despite severe losses, this regiment, armed with 122mm and 152mm howitzers, gave a good accounting of itself in the face of German tanks. Several times when the German tanks broke through the forward Soviet defenses, fire brigades composed of two to three KV-1s would be sent forward to plug the gap.

When, by the end of the day, the Germans broke off their attacks, Ryabyshev remembers hearing cannonade coming from northeast. He was hoping that this was the sound of the IX and XIX Mechanized Corps attempting to link up with him at Dubno. He said, "Everything was quiet behind the left flank of our divisions, where the units from Maj. Gen. I. I. Karpezo's XV Mechanized Corps were supposed to operate. We still have not received any instructions from Gen. R. N. Morgunov, who was supposed to have been coordinating actions of VIII and XV Mechanized Corps."[28]

What's worse, when the VIII Mechanized Corps shifted northeast against Dubno, it opened an undefended gap between the left flank, the 7th Motorized Rifle Division, and the right flank, XV Mechanized Corps' 212th Motorized Division. The 7th Motorized Rifle Division became surrounded from three sides; by German 75th Infantry Division from the north, 11th Panzer Division from east and now the 57th Infantry Division, which got into the unoccupied gap, from the west. In order to prevent his division from being completely cut off, Ryabyshev ordered its retreat through the narrow corridor to the southeast.

After the main body of the VIII Mechanized Corps ceded the blood-soaked ground, the 16th Panzer Division finally had a chance to consolidate gains, rest, and reorganize.

While the 16th Panzer Division was slowly grinding down Ryabyshev's corps, its sister 11th Panzer Division was having a tough time in Ostrog. This division moved far forward, and when Task Force Popel cut its resupply line, it began experiencing difficulties. Its lead elements were being bloodied just beyond Ostrog in a tough contest with Task Force Lukin, while its rear echelons found themselves pressed hard by Commissar Popel's group at Dubno: "At the same time, it had to deal with constant strong enemy attacks against Ostrog bridgehead, while behind them, in the area of Dubno, the German troops had to contend with strong enemy motorized forces with tanks."[29]

Disruption in supply caused severe concerns for 11th Panzer Division, especially with fuel and ammunition. A temporary airlift by several He-101 squadrons attempted to resupply division's forward units, but the amount delivered was insufficient to cover the expenditure of vital supplies.

The Soviet Air Force, despite being much-maligned in recollections of many Soviet memoir writers for its conspicuous absence, nonetheless made a significant impression on Gustav Schrodek. While not always extremely effective in delivering their payloads on target, it had a demoralizing effect on soldiers of the 11th Panzer Division. Recollections of Gustav Schrodek attest to that:

> It started raining during the night, raising hopes that today it would cause the Russian fliers to cancel their activity. But it was not to be. The rain stopped at daybreak, and the Soviet airplanes again emerged immediately afterwards, falling upon column after column of rolling units from 11th PD, which continued arrived at Ostrog during the day. . . . For their part, the tank crews, in order to protect themselves from attacks from the air, would dig foxholes, over which they would position their well-camouflaged tanks. They weathered these air attacks in these pits. Unfortunately, further personnel loses could not be avoided. *It can not be denied that the Soviet opponent, here at least, has the absolute air supremacy. . . . Never in its history did the 15th Panzer Regiment experience so many air attacks as here, in and around Ostrog* [emphasis added].[30]

This last sentence would come as a great surprise to majority of Soviet servicemen who survived the first stage of the war, being left to the un-tender mercies of the *Luftwaffe* without their own air force's interference. Overall, the limited Soviet aviation assets still available to the South-Western Front conducted almost four hundred sorties during the day in the face of overall German air superiority.

CHAPTER 12

Fall Back to Old Border, June 29–30

JUNE 29, 1941

South-Western Front, Colonel General Kirponos Commanding

IT RAINED HEAVILY ALL NIGHT, adding to the misery of both warring sides. In the drizzly morning of June 29, under the overcast sky, Major General Potapov's Fifth Army held the line of Goryn River from the area of Klevan, northwest of Rovno, following the turns in the river south to Goscha. From there south to Mogilyani, a distance of roughly fifteen miles, the area was occupied only by small Soviet reconnaissance patrols. The Mogilyani village was the extreme right flank of Task Force Lukin, still containing the Germans in their bridgehead on the east bank of Goryn River opposite Ostrog.

However, looking southwest from Ostrog, the situation looked tenuous for the Soviet troops. The area between Ostrog and Dubno was virtually unoccupied by Soviet forces for almost twenty miles west to Dubno-Kremenets road. The XXXVI Rifle Corps was deployed from the east bank of Ikva River to Kremenets. Going south along the Ikva River, the 14th Cavalry Division extended the line southwest to Dunayev.

The XV Mechanized Corps was in a vulnerable position at Lopatin, northwest of Brody. The XXXVII Rifle Corps was hurrying from Busk, southwest of Brody, to shore up the escape corridor for the XV Mechanized Corps.

As the Sixth, Twenty-Sixth, and Twelfth Armies continued falling back from the Lvov pocket, the fighting came uncomfortably close to Tarnopol. In late morning of June 29, Kirponos and Purkayev made the decision to move the headquarters of the South-Western Front farther east to Proskurov (modern day Khmelnitskiy). The evening was spent hastily packing up the headquarters, and the large convoy departed for Proskurov during the night of June 29–30. As during the previous move just one week and lifetime ago, Colonel Bagramyan was assigned to stay behind with a small staff at Tarnopol. He was to follow the main body of the Front headquarters element in the morning of June 30, after receiving the word that it arrived at Proskurov. The vacated command post of the South-Western Front in Tarnopol was to be occupied by the headquarters of the Sixth Army.

Russian historian A.V. Isayev described the German wedge impaled between the Soviet Fifth and Sixth Armies as a giant trapezoid. Its base, anchored on Kivertsi in the north and Brody in the south, was roughly forty-five miles long. The sides of the trapezoid stretched approximately sixty miles, with its top following Goryn River for about twenty-five miles.

Stavka continued demanding energetic offensive actions from Kirponos' command. The only formation available to Kirponos still capable of conducting limited offensive operations was Lieutenant General Potapov's Fifth Army. Its location, occupying the lines of Stokhod and Styr Rivers, threatened the left flank of German group of forces at Rovno. Since German command shifted its forward panzer divisions south to deal with the threat posed by the VIII Mechanized Corps, the northern side of Isayev's trapezoid was the only visible location where the Soviet Fifth Army could achieve some small measure of success.

Under pressure from Moscow, on June 29 Kirponos gave Potapov orders to attack on July 1 from Tsuman-Klevan area "towards the south with the goal of cutting off the moto-mechanized enemy group of forces, which crossed Goryn River at Rovno, from their bases and reinforcements and liquidate the breakthrough."

The forces available to the Fifth Army were the XV Rifle Corps (two rifle divisions), XXXI Rifle Corps (two rifle divisions), XXII Mechanized Corps (one tank and one motorized rifle divisions), XXVII Rifle Corps (one and one-third rifle divisions), 1st Antitank Artillery Brigade, the 289th Howitzer Regiment from Stavka's reserves, and 1st Separate Armored Train Detachment. The XXVII Rifle Corps was in most difficult position—it was attempting to prevent the German 298th Infantry Division from expanding its beachhead at the railroad bridge in Rozhysche the previous day. The 135th Rifle Division from this corps was reinforced by the remains of the 19th Tank Division from the XXII Mechanized Corps. This tank unit, which higher echelon commanders insisted on calling a division, had in reality a paltry sixteen T-26 tanks with six field guns, plus the remains of division's support service units.

The XXII Mechanized Corps was to be Potapov's strike force in the upcoming offensive. Its unrealistic mission was to attack from the area of Tsuman towards Dubno and capture the town. Of the other two divisions in the XXII Mechanized Corps, the 41st Tank Division still had close to one hundred T-26 light tanks and a dozen of KV-1s, plus twelve cannon. The 215th Motorized Rifle Division had additional fifteen T-26 tanks and twelve more guns.

While the Fifth Army was conducting an organized pullback from Stokhod River and preparing for one last push, the XIX Mechanized Corps with the 1st Antitank Artillery Brigade and the third division from the XXXI Rifle Corps, the 228th, was defending the Rovno-Novograd-Volynskiy highway. During June 29, Feklenko's corps conducted a local counterattack, crossing over to the west bank of small Goscha River and coming within five mile of Rovno's suburbs. Even though pushed back to the river, the XIX Mechanized Corps managed to maintain a small beachhead on the west bank until July 1. In the morning of June 29th, one of Feklenko's tank divisions, the 43rd, still numbered sixty T-26 light tanks and one medium T-34. Within the next several days it lost almost half of these tanks.

On this day, the XIX Mechanized Corps received a welcomed reinforcement of 1,950 men, arriving on foot in Goscha area. These men, all of whom were inducted into the army in May 1941, had not yet completed their basic training and were initially earmarked for the rear echelon support units of the corps. Now, armed only with rifles and ten light machine guns, these untrained men were to be used as infantry.[1]

General Rokossovskiy's IX Mechanized Corps throughout June 29 was defending the line of Olyka-Klevan, mainly against parts of the German 25th Motorized Infantry and 14th Panzer divisions from the south. Its two tank divisions by now numbered only thirty-two tanks and fifty-five cannons. Potapov's orders to the IX Mechanized Corps concerning the counterattack on July 1 directed Rokossovskiy to utilize his two tank divisions to assist the XXII Mechanized Corps, while withdrawing his 213th Motorized Rifle Division to the area east of Kivertsi to become army's reserve. The headquarters of Potapov's Fifth Army were set up in Kostopil.

VIII Mechanized Corps, Lt. Gen. D. I. Ryabyshev Commanding

During the night of June 28–29, after an attempt by the 7th Motorized Rifle Division to break through to Popel's group near Dubno petered out, Lieutenant General Ryabyshev called for a meeting with his senior commanders. The meeting, held at the command post of the 7th Motorized Rifle Division, had a depressing background: "Vehicles destroyed by Fascist aviation were burning, as well as the German tanks knocked out by our artillery and tankers, were [scattered] throughout our positions."[2]

The VIII Mechanized Corps became separated into three distinct parts, strung out along the Brody-Dubno highway. Commissar Popel, with the 34th Tank Division and parts of 12th Tank and 7th Motorized Rifle divisions, was bottled up in the immediate vicinity southwest of Dubno. Only ten miles away, which became an inseparable gulch, Lieutenant General Ryabyshev was in direct command of the main bodies of 12th Tank and 7th Motorized Rifle divisions. The command post of the VIII Mechanized Corps, along with majority of corps' rear echelon elements, was further fifteen miles southwest.

Both of division commanders present at the meeting, Gerasimov from the 7th Motorized Rifle and Mishanin from the 12th Tank, reported that ammunition and fuel were alarmingly low and people were extremely exhausted. Mishanin himself was not in good shape after his ordeal of being buried by collapsing wall. He was suffering from a concussion and lost his voice. Mishanin's deputy delivered his report for him.

As if Ryabyshev did not have enough on his plate, a further dilemma presented itself during the command staff meeting. A Soviet pilot bailed out of his burning aircraft and landed among positions of the 12th Tank Division. The badly burned flier was able to report that he was delivering written orders to Ryabyshev from the headquarters of the South-Western Front. The packet containing the orders burned up along with man's aircraft, and he did not know what the packet contained. The pilot could only report that the scheduled offensive on July 1 was cancelled.

General Ryabyshev felt himself faced with a difficult predicament: "Not having written orders, I doubted that the offensive has been cancelled. At the same time, the cancellation of general offensive did not give the right to retreat. What to do? Continue with the mission, assigned by the Front, to advance to vicinity of Dubno? The fight during the day demonstrated that we cannot break through to link up with the mobile group. To stay put and continue fighting completely surrounded, with limited ammunition and fuel, was at the very least not smart, because this would have led to complete destruction of the corps."[3]

Ryabyshev did not have communications with Popel; not only were the roads cut, but also "the cipher clerk was killed, [and] during one of the bomb strikes cipher books burned up. We did not have ciphering instructions. Therefore, we lost the ability to use radio."[4] This short paragraph underscored the casualties inflicted by German air attacks on the infrastructure of Ryabyshev's corps. Like the systematic destruction of the Soviet airfield network throughout the border districts, the Germans were now systematically destroying the ability of Soviet tactical echelons to conduct an organized battle.

Faced with a certain destruction of the main body of his command should he stay put, Ryabyshev made the difficult decision to retreat while the German encirclement of his corps was still porous. Plans were quickly made to break out southwest in the direction of Radzivilov, along the Dubno-Brody highway, and take up defensive positions on the heights northeast of the town.

Throughout the night, fighting in the area of the VIII Mechanized Corps was sporadic. The Germans mainly limited themselves to air attacks and some local probes, while bringing up more units from their infantry divisions. Ryabyshev's main body maintained a low profile, preparing for the breakout that was to happen after dark.

The breakout attack began at 2200 hours. Twenty KV-1s and T-34s from the 12th Tank Division charged along both sides of the highway, puncturing a hole in the thin line of German outposts. Lighter Soviet tanks and dismounted riflemen from the same division followed in the wake of heavy tanks and expanded the breach to over two miles.

However, the German defenses quickly came alive, and a heavy artillery barrage fell on the Soviet troops escaping through the narrow gap. Following the lead elements, Ryabyshev's and Mishanin's tanks raced south slightly apart. Ryabyshev remembered seeing Mishanin's tank suddenly burst in flames. Mishanin was the only person to make it out of the tank. Wobbling, he ran into the darkness. This was the last time Ryabyshev saw General Mishanin. He was reported killed, and his body was not recovered.

Ryabyshev himself narrowly escaped Mishanin's fate. After making it through the German artillery barrage his tank had its "turret jammed, cannon barrel damaged. We counted sixteen direct hits on the armor. Luckily . . . the vehicle could move under its own power."

Other than subjecting the retreating Soviet units to running the gauntlet of artillery barrage, the Germans did not pursue, and the rearguard 7th Motorized Rifle Division was able to retreat in good order. As one unit after another appeared out of the darkness, Ryabyshev directed them to the new defensive positions north of Radzivilov.

Unbeknown to Ryabyshev, two divisions from the XXXVI Rifle Corps, the 140th and 146th, sat idle along the Ikva River, less than ten miles from both Ryabyshev's and Popel's groups. Both of these divisions, given halfway active leadership and adequate knowledge of situation, could have been used to link up with the VIII Mechanized Corps and create a significant threat to Dubno. None of this was done, and two invaluable rifle divisions sat on their hands as spectators.

Task Force Popel at Dubno, Corps Commissar N. K. Popel Commanding

Throughout June 29, German forces attempted to push Popel's task force from the Dubno-Brody highway and relieve pressure on the rear echelons of 11th Panzer Division. Popel, occupying a narrow strip of land roughly six miles long and two miles wide, jammed between the Brody-Dubno highway and the Ikva River, from Ptycha to Tarakanov, was surrounded by four German divisions. The 44th Infantry Division was north of it, the 111th Infantry Division firmly held Dubno and extended southeast, the 16th Panzer Division was pressing from the south, and the 57th Infantry Division was coming up from the west.

Despite severe pressure, Popel's men hung on to their positions. Halder noted: "The Russian VIII Corps is bottled up. Some of their tanks seem to have run out of fuel; they are being dug in and used as pillboxes."[5] Offensive capability of the 34th Tank Division, which comprised the core of Popel's task force, was spent in fighting during the previous day. Sounds of combat coming from less than twenty miles away led Popel to believe that the rest of the VIII Mechanized Corps was attempting to link up with him. However, by the time the rumble of artillery died down in the south after midnight, Commissar Popel realized that his group was on its own. There was still one communications truck with a radio available to Popel. Unfortunately, he was not able to raise any Soviet unit.

Popel's force still numbered over ten thousand men, an overwhelming majority of whom came from the VIII Mechanized Corps. In addition, several small detachments from other units that became separated from their commands linked up with Popel's task force. Fortunately, at least for the immediate future, there was food—a small warehouse with flour was discovered at the Ptycha railroad station, and Popel's supply officers put the local peasant women to work baking bread.

While dashing itself to pieces against a tightening German ring, the VIII Mechanized Corps caused consternation at German headquarters:

> Army Group South reports still heavy fighting. On the right shoulder of Panzer Group 1, behind the sector of 11th Panzer Division, a deep penetration by Russian Eight Armored Corps in our lines apparently has caused a lot of confusion in the area between Brody and Dubno and temporarily threatens Dubno from the southwest. This would have been very undesirable in view of the large dumps at Dubno. Also in battle zone of Panzer Group 1, enemy elements with tanks are still active behind the front, sometimes even covering large distances.[6]

XV Mechanized Corps,
Col. G. I. Yermolayev Commanding

The situation of the XV Mechanized Corps was temporarily threatened by the German reserve 9th Panzer Division moving past the northern flank of the Soviet Sixth Army. Its path lay straight at the undefended left flank of the XV Mechanized Corps. Fortunately, this corps was given orders on June 29 to begin pullback.

The vulnerable left flank of the XV Mechanized Corps was held by the 8th Tank Division detached from the IV Mechanized Corps. It fought a sharp rear-guard action with fresh German units, allowing the rest of the XV Corps to slip through the narrow gap between the 9th Panzer Division in the south and several German infantry divisions in the north.

Task Force Lukin at Ostrog,
Lieutenant General Lukin Commanding

Throughout June 29 and lasting through July 2, General Lukin's force, supported by direct fire from the 404th Artillery Regiment and the Heavy Armored Train #31, continued clinging to the area immediately east of Ostrog. Two Soviet battalions which became surrounded in Ostrog were not able to break out and were wiped out by the Germans. Lieutenant Colonel A. I. Podoprigora, shattered by horrific casualties suffered by his 381st Regiment, shot himself.

JUNE 30, 1941

South-Western Front,
Colonel General Kirponos Commanding

In the early hours of June 30, Colonel Bagramyan received a telephone call from Proskurov informing him that the headquarters of the South-Western Front successfully completed the move and were ready to resume operations. It was time now for Bagramyan and his small detachment to follow suit.

The rain, which was intermittent on June 28, now was falling in sheets, and the dirt roads outside Tarnopol became difficult to navigate. Luckily, Bagramyan's small convoy soon hit cobblestone-paved highway, and the going, although bumpy, became easier. It was roughly sixty miles from Tarnopol to Proskurov, and they made it there without incident until Bagrmayan's ZIS-101 car, a mix of cloned 1932 Buick and 1935 Plymouth, hit a washed-out patch of road and slid into a ditch. Not having any means to extricate the vehicle themselves, Bagramyan hitched a ride on another vehicle in his convoy after leaving his driver and several men to wait for help.

Once in Proskurov, an important hub of several major roads, and reunited with the rest of the headquarters staff, Bagramyan was brought up to speed on the situation of the Fifth Army. Liaison officers who returned from the various corps of the Fifth Army reported that orders about the offensive on July 1 had been distributed, and measures were being taken to prepare for the offensive. Despite being under heavy German pressure, the Sixth, Twenty-Sixth, and Twelfth Armies from the Lvov pocket were falling back in relatively good order and taking up positions along the Brody-Zolochev-Berezhany line.

Soviet aviation, as attested by Gustav Schrodek, was continuing to operate a little more effectively. The IV Long-Range Bomber Corps under Col. V. A.

Sudets was supporting operations of the South-Western Front. In the environment where Soviet fighter regiments took horrific losses, bomber aviation often had to operate without fighter support. This reflected in high casualty rates among bomber units: "The bombers flew without reliable [fighter] cover. Each time they were attacked by Fascist fighters and air-defense artillery. The [IV Air] Corps was suffering casualties, but time and time again the heavy planes would take to the air and fly east."[7]

Several Soviet reconnaissance aircraft also managed to fly in daytime to the border and make it back with reports, a significant feat. Unsurprisingly, they reported continuous movements of follow-on German echelons crossing into the Soviet territory. Between 0700 hours and 1000 hours, reconnaissance flights also reported small German tank columns moving from Rovno area towards Ostrog.

Everybody at the headquarters of the South-Western Front by now realized how precarious situation at Ostrog was:

> It was clear that if Task Force Lukin could not hold, the enemy will get far into the rear of the main forces of our Front. This threat concerned each of us. One thought underlined all conversations: the border battle was lost; the troops had to be pulled back to the line of the old fortified districts. But nobody dared to voice it out loud. Everyone understood that the fortified districts, located along the old state border, were still not ready to receive troops and provide a stiff defense.[8]

It was apparent that Stavka in Moscow evaluated the situation in the northern Ukraine along the similar lines. On this day, the Central Committee of the Communist Party created the State Defense Committee, GKO (Gosudarstvenniy Komitet Oborony). Josef Stalin, as expected, placed himself at the head of this newly created body, which now concentrated all the power in the USSR. Directives of the GKO became equal to laws and were to be obeyed and carried out by all individuals and organizations.

With the approval of the GKO, the Soviet High Command ordered Colonel General Kirponos to begin the withdrawal to the fortified districts deeper in Ukraine. These five districts, named after towns of Proskurov, Starokonstantinov, Shepetovka, Novograd-Volynskiy, and Korosten, represented the last chance of halting Army Group South before it reached Kiev. The withdrawal was to be accomplished by July 9.

Colonel Bagramyan remembered that staff officers at the headquarters of the South-Western Front could breathe easier. Everyone understood that withdrawal was necessary several days ago, but, he reported,

> Those of us who had frequent contact with the Front commander during these days understood clearly that demands of [latest] orders—to withdraw to the line of old fortified districts—completely mirrored [Kirponos'] intentions. Only Kirponos' inherent servility, some special convictions in not questioning orders, did not allow him to ask Moscow by himself about permission for such a pullback.[9]

Kirponos' command group now feverishly set to planning for withdrawal. Before, the attack of the Fifth Army on July 1 was treated as an unnecessary evil—a sacrifice to the demands from Moscow. Now, the Fifth Army would be attacking to pin down the German advance, allowing the main forces of the South-Western Front begin their withdrawal.

While the strike force of the Fifth Army, namely the 41st Tank Division, would launch its lonely attack, other units would begin the pullback on staggered timetable. The XV Rifle Corps of the Fifth Army in the north and the Twelfth Army in the south were still located much farther west than the rest of the forces of the South-Western Front. These formations were to begin their retrograde movement during the night of June 30–July 1. The Sixth and Twenty-Sixth Armies were to move in their turn the next night. The retreat was to be conducted in stages, with each army defending intermediary positions in order to ensure smooth pullback and to slow down pursuing Germans.

One of the major difficulties facing the Soviet withdrawal was lack of strength in-depth. Kirponos, Purkayev, and Bagramyan clearly realized that if Germans pursued aggressively, which they were sure to do, any breach in the Soviet lines could lead to encirclement of other retreating formations. There were practically no reserves left to plug the gaps. While Purkayev and Bagramyan wanted to slow down the rate of retreat in order to allow Soviet forces to leap-frog one another on the way east, Kirponos insisted on withdrawing as fast as possible.

As an intermediate solution, each army was instructed to conduct a phased withdrawal as it saw fit. The Front-level reserves were to be formed from depleted IV, VIII, and XV Mechanized Corps, which received withdrawal orders a day earlier, and two rifle divisions from the XLIX Rifle Corps. Around midnight, the finalized orders, maps, and instructions were signed, and liaison officers were sent out to deliver them to their respective commands.

Bagramyan writes:

> Before the war, why hide the sin, we were mainly practicing offensive operations. And to such an important maneuver as retreat, we did not assign appropriate significance. Now we were paying for it. Commanders and headquarters ended up being insufficiently prepared to organize and carry out retreat maneuvers. Now, during the second week of the war, we had to basically re-learn the most difficult science—the science of retreat.[10]

Below are excerpts from the situation overview section of orders issued in the evening of June 30 by Colonel General Kirponos to the forces of the South-Western Front:

1. Mobile enemy units, after fierce fighting, captured the area of Dubno, Ostrog, Rovno.
2. Armies of the South-Western Front are withdrawing by July 9th, 1941, to the line of Korosten, Novograd-Volynskiy, Shepetovka, Starokonstantinov, and Proskurov fortified districts; where, anchored on these fortified districts, [they] will organize a determined defense by field forces, paying particular attention to artillery and anti-tank means.
3. The 5th Army—previous composition, plus 196th Rifle Division of the 7th Rifle Corps.[11] While continuing cooperation with the 6th Army to liquidate the breakthrough in Rovno direction, organize strong defenses along the first line of Novograd-Volynskiy fortified district. The right flank of the army is to begin the withdrawal to the line of Sluch River. The withdrawal is to begin with nightfall on July 1st, 1941. [It is] to reach the line of Sluch River by morning of July 5th, 1941. The intermediate line of Styr River, Chartorysk, Tsuman, Klevan to be reached by midday on July 2nd, 1941, the intermediate line of Antonovka railroad station, Goryn River, Kostopol, Goryn River to be held until July 4th, 1941.[12]

After these orders were sent out, Kirponos listened to the report by General Sovetnikov, his deputy in charge of fortified districts. According to Sovetnikov, only Korosten, Novograd-Volynskiy, and Letichev fortified districts could be considered combat ready. They were occupied by small but permanent garrisons composed of machine-gun and artillery units. Upon arrival of field units, their defensive capability would rise drastically. As far as the other fortified districts were concerned, they were neither combat ready nor had sufficient garrisons and would have to be practically rebuilt anew.

Sovetnikov was seconded by chief of engineers of the South-Western Front, Gen. A. F. Ilyin-Mitkevich, who was in charge of reconstruction of the old fortified districts. He mentioned that even though the bunkers and strong-points were being taken out of mothballs, there were no weapons for them. Ilyin-Mitkevich expressed hope that the retreating field units would be able to deploy their organic weapons there.[13]

The situation in the area of operations of Major General Rokossovskiy's IX Mechanized Corps remained steady throughout the day. After beating back a determined German attack in the area of Klevan, Rokossovskiy's command continued preparing for simultaneous attack and withdrawal for the next day. Major General Feklenko's XIX Mechanized Corps was engaged in minor local actions as well.

Task Force Popel,
Corps Commissar N. K. Popel Commanding

June 30 started off quiet in Popel's area of operations. The rains of previous days ended, and, waiting for attack that they knew must come, Soviet soldiers huddled in stifling June heat. The good weather brought renewed German air and artillery attacks:

> Our forward positions disappeared in smoke and dust. Clouds obscured the sun. The barrage was then shifted into our rear. . . . We did not notice, did not hear, when the aviation appeared. As if cannons of gigantic calibers joined in the artillery barrage . . . . We are even more defenseless under bombs, more so than under [artillery]. We do not have aid defense artillery. Not even one gun.[14]

German aviation and artillery worked over the Soviet positions for two endless hours. Especially hard hit were positions near the Ptycha village, in the southwestern sector. The rear echelon units of the 34th Tank Division were also hit hard. During the previous day, Popel's men managed to tow a small number of disabled tanks to a central location. Since a majority of them were already heavily damaged, no attempt to disperse or camouflage them were taken, and the Germans further bombed them into oblivion.

The inevitable tank and infantry attack followed the bombardment. As Popel expected, the most severed fighting took place at Ptycha. The large village changed hands several times, until the smoking ruins of it finally and firmly remained in German hands. This fighting cost the Soviet side the only one field artillery battery available in Ptycha sector. The carnage was terrible: "Vehicles were burning. Cannon barrels of artillery pieces pounded into the ground were sticking up into the air, overturned half-tracks .... And everywhere—near vehicles, artillery positions, half-tracks—corpses of our and German soldiers."[15]

In the early evening, after the fall of Ptycha, German pressure increased on the Mlynov sector held by a unit from the 34th Tank Division. One of the battalions from its 67th Tank Regiment was almost completely wiped out by a combined attack of German aircraft and panzers. This fight cost the life of Popel's friend, commissar of the 67th Tank Regiment, Ivan K. Gurov. He had to identify his friend's body under trying emotional circumstances: "We began breaking though to the still, slightly smoldering tank. . . . Through the opened front hatch I saw three blackened skeletons." Popel's driver, Korovkin climbed inside the mammoth T-35 tank and among the carnage found a charred Order of the Red Banner, with its enamel melted off. This was an award Ivan Gurov received during the war with Finland.[16]

After enduring punishing air and artillery attacks throughout the day, during the night of June 30–July 1, Popel's command attempted to break out. The task force split into two groups, the combat and the rear echelon ones. In a sudden attack the combat group broke through the still-porous German defenses around Ptycha, allowing the rear echelon convoy, carrying wounded, to slip south around the eastern edge of the village. A small detachment from the 27th Motorized Rifle Regiment commanded by Col. Ivan N. Pleshakov brought up the rear of the almost-helpless convoy.

After the convoy with noncombatants departed, the still-combat-capable group remained with Popel east of Ptycha to cover the retreat. By now, according to Popel, this force consisted of around one hundred tanks, with roughly twenty to twenty-five rounds each and a half-tank of fuel. A handful of riflemen rode on each tank.

Generaloberst Halder noted in his war diary the end of Soviet threat at Dubno: "The situation at Dubno is straightened out. Still, 16th Panzer Division and 16th Motorized Division were not inconsiderably delayed by the episode, and 44th, 111th, and 299th divisions, which were brought up behind the III Panzer Corps, will be stalled for some days; this greatly delays and hampers the follow-up of infantry behind III Corps."[17]

Neither Popel nor any of his officers knew that their corps already abandoned its positions and retreated southeast. While the convoy with wounded from Popel's task force was probing its way south, the main body of the VIII Mechanized Corps was licking its wounds north of Radzivilov. According Ryabyshev, after the first week of the war his corps was down to 19,000 men, 207 tanks, and 21 armored cars. These numbers did not include Popel's task force. Among surviving tanks were forty-three KV-1s, thirty-one T-34s, sixty-nine BT-7s, fifty-seven T-26s, and seven T-40s. Despite being down by one third of its pre-war strength, the VIII Mechanized Corps still retained a significant punch of fifty-four modern KV-1 and T-34s. To put things in perspective, the 207 tanks still available to Ryabyshev on June 30 were almost the same number of tanks that Rokossovskiy's IX Mechanized Corps started the war with; and Rokossovskiy did not have any modern tanks. Especially severe was the loss of almost all the artillery, mainly due to air attacks. In his memoirs, Ryabyshev stated that by June 30, not counting Popel's detached force, the VIII Mechanized Corps sustained losses of 635 killed and 1,673 wounded—a highly unlikely and, obviously, lowered number.[18] Other than plainly overestimating his strength at nineteen thousand, a doubtfully high number, Ryabyshev must have absorbed whatever straggling detachment of Red Army men he could lay his hands on.

In an interesting detail, both Ryabyshev and Popel wrote in their memoirs that both were subjected to several instances when someone claiming to be one of them attempted to contact the other by radio. According to the two memoirists, the speaker spoke fluent Russian, but when challenged could not provide proof to the authenticating questions. In this fashion, the false "Popel" did not know the name of Ryabyshev's dog, and false "Ryabyshev" did not know the make of Popel's hunting rifle. Since both writers independently mention these episodes, they seem like attempts by German intelligence to exploit the confusing situation at the front.

XV Mechanized Corps

Colonel Yermolayev's corps spent most of the day in the vicinity of Zolochev, collecting stragglers, men and machines both, and getting ready to retreat eastwards. Its 10th Tank Division fought a sharp skirmish with German reconnaissance units before setting off itself. Retreat of the 37th Tank Division was also interrupted when it became embroiled in a rear-guard action in support of the 141st Rifle Division from the XXXVII Rifle Corps. After conducting several local counterattacks, the tanks of the 37th Tank Division resumed their pullback.

After 2000 hours, hoping to use the cover of darkness to slip east, the gigantic convoy of the XV Mechanized Corps entered onto the highway east of Zolochev. This was a mistake. Enjoying uncontested air superiority, German aircraft quickly found the defenseless convoy. Under relentless pounding from the air, the highway east of Zolochev turned into a gigantic funeral pyre of retreating Soviet vehicles.

There was one bright spot during that day. Almost a thousand survivors from the 87th Rifle Division under command of Colonel Blank made it through German lines and linked up with the XV Rifle Corps. These men made an incredible journey of over one hundred miles through the nightmare of constant encirclements, bringing out their division's flag with them.

CHAPTER 13

The Last Convulsion, July 1–2

Fifth Army, Major General Potapov Commanding

AS A MAJORITY OF FORCES, PARTICULARLY ITS INFANTRY and rear echelons, continued pulling back to the 1939 border, the units of the Fifth Army designated to participate in the last-ditch effort to slow down the armored spearhead of Army Group South attacked as scheduled in the morning of July 1. Reacting to the crisis situation south of Dubno during the previous two days, the German command shifted several divisions to the threatened sector, presenting the Soviets with a golden opportunity to inflict some telling damages on the left flank of the German advance.

Initially, the attack went surprisingly well, exceeding meager expectations. The two tank divisions of Maj. Gen. K. K. Rokossovskiy's IX Mechanized Corps contended throughout the day with parts of German 25th Motorized Infantry Division. The 20th Tank Division under Col. M. E. Katukov advanced approximately seven miles by 1500 hours. It could go no farther and by the end of the day returned to its starting positions. Its sister 35th Tank Division advanced roughly four miles before similarly being halted and forced to retreat by nightfall. In an after-action report, the command of the 20th Tank Division claimed up to 1,000 Germans killed, and ten tanks and two artillery batteries destroyed. It stated its own losses at highly doubtful only two hundred men killed and wounded. Still, there were flashpoints of heavy fighting, such as the plight of one German infantry battalion being temporary surrounded in the Bronniki village and losing 153 killed and unknown number of wounded.[1]

Repeating the mistake of the first counteroffensive of the South-Western Front just few short days before, this second attack also suffered from a lack of coordination between Soviet armored formations. By 1500 hours the offensive of the IX Mechanized Corps began petering out, brought to a halt by strong German defenses. However, 1500 hours was the time when the XXII Mechanized Corps went forward. Its 19th and 41st Tank Divisions advanced in the first echelon, supported by the 215th Motorized Rifle Division.

The 41st Tank Division initially met with surprising success, pushing back forward German elements and coming within ten miles north of Dubno by 1030 hours on July 2. Casualties were high on both sides, and the combat eventually ground to a halt in the afternoon of July 2.

Its sister division, the 19th Tank, which by now was relatively well reorganized after the drubbing it received on June 24, started out well. Steadily moving forward, it reached the vicinity of Mlynov in late morning of July 2. However, around 1400 hours, the 19th Tank Division was itself suddenly attacked by the SS Division *Adolf Hitler* in its right flank and rear and was forced to retreat with heavy casualties. The command group of the 19th Tank Division, including its commander, Maj. Gen. K. A. Semenchenko, was encircled. It was able to break out only seven days later.

Following behind the two tank divisions, the 215th Motorized Division had the mission of protecting the left flank and rear of the XXII Mechanized Corps. While not heavily engaged in fighting, it was subjected to strong artillery and air strikes and suffered heavy casualties.

The third armored formation belonging to the Fifth Army, the XIX Mechanized Corps under Major General Feklenko, was already on the east bank of the Goryn River and was in no shape to advance, barely holding back German attempts to sweep it aside.

The XXVII Rifle Corps, while being still called a "corps," numbers-wise was less than a division. It consisted of remains of the 135th Rifle Division and the survivors of the 16th Rifle Regiment from 87th Rifle Division, plus everybody from the rear support units who could be placed in line. It is of no surprise that the XXVII Rifle Corps was brought to a halt after advancing barely a mile in the early afternoon on the 1st of July.

The counterattack of the Fifth Army in direction of Dubno, especially the almost-twenty mile penetration by the XXII Mechanized Corps, worried the German command about the rear echelons of the III Motorized and LV army corps. Since the main bodies of these two corps were locked in combat with the Soviet VIII Mechanized Corps around Dubno, the German command hurriedly moved uncommitted forces against the XXII and IV Mechanized

Corps. They consisted of the 670th Separate Antitank Battalion, a reinforced panzer regiment, a reconnaissance battalion from the 16th Panzer division, and the SS Motorized Division *Adolf Hitler*. The latter, after moving through Lutsk, slammed into both XIX and XXII Mechanized Corps and forced them to retreat. The 25th Motorized and parts of 14th Panzer Divisions were moved against the IX Mechanized Corps. As the result of the rapid enemy reactions and counter-moves, the advance of the Fifth Army in the direction of Dubno had only limited results. Attack of the XXXI Rifle Corps in the direction of Lutsk was unsuccessful as well.

Halder noted these events: "A heavy enemy attack was repulsed with severe enemy losses west of Rovno; III Corps (northern wing of the armored group) temporarily stalled; central sector and southern wing advancing."[2]

By the morning of July 2, all of the Fifth Army was in general retreat. The northern arm of this army, composed of the XV and XXXI Rifle corps, received their pullback orders late and by the morning of July 2 were still occupying their positions along the Stokhod River, far west of the rest of the Fifth Army. Once the orders were received, a week-long race to the east began along the bad roads, made even worse by the frequent rains. Even though falling back at a fast pace, these units retreated in a relative good order. The German pressure in this sector was the least obtrusive. The German armored forces had been shifted south to Rovno and Dubno, and pursuit of the northern wing of the Fifth Army was conducted by German infantry divisions. However, difficult, marshy, water-logged terrain in this area of northern Ukraine heavily favored the defender, and Potapov was able to extricate these two corps without major problems.

However, the southern portion of Potapov's army was in tatters. The remains of the three mechanized corps, the IX, XIX, and XXII, suffered heavily the previous day and, having already lost the majority of their armored vehicles, were effectively infantry formations. The XXVII Rifle Corps, barely at division's strength, continued melting away.

Task Force Popel, East of Dubno

In the morning of July 1, using the slight cover of early morning fog, Commissar Popel's command continued navigating its way through the German line's encirclement. They proceeded in several distinct groups: Lt. Col. Petr I. Volkov's 24th Tank Regiment from 12th Tank Division, Maj. A. P. Sytnik's 67th Tank Regiment from the 34th Tank Division, Capt. V. F. Petrov's 68th Tank Regiment from the same division, and Popel's command element.

After successfully negotiating a swampy area, their strung-out columns were taken under fire by several German artillery batteries. Even though the German gunners could not clearly see in the foggy morning, their shells were beginning to find their targets. One of the first Soviet vehicles hit was Popel's own T-34.

Several rounds that hit his tank did not penetrate tank's sloping armor, but jammed its turret and knocked out a track. While his tank was being repaired, Popel commandeered a passing KV-1 tank and arrived at the first rally point. Slowly, in small groups or in whole units, Popel's command filed past him and continued on.

Very soon German aviation joined in the fray, and Soviet losses began to mount. After leaving behind a rear guard under Senior Battalion Commissar Yefim I. Novikov, Popel ordered everyone to break out at top speed. Besides artillery and aviation, units from German 16th Panzer Division quickly reacted to the Soviet maneuver and pressed on in the earnest, attempting to cut off as many Soviet forces as possible.

In his memoirs, Popel shows glimpses of the mad dash through the nightmare of exploding artillery shells and dropped bombs, shots traded at point-blank ranges by Soviet and German tankers:

> Everything that happened then is recalled as if in a nightmare. Separate incidents, scenes, appear in the shroud of bloody fog. As much as I want to, I can not coherently present this incomparable slaughter which lasted all day. . . . One of our T-34s flared up like a torch, darting around a field. Over a dozen Pz IVs at the same time gang up on a KV. We are shooting German vehicles point blank. When ammunition runs out, we ram them. . . . Volkov's vehicle began burning like a bonfire. With great difficulty he climbed out of it. Wounded leg failing him, Volkov fell and lost consciousness. Nobody followed him out of the burning tank.
>
> Sytnik's KV, in the heat of battle, rushed ahead of others. Rammed several Pz IIIs. [His] vehicle became a pile of shapeless metal. He began retreating with its crew deeper into the thickets.
>
> The thick grass turned yellow all around. The fog is clinging to it. Nonstop thunder fills the air, rolling around the forest. You can't tell where are our tanks, where are the German ones. Everywhere are black metal boxes, spewing out flames. . . .
>
> We are fighting since pre-dawn. People's nerves have atrophied, the self-preservation instinct is turned off. Some completely ignore bombs or shells.

[They] climb out of tanks, jump out of the trenches, without stooping they are going forward until felled by a bullet or a shell fragment.[3]

Finally, a handful of tanks, one ambulance, and three staff cars break through, followed by a number of men on foot and clinging to the vehicles. In the gathering darkness, Popel called for a halt to allow his men some rest and to wait for stragglers. In ones or twos, sometimes in small groups, Soviet soldiers on foot continue dribbling in. An officer brought news of Commissar Novikov's death, leading the rear-guard until the end.

Bone-tired Commissar Oksen and several soldiers, without having a chance to rest, set off to find a local guide. Their location was almost at the edge of the only map available to Popel, and he desperately needed someone to show him the way out of the unfamiliar locale. Ruefully Popel noted later: "Our [VIII Mechanized] Corps did not have [local] maps. We weren't planning on retreating."[4]

Oksen managed to soon locate two local civilians who showed them the way deeper into the forest. Before setting off, they pushed the last four-wheeled vehicles into a ravine, and now only a handful of severely damaged tanks were available to Popel's group. After traveling through difficult terrain for a short period of time, they halted for the night in another deep ravine, one of many criss-crossing the area.

While Popel's task force was navigating through the nightmare of its escape, Lieutenant General Ryabyshev sent out several strong recon detachments trying to find Popel. They were unsuccessful and turned back after running into Germans seemingly everywhere. The bulk of Ryabyshev's command received an unexpected gift of a full day's rest in the immediate vicinity of Tarnopol:

> Being in the reserve of the Front Commander, the 8th Mechanized Corps was putting itself back into shape in a relatively quiet environment. Soldiers were repairing tanks, trucks, weapons, and for the first time in [ten] days of fighting and exhausting road marches, our men had an opportunity to catch up on sleep.[5]

South-Western Front,
Colonel General Kirponos Commanding

On July 1, the attention of command group of the South-Western Front was focused not on the attack by the Fifth Army, but on timely pullback by the other three armies belonging to the Front. Especially concerning was situation

249

of the Sixth Army under General Muzychenko, on which Kirponos placed high hopes of reducing the poorly defended gap between him [Muzychenko] and Potapov. The offensive of the Fifth Army was now relegated to the lowly status of an afterthought: "Therefore, in the new orders, we reluctantly admitted that the offensive capabilities of the Front are exhausted. Even though [operational orders] mentioned the counteroffensive by the forces of the Fifth Army, the orders were, in fact, laced with the spirit of the defensive."[6]

As the Germans continued pressing on to Shepetovka, they pried the Soviet Fifth and Sixth Armies farther and farther apart. Operational command of XXXVI and XXXVII Rifle Corps, as well as the 14th Cavalry Division, was given to Muzychenko. However, Muzychenko was not able to establish contact with these formations, and they moved back in the general chaos of the retreat.

Kirponos in no uncertain terms ordered Muzychenko to get control of the situation:

> I am ordering you to immediately take control of 36th Rifle Corps, 14th Cavalry Division and 37th Rifle Corps, which were assigned to your command, and take decisive measures to restore situation along the line of Kremenets–Novi Pochayiv. You can also utilize the 2nd Anti-Tank Artillery Brigade for these purposes. If situation calls for it, you are permitted to utilize the 15th Mechanized Corps, but only as the last resort.[7]

Kombrig (Brigade Commander, an old rank) S. P. Zdybin, commanding the XXXVII Rifle Corps, reported that the 14th Cavalry Division, which was defending Kremenets, already vacated the town, exposing the right flank of the XXXVII Rifle Corps. By 1100 hours Germans began flanking Zdybin's formation.

The XV Mechanized Corps, with the 8th Tank Division from the IV Mechanized Corps still attached to it, became embroiled in combat on the right flank of the Sixth Army, even without Muzychenko's orders. Its divisions were stretched along the Zolochev-Podkamen axis facing northwest, slowly falling back under steady German pressure. Despite poor weather, German air attacks were unrelenting, and especially hard-hit were the 37th Tank and 212th Motorized Rifle divisions. In conjunction with the air attacks, German pressed hard overland and fractured positions of the two Soviet divisions, inflicting heavy casualties on them. Commander of the 212th Motorized Rifle Division, Maj. Gen. Sergey V. Baranov, was wounded and taken prisoner. He later died in German captivity. His chief of staff, Col. Mikhail A. Pershakov, and commander of the 74th Tank Regiment, Colonel Koyuntin, were missing in action and presumed dead.

At midnight on July 1, the staff of the South-Western Front issued an intelligence estimate summarizing conclusions of the Front's command group:

1. The enemy continues to exploit the success of the moto-mechanized group in the easterly and south-easterly directions from vicinity of Rovno-Ostrog, while at the same time attempting to cut off the withdrawal routes of units from Lvov direction.
2. [Enemy] created a large group of forces for actions against the center of the South-Western Front.[8]

On July 2, the Germans captured Tarnopol, which was vacated by the headquarters of the South-Western Front just days before, breaching the defense lines of the Sixth Army. The pressure on the Soviet Sixth Army was great, and it seemed like its commander Muzychenko was not up to the task:

Looking at the combat reports which we received from him, it was obvious that the command of the 6th Army did not even approximately know situation of its neighbors. Corps commanders, out of contact with the army headquarters and not receiving regular information about neighbors' situation, were acting without cooperation, on their own responsibility.

In order to plug up this serious development, Kirponos committed his last reserves—the two rifle divisions of the XLIX Rifle Corps and the XXIV Mechanized corps. The XXIV Mechanized Corps set up its positions in the area of Volochiysk, directly across the Tarnopol-Proskurov highway. The XLIX Rifle Corps took up positions along the line of Yampol-Teofil-Ulyanovo.

The Nineteenth Army, which was supposed to occupy and defend the immediate vicinity of Kiev, was ordered north to Byelorussia.[9] In case the Germans would achieve a significant breakthrough at Tarnopol and head for Kiev, orders were sent to the military commandant of Kiev garrison to take rapid measures in manning and arming the Kiev Fortified District. Nikita S. Khrushchev departed Kirponos' headquarters in order to personally oversee preparations to defend Kiev.

Muzychenko's Sixth Army was in dire straits, its planned orderly withdrawal disintegrating into a series of desperate rear-guard actions and breakouts from encirclements into which the front lines of the Sixth Army fractured. The IV Mechanized Corps under Maj. Gen. Andrey A.

Vlasov conducted a series of stubborn rear-guard fights, allowing various parts of the Sixth Army to fight their way clear. The XXXVI Rifle Corps, along with the 14th Cavalry Division, after suffering heavy casualties, finally broke out of its encirclement and headed for the Yampol area, attempting to link up with the left flank of the IVIX Rifle Corps. The XXXVII Rifle Corps was barely hanging on to its positions in the area of Noviki-Ivachuv. The VI Rifle Corps and the 3rd Cavalry Division were surrounded in the area of Tarnopol, and there were no news from them. A counterattack of the 10th Tank Division from the XV Mechanized Corps temporary slowed down the Germans at Tarnopol. The rest of the XV Mechanized Corps continued retreating from the city. The Twelfth and Twenty-Sixth armies were falling behind the Sixth Army, creating another gap, this one on the left flank of the Sixth Army. Approach of the Germans towards Proskurov itself forced Kirponos to order evacuation of Front's headquarters to Zhitomir.[10]

Task-Force Lukin, Ostrog

While the attack of the Fifth Army allowed its rear echelons orderly retreat and prevented the Germans from conducting their own offensive operations, the outcome of the border battle was clear. At Ostrog, the makeshift task force under General Lukin, bled dry after accomplishing all that it could, was at its strength's end. It was now not the question of "if" the Germans could break into the operational maneuver areas east of Ostrog, but "how soon." Behind Lukin lay almost-undefended Shepetovka with its convenient highway and railroad nexus.

Still, Gustav Schrodek readily admitted that his 11th Panzer Division continued to have a difficult time with Lukin's group:

> During the afternoon of July 1, the 11th Panzer Division was still in the tough, embittered fight defending the Ostrog bridgehead. As a strong thunderstorm turned all roads into a morass, the raging four-day-long tank battle between Dubno and Werba came to an end. All enemy attacks broke down despite Russian partial materiel superiority of tank equipment and willingness to fight despite bloody losses.[11]

At this critical time, General Lukin was called away by Moscow to rejoin his Sixteenth Army on the Western Front. Bagramyan described the effect Lukin's recall had on his task force: "At this time we realized that everything was hinging on willpower and energy of this man. He was gone, and his heroic depleted group, which for a whole week pinned down huge enemy forces, practically ceased to exist as a military formation. Its component units were absorbed into the Fifth Army."[12]

Bagramyan further noted that Kirponos was planning to replace Lukin's group with the VII Rifle Corps, which was being transferred from the Southern Front. However, two rifle divisions of this corps did not arrive in Shepetovka area in time. The XLIX Rifle Corps under command of Maj. Gen. I. A. Kornilov, one of the last available reserve units, was ordered to proceed in all haste from Volochiysk, east of Proskurov, to take up positions in the Izyaslav and Starokonstantinov fortified districts.

On July 2 Lt. Gen. D. I. Ryabyshev's VIII Mechanized Corps arrived in Proskurov. The retreat there was conducted under difficult conditions along the road from Tarnopol. The march was led by the 7th Motorized Rifle Division, followed by the corps headquarters and rear echelons, with the rear brought up by the battered 12th Tank Division.

Ryabyshev recorded one episode of the aftermath of an attack by German aviation:

> Enemy dive bombers periodically appeared in the air. After dropping bombs, they would fly along the column, strafing it with machine guns. Our planes were nowhere to be seen. The whole burden of fighting the enemy aircraft fell on antiaircraft artillery and machine guns. After noon, a column moving ahead of us suddenly stopped. Five, ten minutes went by, and we were still standing.
>
> We could hear shell explosions. Sensing something wrong, I hurried forward in my KV and soon saw four burning trucks loaded with shells. These shells would explode, terrifying the poor refugees. It was impossible to go around these vehicles: an impassable swamp stretch for almost a mile to the right and a relatively high hill with steep slope rose up to the left. There was no time to wait until the vehicles would completely burn out and shells stop exploding. Only the tanks would be able to climb the mountain; the wheeled vehicle would not have made it. The column could not remain on the road for long—the enemy bombers could return at any moment. Before I had a chance to make a decision, I heard from my driver:
>
> "Quickly, Comrade General, close your hatch!"
>
> I lowered myself into the turret and closed the hatch tightly. KV, picking up speed, charged the burning vehicles. The distance rapidly shrunk. Another moment—and tank hit with its armored chest one truck,

then second one, third one. . . . The vehicles flew in all directions. The shells stopped exploding. The traffic jam disappeared.

In the heat of the moment, I bawled out the driver for his risky stunt, totally without my consent. At a later date I appreciated his initiative and bravery and was sorry that I did not put him in for an award. At that difficult time, under the influence of difficulties and failures, the ability to appreciate bravery became numb.

After liquidating the traffic jam, the troops and refugees continued on. I decided to reach the head of the 7th Motorized Rifle Division's column, but it wasn't that easy. The enemy aviation constantly bombed us. Vehicles and refugees' wagons were constantly breaking down. The infantrymen . . . would push into the ditches the damaged vehicles, wagons, dead horses and continue the march.[13]

Shortly before Proskurov, Ryabyshev's column linked up with column of wounded which Popel sent out with Pleshakov.

After making his report to General Purkayev, Ryabyshev received his next set of orders—to move to Kazatin to rest and reorganize. With great difficulty, Ryabyshev and his staff officers managed to cobble together a train and load his 134 tanks and 5 tractors.[14]

While Ryabyshev was withdrawing the main body of his corps, Commissar Nikolai Popel with his group remained in the deep ravine just east of Verba, near the Ikva River. He spent three days there, gathering survivors which were wandering through the surrounding woods and organizing his force into companies and battalions. By the end of the third day, July 4, Popel had slightly over nine hundred men with him. The majority of these men belonged to the VIII Mechanized Corps, but some were soldiers separated from a variety of other units. There even was a small group from 124th Rifle Division, which was surrounded near Vladimir-Volynskiy during the second day of the war. This tiny cluster of men got caught up in the ebb and flow of the chaotic events and linked up with Popel's unit, over one hundred miles from where 124th Rifle Division was destroyed.

In his own turn, after covering approximately one hundred miles, fighting almost every step of the way and suffering severe privations, Popel's command rejoined the Red Army on July 23, near a small village of Belokorovichi, southwest of Novograd-Volynskiy.[15] The border battle was over.

Conclusion

SETTING OUT TO FINISH THE LAST SECTION, I scanned through reams of information and books that I have gathered for my research. I felt that an analysis was needed to summarize why the large numbers of Soviet mechanized formations were defeated with such an almost contemptuous ease by their German opponents. My glance fell across a report written on August 5, 1941, by Major General Morgunov, chief of armored forces of the South-Western Front. By the time of writing of his report, not only was the border battle lost, but the line of old fortified regions was pierced as well. In his report, General Morgunov succinctly outlined a majority of main causes leading to the defeat of Soviet mechanized formations in the initial period of the war. What happened to Red Army tank units in Ukraine was mirrored along the whole front.

Below, shortened and edited, are excerpts from Morgunov's report:

1. From the very first day of war, the mechanized corps were employed incorrectly, because, while the mechanized corps (I'm not talking about all of them) were really a Front-level asset, all of them were assigned to [field] armies. Naturally, cases of reassignment of an individual mechanized corps directly to an army should have been possible, but [only] in instances when situation really demanded it, and this should have been done by grouping them into strike forces.

2. All operations of mechanized corps were conducted without thorough reconnaissance; some units were completely unaware what was happening in their immediate vicinity. There was absolutely no aerial reconnaissance assigned specifically for mechanized corps. Control of the mechanized corps by commanders of all-arms [armies] was poorly organized; units were widely separated ... and by the time of the

offensive were not in contact with each other. Headquarters of armies were completely not ready to control such large mechanized formations as the mechanized corps. Infantry, as a rule, acted independently, and the overall situation did not permit organization of combined operations.

3. Headquarters of armies completely forgot that equipment has a limited lifespan, that it needs maintenance, minor repairs, refueling and re-arming.... Mechanized corps completely lacked air cover during the road marches, as well as after combat....

4. Information top-to-bottom, as well as with neighboring units, was established very poorly. The war, from the very beginning, assumed fluid character; the enemy turned out to be more mobile. The main feature of his actions is the wide use of encirclements and flank attacks. [Germans] avoid head-on attacks and immediately would employ mobile antitank assets . . . while encircling around one or (in most cases) both flanks. Our command personnel were poorly trained during peacetime for these very operations; trying, therefore, to defend in close contact with neighbor, while there were no adequate forces to establish such a defense....

There were many shortcomings committed directly by commanders of mechanized formations, such as:

1. Headquarters of mechanized corps, tank divisions, and regiments did not yet possess operational-tactical know-how; they could not reach right conclusions and completely failed to understand plans of army and front commanders.

2. Command personnel is lacking sufficient initiative.

3. Not all the mobile assets, which the corps possessed, were utilized.

4. There was no maneuverability—there was listlessness, sloth in carrying out orders.

5. Operations, as a rule, were demonstrated by head-on attacks, which led to unnecessary loss of equipment and personnel. This happened because commanders at all levels neglected reconnaissance.

6. Inability to organize combat operations along the routes which would interfere with enemy movements, who advanced mainly along roads.

7. Obstacles were not utilized; cooperation with combat engineer troops was nonexistent.

8. The was no attempt to deny the enemy the opportunity to bring up fuel and ammunition. Ambushes along the main enemy routes of advance were not employed.

9. Enemy pressure on [our] flanks led to fear of being encircled, while the tank units should not fear encirclements.

10. Large population centers were not utilized to destroy the enemy and inability to operate in them was discovered.

11. Control, starting from platoon commander to senior commanders, was poor; radio was seldom utilized; too much time was wasted on encoding and decoding [of messages].

12. Crews were extremely poorly trained in preventive maintenance: there were cases when crews abandoned their vehicles with ammunition still in them; there were individual cases when crews left their vehicles and retreated.

13. All units lacked [sufficient] means of evacuation; the ones that did have them, could support mechanized corps and tank divisions only during offensive operations.

14. Personnel was not familiar with new equipment, especially KV and T-34; and was completely untrained in conducting repairs in field conditions. Repair facilities of tank divisions turned out to be incapable to conduct repairs during retrograde operations.

15. Large percentage of command personnel did not know missions, did not have maps, which led to instances when not just individual tanks, but whole units would wander around aimlessly.

16. Existing organization of rear echelons is too cumbersome: commander's technical deputy, instead of working with combat materiel, as a rule, would remain behind in the rear echelon. The rear support echelons need to be reduced, leaving only those vehicles employed in delivering fuel, ammunition, and food.

17. There was no, as a rule, army-level staging areas for emergency vehicles, and nobody oversaw their operations. Lack of organic evacuation assets on army and front levels, led to inability to evacuate combat equipment.

18. Headquarters turned out to be poorly trained, staffed, as a rule, with officers not having experience of working in tank units.

19. [Too] many people oversaw mechanized formations: front would assign missions, army would assign missions, commanders of rifle corps would assign missions. Employment of the 41st Tank Division of 22nd Mechanized Corps is the vivid demonstration of this issue.

20. Some commanders of mechanized corps turned out to be not up to the task and completely lacked understanding about mechanized corps operations.

Given the reasons above, the Soviet defeat in the battle for northwest Ukraine was unavoidable. Battles are not fought by abstract concepts of corps and division, moved with chess-like precision on a map top. Battles are chaotic conglomerations of very tangible human and mechanical factors with very distinct limits, all wrapped up in a blanket of confusion and lack of information.

The Red Army of 1941 could be described being akin to mythological golem, large, scary, and formidable, but with no soul and very little brain. The brutal purges of late 1930s ripped the very soul out of the Soviet officer corps. Besides sheer loss of life and destroyed careers, the spirit of innovation and initiative was lost along with a significant portion of the upper crust of Red Army's commanders. Golem's puppet strings ended up in the inept hands of Stalin's cronies from the heady days of the Russian Civil War.

An underlying factor of Soviet efforts during the battle in Lutsk-Dubno-Brody triangle was an utter lack of coordination and gaping information void. Over one hundred thousand Soviet soldiers and well over three thousand tanks and armored cars moved to the sound of the guns without any tangible efforts to coordinate their operations. They were fed into the grinder piecemeal.

Enjoying strategic initiative, German commanders achieved numerical and qualitative superiority at the time and place of their choosing. While all the German divisions crossing into the Soviet Union on June 22 were viable and combat-capable formations, the majority of their Red Army counterparts were pale facsimiles of same. This point merits a closer look.

The basic maneuver block tasked with combat operations was a division. Eighteen German divisions from the Sixth Army and Panzer Group [1] were directly involved in the battle of the Bloody Triangle. I am considering this battle as lasting from June 22 to July 2, in the area from Vlodava in the north to Krystonopol in the south and east to Ostrog. These eighteen divisions are broken down into ten infantry divisions, one security division, two motorized divisions, and five panzer divisions. The five panzer divisions numbered roughly 650 tanks between them, with an additional approximately 100 tank destroyers and assault guns in four separate battalions.

Opposing this German group of forces was the Soviet Fifth Army, with additional reserve infantry and mechanized corps, consisting of twenty-eight divisions total. These forces were broken down into eleven rifle divisions, eleven tank divisions, and six motorized rifle divisions.

There were several more corps on the Soviet side and several more divisions on German sides, which were in close proximity to Dubno battle, but did not take immediate action in these particular events. I do not include them in this total.

Table 20.
Soviet Divisions in Dubno Battle

Corps	Tank	Divisions: Mechanized Rifle	Rifle
VIII Mechanized	12th, 34th	7th	
IX Mechanized	20th, 35th	131st	
XV Mechanized	10th, 37th	212th	
XIX Mechanized	40th, 43rd	213th	
XXII Mechanized	19th, 41st	215th	
IV Mechanized	8th		
V Mechanized[1]		109th	
XV Rifle			45th, 62nd
XXVII Rifle			87th, 124th, 135th
XXXI Rifle			193rd, 195th, 200th
XXXVI Rifle			140th, 146th, 228th
Total Divisions	11	6	11

If we look at just the number of divisions intimately involved in the struggle of the Bloody Triangle, the Germans are clearly outnumbered. However, qualitatively, Germans held a clear advantage. Each German division was larger in terms of assigned personnel. A German infantry division numbered susteen thousand men and a panzer division, fourteen thousand. Being already on war footing, these divisions were almost at their fully assigned strengths.

Of the Soviet divisions, a overwhelming majority was still on prewar footing, with the average of rifle divisions in the first echelon being around ten thousand men. The rifle divisions from the reserved corps, like the XXXI and XXXVI, numbered closer to eight thousand men.

Qualitatively, the Germans were on top as well. As I have already mentioned, each German division was fully a combat-worthy formation. Their Soviet counterparts, on the other hand, would have to be closely examined to determine which numbers could be called combat-capable.

Based on their time of formation, histories, and tables of organization and equipment, I would rate only six of these divisions as combat capable. I would characterize further nine more divisions as marginally capable of combat operations. I include all five of the rifle divisions from the Fifth Army in this category due to them being close to required personnel and equipment numbers, but lacking in command personnel and training. Divisions like the 37th Tank, belonging to the XV Mechanized Corps, for example, had roughly 90 percent of assigned tank strength, but fully over 80 percent of them (258 out of 316 tanks on hand) were super-numerary BT-7s, which this division was not supposed to have. The rest were chaff, a true cannon fodder, beefing up the Soviet numbers without adding further combat capabilities to the mix.

Table 21.

Combat Capable Soviet Divisions

Combat-Capable	Marginally Combat-Capable
41st Tank Division	34th Tank Division
12th Tank Division	37th Tank Division
8th Tank Division	215th Motorized Rifle Division
10th Tank Division	215th Motorized Rifle Division
7th Motorized Rife Division	45th and 62nd Rifle Divisions
131st Motorized Rifle Division	87th, 124th, and 135th Rifle Divisions

Much lip service has been given to the vaunted invulnerability of Soviet new machines, the medium T-34 and heavy KV tanks. However, this was just that—a myth. In an ancient battle between armor and projectile, the projectile usually won. While the thicker armor of T-34s and KVs could undoubtedly shake off projectile of German panzers and regimental antitank guns, they could do so only at medium to longer ranges. Germans' flexible tactics and initiative quickly developed an effective antidote to the new Soviet machines.

Faced with an attack by Soviet tank formations, the lighter German tanks would fall back, drawing the Soviet units behind them in pursuit onto the waiting ambush of heavier 105mm and 150mm artillery from corps and army assets. The famous 88, a versatile air-defense gun, showed itself remarkably efficient in dispatching the dreaded Soviet tanks. At the same time, the more-maneuverable German panzers would double back and take the winded Soviet tank units from their vulnerable sides and rear.

Even as the Germans initially had difficulties with the new Soviet machines, they had no problems with disposing of the lighter Soviet tanks, the T-26 and BT series, which comprised the majority of Soviet tank formations. The much-maligned German regimental 37mm antitank guns, contemptuously called by their crews as "door-knockers," proved to be quite efficient against the lighter Red Army tanks. The cannons on German panzers proved to be quite adequate to this task as well.

The use of artillery during the battles around Dubno has usually been glossed over. Yet, in a deadly cocktail that contributed to the defeat of Soviet counteroffensive, the German artillery played a major and decisive role. It is with the proper respect that the Russians call artillery "The God of War."

Communications proved to be the weak link that plagued the Soviet tank formations for quite some time. At the beginning of the war, almost the only tanks equipped with radio were the commanders' machines, usually not below company level. The rest had to rely on flag signals and messages relayed by motorcycle riders.

During battles, the Soviet tankers had a tendency to bunch up closer to their commanders in order to be able to better see their signals. The Germans quickly learned to spot and knock out command tanks, usually leaving the remainder of Soviet vehicles as a headless herd. Personally brave, Soviet officers, often up to senior levels, tended to actively participate in the attack or lead it from the front, suffering disproportionate numbers of casualties.

As already pointed out by General Morgunov above, high-level coordination of large-scale operations left much to be desired. Purkayev and Kirponos' plans to utilize six mechanized corps in an early effort to defeat von Kleist's Panzer Group 1 show sound operational thinking. However, it was the execution of these plans that came to naught.

Soviet reliance on civilian communications networks before the war and German timely neutralization of the same left Kirponos' staff without an effective means to coordinate the efforts of forces converging on the border. German *Luftwaffe* further frustrated Soviet attempt to reestablish communications by systematically hunting down and destroying Soviet command posts with their irreplaceable radio equipment.

On par with the lack of communications, the Soviet ability to gather information came up short. German air superiority denied the Red Air Force its ability to conduct aerial reconnaissance, while lack of appropriate equipment, personnel, and training left Soviet ground formations moving blind.

Still, despite all the shortcomings, the Soviet forces in Ukraine gave Germans the first bloody nose, not only slowing down the overconfident *Wehrmacht*, but even halting them for three days at Ostrog. Forced to attack into numerous Soviet formationsecheloned in depth and limited by poor road system, von Kleist's panzers could not achieve the finesse needed to break into operational maneuver room. West of Lutsk, faced with determined defense by gunners of General Moskalenko's 1st Antitank Brigade, the Germans had to give up their attempts of rapid and easy advance up the *Panzerstrasse* to Kiev. Time lost in bypassing and battering aside Soviet forces near Lutsk, and then Rovno, significantly contributed to delaying the blitzkrieg in Ukraine.

The formidable Soviet mechanized corps virtually melted in the cauldrons of war. Of the powerful armored fleet of Kiev Special Military District that greeting the morning of June 22, less than three hundred operational tanks remained by mid-July. Still, the lessons learned and paid for with a premium were instrumental in rebuilding the Soviet armored corps anew. The Battle of Dubno was lost, but Kursk loomed large on the horizon.

Abridged Order of Battle: Army Group South

This abridged version depicts only the major combat formations of the two armies (Panzer Group 1 was an army in all but name) that participated in the Bloody Triangle battle:

Commander: Generalfeldmarschall Gerd von Rundstedt

SIXTH ARMY
Generalfeldmarschall Walther von Reichenau

Army Reserves
    LV (55th) Corps: General of Infantry Vierow
        75th Infantry Division: Lieutenant-General Hammer
        168th Infantry Division: Lieutenant-General Mundt
298th Infantry Division: Major-General Graessner
(under direct control of HQ 6th Army)
        278th Air Defense Artillery Battalion (88mm)
        279th Air Defense Artillery Battalion (88mm)

XVII (17th) Corps: General of Infantry Kienitz
    56th Infantry Division: Major-General von Oven
    62nd Infantry Division: Lieutenant-General Keiner

XXIX (29th) Corps: General of Infantry von Obstfelder
    44th Infantry Division: Lieutenant-General Siebert
    111th Infantry Division: Lieutenant-General Stapt
    299th Infantry Division: Major-General Moser

XLIV (44th) Corps: General of Infantry Koch
    9th Infantry Division: Major-General von Schleinitz
    297th Infantry Division: Lieutenant-General Pfeffer

PANZER GROUP 1

GeneralOberst Ewald von Kleist

Group Reserves
    16th Motorized Division: Major-General Henrici
    25th Motorized Division: Lieutenant-General Cloesner
Motorized Division SS "Liebstandarte Adolf Hitler":
Obergruppenfuehrer Sepp Dietrich

III Motorized Corps: General of Cavalry Mackensen
    13th Panzer Division: Lieutenant-General von Rothkirch
    14th Panzer Division: Major-General Kuehn
    652nd Tank Destroyer Battalion (motorized)
    191st Assault Gun Battalion (motorized)
    eight motorized artillery battalions (105mm to 240mm)

ILVIII (48th) Motorized Corps: General of Panzer Troops Kempf
    11th Panzer Division: Major-General Cruewell
    16th Panzer Division: Major-General Hube
    57th Infantry Division: Lieutenant-General Bluemm
    197th Assault Gun Battalion
    six motorized artillery battalions (105mm to 240mm)

XIV (14th) Motorized Corps: General of Infantry von Wietersheim
    9th Panzer Division: Lieutenant-General von Hubicki
    Motorized Division SS "Wiking": Brigadenfuehrer Steiner

Kiev Special Military District Order of Battle

Commander: Col. Gen. M. P. Kirponos
Political Deputy: Corps Commissar N. N. Vashugin (later Nikita Khruschev)
Chief of Staff: Lt. Gen. M. A. Purkayev
Deputy Commander: Lt. Gen. F. S. Ivanov
Deputy Commander: Lt. Gen.V. F. Yakovlev
Deputy Commander, District Armored Forces: Maj. Gen. R. N. Morgunov
Deputy Commander, District Air Forces: Lt. Gen. E. S. Ptukhin
Deputy Commander, Intelligence: Col. G. I. Bondarev

FORCES DIRECTLY SUBORDINATED TO HQ KIEV SPECIAL MILITARY DISTRICT

Armor

IX Mechanized Corps (20th, 35th Tank Divisions,
    131st Motorized Rifle Division)
XV Mechanized Corps (10th, 37th Tank Divisions,
    212th Motorized Rifle Division)
XIX Mechanized Corps (40th, 43rd Tank Divisions,
    213th Motorized Rifle Division)
XXIV Mechanized Corps (45th, 49th Tank Divisions,
    216th Motorized Rifle Division)
1st Separate Armored Train Detachment (35th Heavy and 15th,
    17th Light Armored Trains)

Infantry

VII Rifle Corps (147th, 196th, 206th Rifle Divisions)
XXXI Rifle Corps (193rd, 195th, 200th Rifle Divisions)
XXXVI Rifle Corps (140th, 146th, 228th Rifle Divisions)
XXXVII Rifle Corps (80th, 139th, 141st Rifle Divisions)
XLIX Rifle Corps (190th, 197th, 199th Rifle Divisions)
LV Rifle Corps (130th, 169th, 189th Rifle Divisions)

Additional ground forces

V Cavalry Corps (14th Cavalry Division)
1st Airborne Corps (three brigades)

Aviation

17th Bomber Division
18th Bomber Division
19th Bomber Division
36th Fighter (PVO) Division
315th Air Reconnaisance Regiment
316th Air Reconnaisance Regiment
Separate Medical Evacuation Squadron

Fortified districts

1st (Kiev) Fortified District
3rd (Letichev) Fortified District
5th (Korosten) Fortified District (two to seven separate
    machine-gun battalions)
7th (Novograd-Volynskiy) Fortified District (one machine-gun
    and one artillery battalion)
13th (Proskurov) Fortified District
14th (Starokonstankinov) Fortified District
15th (Shepetovka) Fortified District
16th (Ostropol) Fortified District

Air Defense Command

(PVO: Protivo-Vozdushnaya Oborona)
Kiev PVO District (3rd PVO Division, 135th and 141st Separate Air Defense
    Artillery Battalions, 4th Early Detection Regiment)
Lvov PVO District (4th PVO Division, 11th PVO Brigade, 19th Early

Detection Battalion, 146th Separate Air Defense Artillery Battalion)

Rovno PVO District (256th, 286th, 374th, 87th Separate Air Defense Artillery Battalions, 29th Early Detection Battalions)

Stanislav PVO District (227th, 85th, 334th Separate Air Defense Battalions, 4th Early Detection Battalion)

Ternopol PVO District (186th Air Defense Artillery Regiment, 34th, 126th Separate Air Defense Artillery Battalions)

Zhitomir PVO District (139th, 254th Separate Air Defense Artillery Battalions, 22nd Early Detection Battalion)

Vinnitsa PVO District (375th Separate Air Defense Artillery Battalion, 122nd Air Defense Machine Gun Company, 14th Early Detection Battalion)

5th Searchlight Regiment

Rear Echelon Support Services

Transportation: Special Railroad Corps (seven regiments); one transportation (truck) regiment; Transportation Depot

Artillery Supply: nineteen ammunition depots, one artillery weapons systems depot

Fuel: One distribution depot; forty-two storage depots; one laboratory; one repair depot

Supply: sixteen food storage depots; one bread-baking factory; four equipment/uniform depots; three repair depots

Medical: seventeen hospitals; five medical supply/equipment depots; four laboratories

Veterinary: two vet hospitals; two vet laboratories; two vet supply/equipment depots

FIFTH ARMY

Commander: Maj. Gen. M. I. Potapov
Political Deputy: Division Commissar M. S. Nikishev
Chief of Staff: Maj. Gen. D. S. Pisarevskiy

XV Rifle Corps (45th, 62nd Rifle Divisions)
XXVII Rifle Corps (87th, 124th, 135th Rifle Divisions)
XXII Mechanized Corps (19th, 41st Tank Divisions, 215th Motorized Rifle Divisions)
39th Fighter Division

14th Mixed Air Division
62nd Bomber Division
1st Antitank Artillery Brigade (Reserves of High Command)
589th Howitzer Artillery Regiment (Reserves of High Command)
87th, 295th, 374th Separate Air Defense Artillery Batttalions, PVO
22nd Early Detection Battalion
2nd (Vladimir-Volynskiy) Fortified District
(19th, 20th, 145th, 146th Separate Machine-Gun Battalions,
    85th, 92nd Separate Artillery Battalions)
9th (Kovel) Fortified District (47th, 201st Separate Machine-Gun Battalions)
Two sections of 4th (Strumilov) Fortified District

SIXTH ARMY

Commander: Lt. Gen. I. N. Muzychenko
Political Deputy: Division Commissar N. K. Popov
Chief of Staff: Brigade Commander N. P. Ivanov
    (rank equivalent to Major-General)

VI Rifle Corps (41st, 97th, 159th Rifle Divisions)
IV Mechanized Corps (8th, 32nd Tank Divisions,
    81st Motorized Rifle Divisions)
3rd Cavalry Division
15th Mixed Air Divisions
16th Mixed Air Divisions
3rd Antitank Artillery Brigade (Reserves of High Command)
135th Artillery Regiment (Reserves of High Command)
324th Howitzer Artillery Regiment (Reserves of High Command)
4th (Strumilov) Fortified District (35th, 42nd Separate
    Machine-Gun Battalions)
6th (Rava-Russkaya) Fortified District (21st, 36th, 141st Separate
    Machine-Gun Battalions)

TWELFTH ARMY

Commander: Maj. Gen. P. G. Ponedelin
Political Deputy: Brigade Commissar I. P. Kulikov
Chief of Staff: Maj. Gen. B. I. Arushanyan

XIII Rifle Corps (44th, 192nd Rifle Divisions)

XVII Rifle Corps (60th, 96th Mountain Rifle Divisions, 164th Rifle Division)

XVI Mechanized Corps (15th, 39th Tank Divisions, 240th Motorized
    Rifle Division)

58th Mountain Rifle Division

44th Fighter Division

64th Fighter Division

4th Antitank Artillery Brigade (Reserves of High Command)

168th Howitzer Artillery Regiment (Reserves of High Command)

37th Engineer Regiment

20th, 30th Separate Air Defense Artillery Battalions, PVO

293rd Separate Communications Battalion

46th Early Detection Battalion

10th (Kamenets-Podolskiy) Fortified District
    (31st, 149th Separate Machine-Gun Battalions)

11th (Chernigov) Fortified District

12th (Mogilev-Podolskiy) Fortified District

TWENTY-SIXTH ARMY

Commander: Lt. Gen. F. Y. Kostenko

Political Deputy: Brigade Commissar D. E. Kolesnikov

Chief of Staff: Col. I. S. Varennikov

VIII Rifle Corps (99th, 173rd Rifle Divisions, 72nd Mountain Rifle Division)

VIII Mechanized Corps (12th, 34th Tank Divisions, 7th Motorized
    Rifle Division)

63rd Fighter Division

46th Mixed Air Division

2nd Antitank Artillery Brigade (Reserves of High Command)

376th Howitzer Artillery Regiment (Reserves of High Command)

34th, 259th Separate Air Defense Artillery Battalions
    (Reserves of High Command)

6th, 12th Separate Machine-Gun Companies

8th (Peremyshl) Fortified District (52nd, 150th Separate
    Machine-Gun Battalions)

FORCES LOCATED ON THE TERRITORY OF KIEV SPECIAL MILITARY DISTRICT, BUT NOT SUBORDINATE TO IT

Reserves of High Command
1st Air Corps (40th, 50th Bomber Divisions, 56th Fighter Division)
2nd Air Corps (35th, 48th Bomber Divisions, 67th Fighter Division)
5th Antitank Artillery Brigade (Reserves of High Command)

Internal Security Troops (NKVD)
4th NKVD Motorized Rifle Division
10th NKVD Railroad Division
21st NKVD Cavalry Regiment
4th, 16th, 56th, 64th, 66th NKVD Rifle Regiments

Border Guard Troops (NKVD), 20,000+ men
    (individual detachments rounded to nearest hundred)
Commander: Maj. Gen. A. V. Khomenko
HQ located in Lutsk, 200 men
98th (Lyuboml) Detachment: 1,600 men
90th (Vladimir-Volynskiy) Detachment: 1,900 men
91st (Rava-Russkaya) Detachment: 2,100 men
92nd (Peremyshl) Detachment: 2,300 men
93rd (Liskov) Detachment: 2,100 men
94th (Skolensk) Detachment: 2,200 men
95th (Nadvornya) Detachment: 2,200 men
97th (Chernovski) Detachment: 3,000 men
Separate (Kolomiya) Detachment: 500 men
20th (Slavuta) Detachment: 1,600 men
22nd (Volochisk) Detachment: 1,100 men

Order of Battle of Soviet Mechanized Corps

VIII Mechanized Corps, Twenty-sixth Army, Kiev Special Military District, HQ in Drogobych

Commander; Lt. Col. Dmitriy I. Ryabyshev
Political Deputy: Brigade Commissar Nikolay K. Popel
Chief of Staff: Col. Fedor G. Katkov

12th Tank Division: Col. Petr S. Fotchenkov
23rd Tank Regiment
24th Tank Regiment
12th Motorized Rifle Regiment
12th Howitzer Regiment
Support units
34th Tank Division: Col. Ivan V. Vasilyev
67th Tank Regiment
68th Tank Regiment
34th Motorized Rifle Regiment
34th Howitzer Regiment
Support units
7th Motorized Rifle Division: Col. Aleksandr V. Gerasimov
27th Motorized Rifle Regiment
300th Motorized Rifle Regiment
405th Tank Regiment
23rd Artillery Regiment
Support units
2nd Motorcycle Regiment

IX Mechanized Corps, Kiev Special Military District, HQ in Novograd-Volynskiy

Commander: Maj. Gen. Konstantin K. Rokossovskiy
Political Deputy: Brigade Commissar Dmitriy Kamenev
Chief of Staff: Maj. Gen. Aleksei G. Maslov

20th Tank Division: Col. Mikhail Katukov
39th Tank Regiment
40th Tank Regiment
20th Motorized Rifle Regiment
20th Howitzer Artillery Regiment
Support units
35th Tank Division: Col. Nikolay A. Novikov
69th Tank Regiment
70th Tank Regiment
35th Motorized Rifle Regiment
35th Howitzer Regiment
Support units
131st Motorized Rifle Division: Col. Nikolay V. Kalinin
509th Motorized Rifle Regiment
743rd Motorized Rifle Regiment
58th Tank Regiment
409th Artillery Regiment
Support Units
32nd Motorcycle Regiment

XV Mechanized Corps/Sixth Army, Headquartered at Brody

Commander: Maj. Gen. Ignatiy I. Karpezo
Executive Officer: Col. Georgiy I. Yermolayev
Political Officer: Brigade Commissar Ivan V. Lutai
Chief of Staff: Maj. Gen. Mikhail K. Nozdrunov
10th Tank Division: Maj. Gen. Sergei Y. Ogurtsov
19th Tank Regiment
20th Tank Regiment
10th Motorized Rifle Regiment

10th Howitzer Regiment
Support Units
37th Tank Division: Col. Fedor G. Anikushkin
73rd Tank Regiment
74th Tank Regiment
37th Motorized Rifle Regiment
37th Howitzer Regiment
Support Units
212th Motorized Rifle Division: Maj. Gen. Sergei V. Baranov
669th Motorized Rifle Regiment
692nd Motorized Rifle Regiment
131st Tank Regiment
655th Artillery Regiment
Support units
25th Motorcycle Regiment

XIX Mechanized Corps, Kiev Special Military District, HQ in Berdichev

Commander: Maj. Gen. Nikolai V. Feklenko
Political Deputy: Regimental Commissar Ivan S. Kalyadin
Chief of Staff: Col. Kuzma G. Devyatov

40th Tank Division: Col. Mikhail V. Shirobokov
79th Tank Regiment
80th Tank Regiment
40th Motorized Rifle Regiment
40th Howitzer Regiment
Support Units
43rd Tank Division: Col. Ivan G. Tsibin
85th Tank Regiment
86th Tank Regiment
43rd Motorized Rifle Regiment
43rd Howitzer Regiment
Support Units
213th Motorized Rifle Division: Col. Vasiliy M. Osminskiy
702nd Motorized Rifle Regiment

739th Motorized Rifle Regiment
132nd Tank Regiment
671st Artillery Regiment
Support Units
21st Motorcycle Regiment

XXII Mechanized Corps, Fifth Army, Kiev Special Military District, HQ in Rovno

Commander: Maj. Gen. Semen M. Kondrusev
Political Deputy: Brigade Commissar Aleksandr P. Sinitsin
Chief of Staff: Maj. Gen. Vladimir S. Tamruchi

19th Tank Division: Maj. Gen. Kuzma A. Semenchenko
37th Tank Regiment
38th Tank Regiment
19th Motorized Rifle Regiment
19th Howitzer Regiment
Support units
41st Tank Division: Col. Petr P. Pavlov
81st Tank Regiment
82nd Tank Regiment
41st Motorized Rifle Regiment
41st Howitzer Regiment
Support units
215th Motorized Rifle Division: Col. Pavlin A. Barabanov
707th Motorized Rifle Regiment
711th Motorized Rifle Regiment
133rd Tank Regiment
667th Artillery Regiment
Support Units
23rd Motorcycle Regiment

Organization of German Motorized Infantry Division

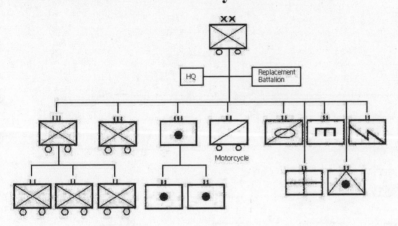

Organization of German Panzer Division

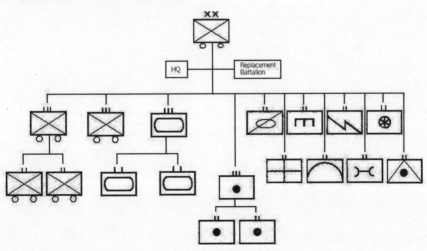

Organization of Soviet Antitank Artillery Brigade

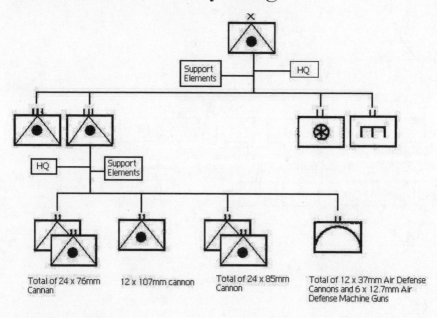

Total of 24 x 76mm Cannan

12 x 107mm cannon

Total of 24 x 85mm Cannon

Total of 12 x 37mm Air Defense Cannons and 6 x 12.7mm Air Defense Machine Guns

Notes: By the start of the war only one brigade was fully complete.

Organization of Soviet Mechanized Corps and Tank Division

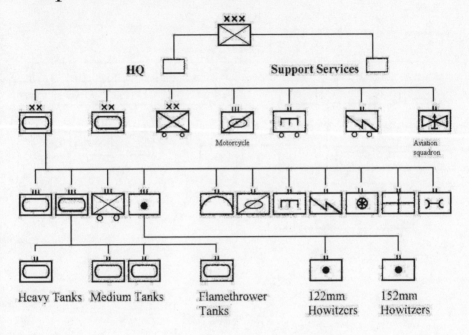

Notes:
1) By the start of the war, none of mechanized corps formed an air force squadron
2) By the start of the war, only some of mechanized corps formed a flamethrower tank battalion.

Organization of Soviet Motorized Rifle Division

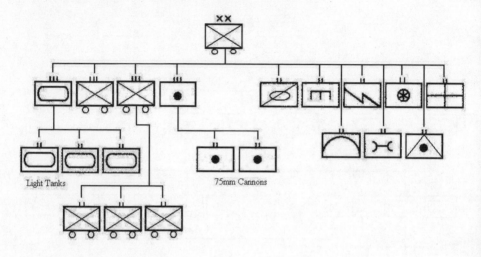

Light Tanks

75mm Cannons

Organization of Soviet Rifle Division

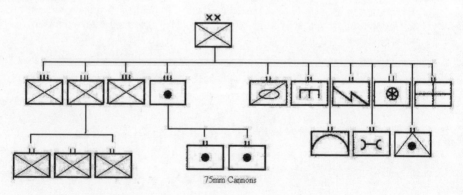

75mm Cannons

Unit Symbols

Symbol	Label		Symbol	Label		Symbol	Label
	Army			Armor			Signals/Communication
	Division			Infantry			Transportation
	Brigade			Reconnaissance			Medical
	Regiment			Field Artillery			Repair
	Battalion			Air Defence Artillery			Aviation
	Motorized			Engineers			Anti-Tank Artillery

Comparative Strength of Armored Units

	Soviet Union	Total per Corps			Total
VIII Mechanized Corps		907	**13th Panzer Division**		92
Heavy Tanks	128		Pz.Kpfw. I	0	
Medium Tanks	100		Pz.Kpfw. II	45	
Light Tanks	626		Pz.Kpfw. III	27	
Recon/Amphibious Tanks	53		Pz.KPfw. IV	20	
Armored Cars	172	172	Armored Cars	13	13
IX Mechanized Corps		298	**14th Panzer Division**		92
Light Tanks	269		Pz.Kpfw. I	0	
Recon/Amphibious Tanks	29		Pz.Kpfw. II	45	
Armored Cars	73	73	Pz.Kpfw. III	27	
			Pz.KPfw. IV	20	
XV Mechanized Corps		732	Armored Cars	11	11
Heavy Tanks	64				
Medium Tanks	127		**11th Panzer Division**		135
Light Tanks	541		Pz.Kpfw. I	0	
Armored Cars	160		Pz.Kpfw. II	44	
			Pz.Kpfw. III	71	
XIX Mechanized Corps		453	Pz.KPfw. IV	20	
Heavy Tanks	5		Armored Cars	8	10
Light Tanks	296				
Recon/Amphibious Tanks	152		**16th Panzer Division**		136
Armored Cars	26	26	Pz.Kpfw. I	0	
			Pz.Kpfw. II	45	
			Pz.Kpfw. III	71	
			Pz.KPfw. IV	20	
			Armored Cars	10	10

	Soviet Union	Total per Corps			Total
XXII Mechanized Corps		712	**9th Panzer Division**		131
Heavy Tanks	31		Pz.Kpfw. I	8	
Light Tanks	679		Pz.Kpfw. II	32	
Recon/Amphibious Tanks	2		Pz.Kpfw. III	71	
Armored Cars	82	82	Pz.KPfw. IV	20	
			Armored Cars	12	12
8th Tank Division/4th MC		258			
Heavy Tanks	50				
Medium Tanks	208				
Light Tanks	67	67			

Overall Totals		**Panzer Group 1 Totals**	
Heavy Tanks	278	Pz.Kpfw. I	8
Medium Tanks	435	Pz.Kpfw. II	211
Light Tanks	2478	Pz.Kpfw. III	267
Recon/Amphibious Tanks	236	Pz.KPfw. IV	100
Tank Total	*3427*	Tank Total	586
Armored Cars	513	Armored Cars	54
		Tank Destroyer	18
		Assault gun	36

German Armored Vehicles

	Tanks*		
	Light Pz. Kpfw. I	Light Pz. Kpfw II	Medium Pz. Kpfw III
Years of production	1934–1943	1935–1944	1936–1944
Crew	2	3	5
Armament			
Cannon version		1x20mm 1x7.92mm mg	1x37/5075mm 2x7.92mm mg
Machine-gun version	2 x 7.92mm		
Weight (in tons)	5.4 to 8.5	8.6 to 9.5	19.5 to 22.3
Length (in meters)	3.96 to 4.44	4.64 to 4.84	5.38 to 6.41
Width (in meters)	1.85 to 2.06	2.24 to 2.28	2.92
Height (in meters)	1.72 to 2.05	1.98 to 2.02	2.44 to 2.51
Ground clearance (in meters)	0.3	0.34	0.39
Armor thickness (in mm)	15	15 to 30	30 to 70
Engine	carburetor	carburetor	carburetor
Engine power (in horsepower)	60	140	260 to 300
Maximum speed, kph			
on wheels			
on tracks	50	40 to 50	40
Maximum range, km			
on wheels			
on tracks	150 to 200	190 to 260	145 to 175
Number produced			
Cannon version		1,900	6,800
Machine-gun version	1,500		

Note: This chart does not include Czech tanks because they did not take part in events described in the book.

Tanks*			Armored Cars	
Medium	Assault Gun	Tank Destroyer	Light	Heavy
Pz. Kpfw IV	Stug III	Panzerjager I	SdKfz. 221/222/223	Sd.Kfz. 232/234
1937–1945	1938–1945	1940–1941	1935–1944	1937–1945
5	4	3	2 to 3	4
1x75mm	1x75mm	1x47mm	1x20mm	1x20/50/75mm
2x7.92mm mg	1x7.92 mg		1x7.92mm mg	1x7.92mm
			1x7.92mm	
25 to 29	24	7	5.25	8.35
5.89 to 7.02	6.85	4.14	4.75	5.82
2.84 3.29	2.95	2.01	1.91	2.23
2.68	2.16	2.25	1.82	2.38
0.39	0.38	3	0.25	0.3
20 to 80	15 to 80	7 to 15	8 to 14	8 to 18
carburetor	carburetor	carburetor	carburetor	carburetor
230 to 300	300	100	90	155
			80	82
40	40	50		
			300	305
150 to 320	150	150		
8,500	10,600	200	800	1,400

Soviet Armored Vehicles

PART I

	Light Tanks		
	BT-2	BT-5	BT-7
Years of production	1932–1933	1933–1934	1935–1940
Crew	3	3	3
Armament			
Cannon version	1x37mm cannon; 1x7.62 mg (optional)	1x45mm cannon; 1x7.62 DT mg	1x45mm or 76mm cannon; 1 or 2x7.62 DT mg
Machine-gun version	2 or 3x7.62 mg		
Weight (in tons)	10.2	11.5	13.8 to 14.6
Length (in meters)	5.35	5.5	5.6
Width (in meters)	2.23	2.23	2.32 to 2.52
Height (in meters)	2.16	2.25	2.4
Ground clearance (in meters)	0.35	0.35	0.4
Armor thickness (in mm)	13	13	10 to 22
Engine	carburetor	carburetor	carburetor
Engine power (in horsepower)	400	400	400–500
Maximum speed, kph			
on wheels	72	72	72–86
on tracks	52	52	52–62
Maximum range, km			
on wheels	200	200	500
on tracks	120	120	350
Number produced		1884	5456
Cannon version	208		
Machine-gun version	412		

Light Tanks

T-26	T-37	T-38	T-40
1931–1939	1933–1936	1936–1939	1940–1941
3	2	2	2
1x35mm/45mm/76mm cannon; 1/2x7.62 mg			1x20mm automatic gun; 1x7.62mm DT mg
2 x 7.62 DT mg	1x7.62 DT mg	1x7.62 DT mg	1x12.7mm and 1x7.62 mg
8.2 to 19.5	3.2	3.3 to 3.8	5.5
4.62	3.37	3.78	4.11
2.44	1.94	2.32	2.33
2.2 to 2.5	1.82	1.62	1.9
0.38	0.28	0.3 0	0.3
13 to 15	6 to 9	9	10 to 15
carburetor	carburetor	carburetor	carburetor
90 to 97	40	40	85
	6 (on water)	6 (on water)	6 (on water)
30 km	35	40 to 46	45
100–240 km	230	220	300
8730	2627	137	
			41
			668

Soviet Armored Vehicles

PART II

	Medium Tanks		Heavy Tanks
	T-34	T-28	T-35
Years of production	1940+	1932–1941	1933–1939
Crew	4	6	11
Armament			
Cannon version	1x76.2mm gun	1x76.2mm gun	1x76.2mm &
	2x7.62mm mg	4 or 6x7.62mm mg	2x45mm guns
			7x mg
Machine-gun version			
Weight (in tons)	26.3 to 32	28	50-55
Length (in meters)	5.92 to 8.1	7.44m	9.72
Width (in meters)	3	2.87m	3.2
Height (in meters)	2.72	2.82m	3.42
Ground clearance (in meters)	0.4	0.56m	0.53
Armor thickness (in mm)	40 to 70	20 to 80	20 to 30
Engine	diesel	carburetor	carburetor
Engine power, (in horsepower)	500	18	500–580
Maximum speed, kph			
on wheels			
on tracks	55	37	30
Maximum range, km			
on wheels			
on tracks	300 to 465	220	150
Number produced			
Cannon version	33800	503	61
Machine-gun version			

Heavy Tanks		Armored Cars	
KV-1	KV-2	BA-20	BA-10
1940–1942	1940–1941	1936–1938	1938–1941
5	6	2 or 3	4
		1x7.62mm mg	
1x76.2mm gun	1x152mm howitzer		1x45mm gun
3 to 4 mg	3x7.62mm mg		2x7.62mm mg
		2013	
44-47	52	2.3 to 2.5	5.1 to 5.4
6.75	7.1	4.1	4.66m
3.32	3.32	1.8	2.1m
2.71	3.24	2.3	2.2m
0.45	0.43	0.24	0.23m
75 to 95	75	6 to 9	10
diesel	diesel	carburetor	carburetor
600	600	50	50
		90 k	53
32-35	34		
		250–450	300
250	250		
2800	334		3311

MAPS

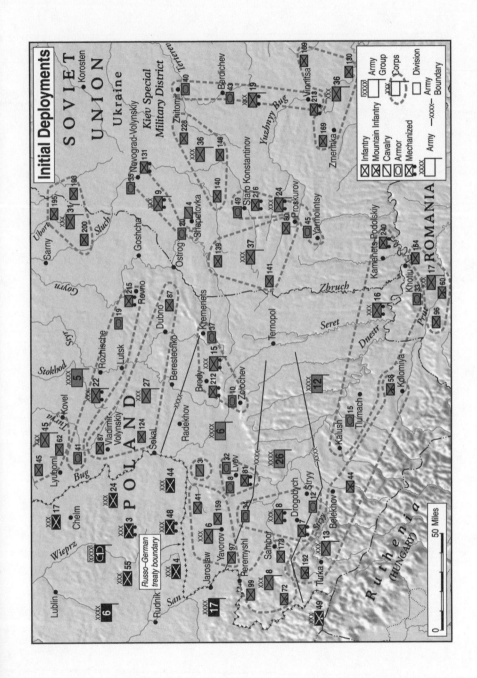

289

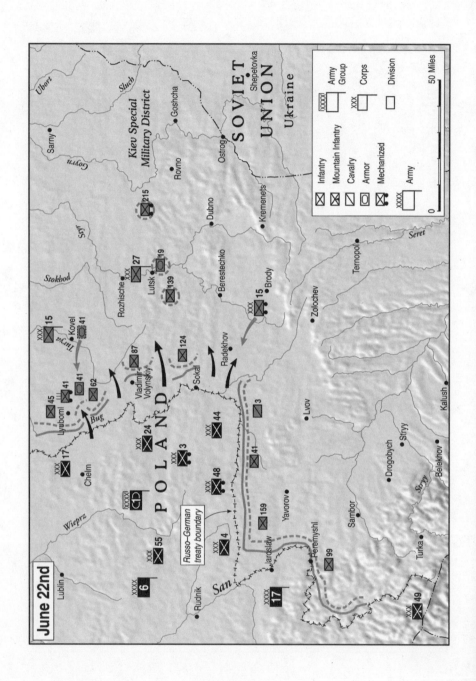

June 22nd

SOVIET UNION
Ukraine

Kiev Special Military District

Russo–German treaty boundary

POLAND

Legend:
- Army Group (XXXXX)
- Corps (XXX)
- Division
- Infantry
- Mountain Infantry
- Cavalry
- Armor
- Mechanized
- Army (XXXX)

50 Miles

Rivers/places: Ubort, Slucb, Sarny, Goshcha, Horyn, Shepetovka, Ostrog, Rovno, Dubno, Kremenets, Seret, Stokhod, Styr, Rozhische, Lutsk, Berestechko, Brody, Ternopol, Zolochev, Kovel, Turya, Vladimir-Volynskiy, Sokal, Radekhov, Lvov, Kalush, Lyubomi, Bug, Chelm, Yavorov, Sambor, Drogobych, Stryy, Belekhov, Wieprz, Jardslaw, Peremyshl, Turka, Lublin, Rudnik, San

Units: 215, 27, 19, 139, 15, 41, 15, 87, 124, 41, 62, 45, 3, 44, 24, 3, 41, 48, 159, 99, 4, 49, 6, 55, 17, 17

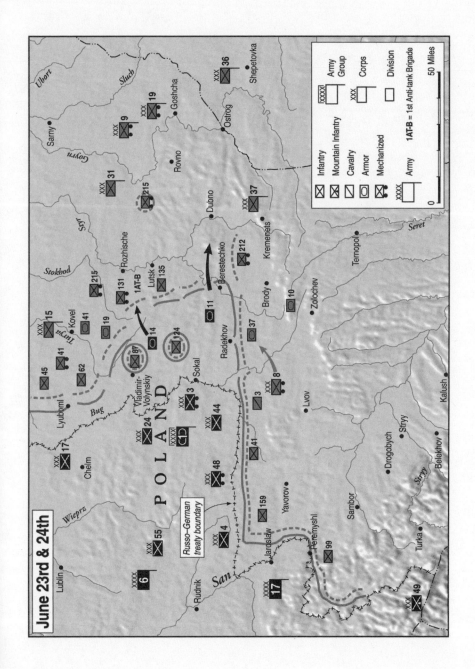

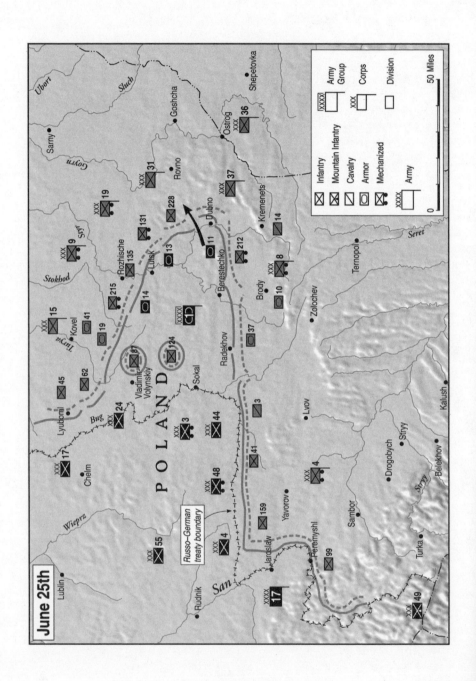

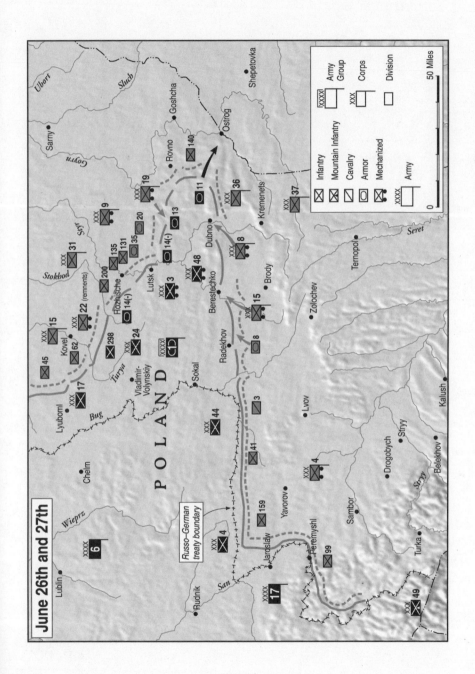

June 26th and 27th

Legend:
- Army Group
- Corps
- Division
- Infantry
- Mountain Infantry
- Cavalry
- Armor
- Mechanized
- Army

50 Miles

Russo–German treaty boundary

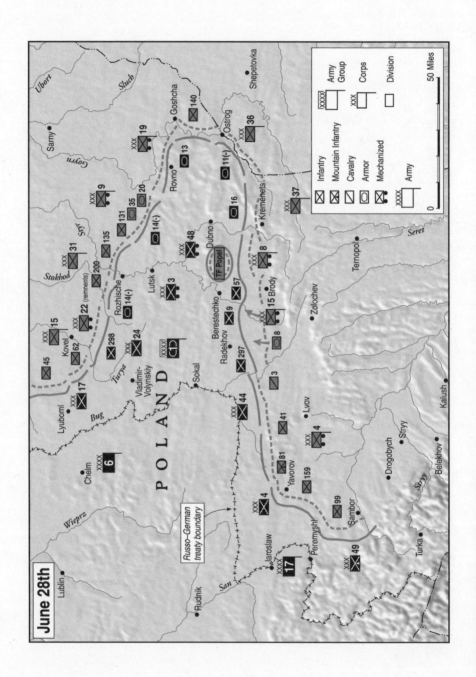

June 28th

Legend:
- Army Group
- Corps
- Division
- Infantry
- Mountain Infantry
- Cavalry
- Armor
- Mechanized
- Army

50 Miles

POLAND

Russo–German treaty boundary

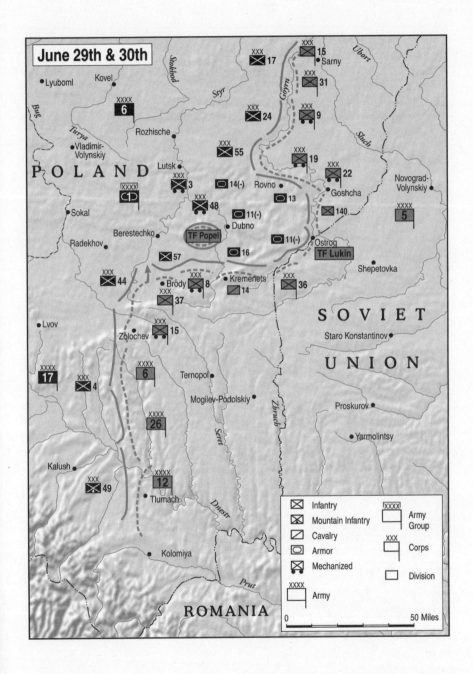

June 29th & 30th

Lyuboml
Kovel
Stokhod
Styr
XXX 17
XXX 15 Sarny
Ubort
Bug
Turya
XXXX 6
Rozhische
XXX 24
Goryn
XXX 31
XXX 9
Sluch
Vladimir-Volynskiy
POLAND
Lutsk
XXX 55
XXX 3
14(-)
Rovno
XXX 19
XXX 22
Novograd-Volynskiy
Sokal
XXXX C1D
XXX 48
11(-)
Dubno
13
Goshcha
140
XXXX 5
Berestechko
TF Popel
16
11(-)
Ostrog
TF Lukin
Shepetovka
Radekhov
57
Kremenets
XXX 36
SOVIET
XXX 44
Brody
XXX 8
14
XXX 37
Lvov
XXX 15
Zolochev
Staro Konstantinov
UNION
XXXX 17
XXX 4
XXXX 6
Ternopol
Mogilev-Podolskiy
Proskurov
XXXX 26
Seret
Zbruch
Yarmolintsy
Kalush
XXX 49
XXXX 12
Tlumach
Dnestr
Kolomiya
Prut

	Infantry		XXXX Army Group
	Mountain Infantry		
	Cavalry		XXX Corps
	Armor		
	Mechanized		Division
XXXX	Army		

0   50 Miles

ROMANIA

295

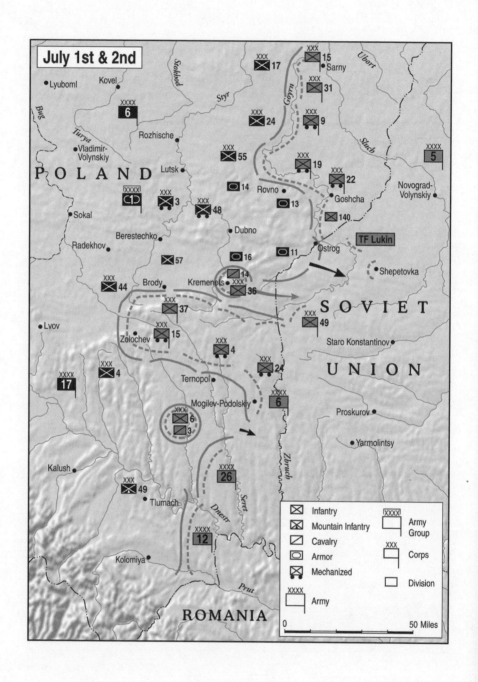

July 1st & 2nd

Lyuboml
Kovel
POLAND
Vladimir-
Volynskiy
Rozhische
Lutsk
Sokal
Berestechko
Radekhov
Dubno
Brody
Kremenets
Lvov
Zolochev
Ternopol
Kalush
Mogilev-Podolskiy
Tlumach
Kolomiya
ROMANIA

Sarny
Novograd-
Volynskiy
Rovno
Goshcha
Ostrog
TF Lukin
Shepetovka
SOVIET
Staro Konstantinov
UNION
Proskurov
Yarmolintsy

6
1
5
17
26
12
6

17
15
31
24
9
55
19
22
3
14
48
13
57
16
11
44
14
36
49
37
4
15
24
4
6
49

Bug
Turya
Stokhod
Styr
Styr
Gorin
Ubort
Sluch
Zbruch
Seret
Dnestr
Prut

Infantry
Mountain Infantry
Cavalry
Armor
Mechanized
Army
Army Group
Corps
Division

0   50 Miles

296

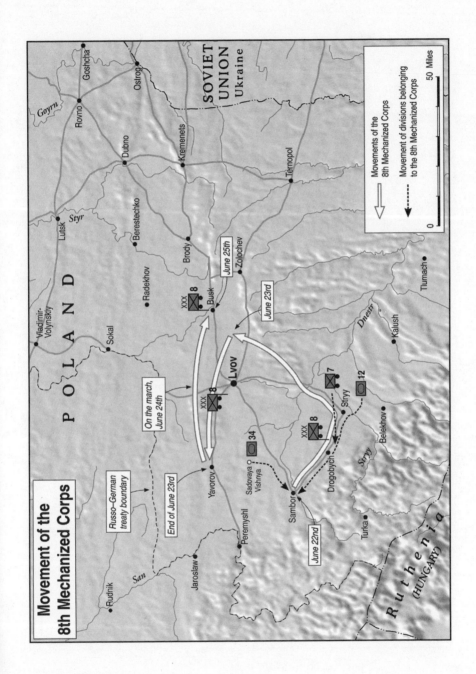

Movement of the 8th Mechanized Corps

SOVIET UNION
Ukraine

P O L A N D

Ruthenia (HUNGARY)

Legend:
→ Movements of the 8th Mechanized Corps
⇢ Movement of divisions belonging to the 8th Mechanized Corps

0 — 50 Miles

Goshcha
Ostrog
Rovno
Goyrn
Dubno
Kremenets
Ternopol
Lutsk
Styr
Berestechko
Brody
Radekhov
Busk
June 25th
Zolochev
June 23rd
Dnestr
Tlumach
Kalush
XXX 8
Sokal
Vladimir-Volynsky
Lvov
7
12 Stryy
Belekhov
On the march, June 24th
XXX 8
8
Stryy
Yavorov
34
Sadovaya Vishnya
XXX 8
Drogobych
Russo-German treaty boundary
End of June 23rd
Peremyshl
Sambor
June 22nd
Turka
San
Jaroslaw
Rudnik

297

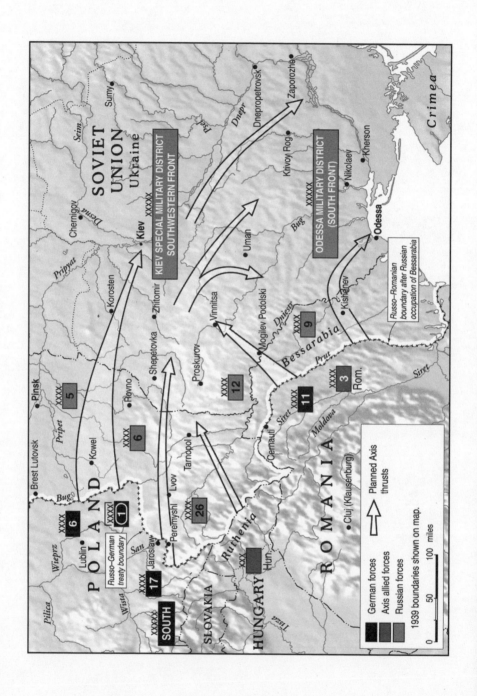

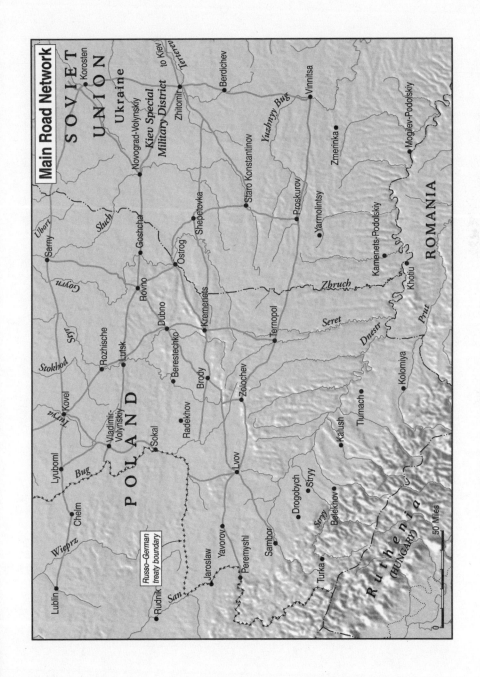

Notes

CHAPTER 1

1. Ihr Schrodek, *Glaube galt dem Vaterland: Geschichte des Panzer-Regiments 15*, 121.
2. Halder, 337.
3. Mackensesn, 4.
4. Halder, 316.
5. Ibid., 297.
6. Guderian, 144.
7. Stolfi, 19.
8. Halder, 345.
9. Ibid., 314.
10. Ibid., 324.
11. Ibid., 345.
12. Ibid., 318.
13. Based on a two-battalion regiment. Nine panzer regiments had three battalions, none of them belonging to Army Group South.
14. Isayev, 73.

CHAPTER 2

1. Habek, 264.
2. Zhukov, 220.
3. Grigorenko, 59.
4. Zhukov, 224.
5. Grigorenko, 90.
6. Ibid., 111.

7. In the Soviet/Russian military, the term "military academy" is applied to learning institutions for officers of field and general grades. The term "military school" is applied to a primary officer training institutions producing lieutenants.
8. Bagramyan, 71.
9. *Kiev Special*, 14.
10. Zhukov, 218.
11. Vladimirskiy, page 26.
12. Habeck, 92–97.
13. Ibid., 186.
14. Drogovoz, 3.
15. RKKA, "The Workers' and Peasants' Red Army," commonly shortened to "The Red Army."
16. *Tank Encyclopedia*, 251.
17. Baryatinskiy, 96.
18. Ibid., 154–155.
19. *Tank Encyclopedia*, 138.
20. Zhukov, vol. 1, 309.
21. Drogovoz, 16.
22. Glantz, 161.

CHAPTER 3

1. Zhukov, 335.
2. Vladimirskiy, 33.

CHAPTER 4

1. Sbornik, vol. 33.
2. Malygin, 24.
3. Sbornik, vol. 33.
4. Malygin, 22.
5. Vladimirskiy, 30.
6. Sbornik, vol. 33.
7. Ibid., vol. 33.
8. Ibid., vol. 33.
9. Flame-thrower tanks.
10. Sbornik, vol. 33.
11. Ibid., vol. 33.
12. Ibid., vol. 33.
13. Ibid., vol. 33.
14. Ibid., vol. 33.
15. Ibid., vol. 33.
16. Ibid., vol. 33.
17. Ibid., vol. 33.
18. Ibid., vol. 33.
19. Ibid., vol. 33.
20. Ibid., vol. 33.
21. Moskalenko, 19.
22. Vladimirskiy, 26.
23. Sbornik, vol. 36.
24. Ibid., vol. 36.
25. Ibid., vol. 36.
26. Sbornik, vol. 33.
27. Sbornik, vol. 33.

CHAPTER 5

1. Churchill, *The Grand Alliance*, 352.
2. *Hitler's War Directives*, 94.
3. Reed, 696.
4. Ibid., 696.
5. Ibid., 697.
6. Whymant, 99.
7. Ibid., 145.
8. Ibid., 184.
9. Ibid., 184.
10. Churchill, *The Grand Alliance*, 370.
11. Perrault, 28.
12. Richardson, 1.
13. Zhukov, 352.
14. Montefiore, 312.
15. Khan, 119.
16. Arkhipenko, 27.
17. Ibid., 21.
18. Bagramyan, 39.
19. Ibid., 42.
20. Ibid., 44.
21. Zhukov, 341.
22. Ibid., 307.
23. Bagramyan, 62.
24. Zhukov, 345.
25. Bagramyan, 63.
26. Ibid., 63.
27. Ibid., 65.
28. Ibid., 66.
29. Zhukov, 332.
30. Popel, 20.
31. Ibid., 22.
32. Arkhipenko, 26.
33. Zhukov, 367.
34. Bagramyan, 76.
35. Ibid., 82.

CHAPTER 6

1. "Bug" is pronounced as "boog."
2. "Ustilug" is pronounced as "oo-stee-loog."
3. *Wehrmacht*'s special forces regiment.
4. Malygin, 5.
5. Ibid., 6.
6. From here on, the Soviet infantry units will be designated as "rifle" in close translation of the Russian terminology.
7. These battalions were 1st/16th Rifle

Regiment, 3rd/96th, and 1st/283rd.
8. Schrodek, 124.
9. In a curious incident, when Ivan Fedyuninskiy was appointed to command the
   XV Rifle Corps in April of 1941, his
   expected promotion to Major-General
   had not come through yet. As the result,
   Colonel Fedyuninskiy was in charge
   of several major-generals in his corps,
   including his second-in-command and
   his division commanders.
10. Fedyuninskiy, 9.
11. Army Group South, 16.
12. Ibid., 16.
13. No relation to Marshal S. K. Timosh-
    enko, Peoples' Commissar for Defense.
14. Irinarkhov, 32.
15. Vasilevskiy, vol. 1, 114.
16. Irinarkhov, 286.
17. Skripko, 109.
18. Ibid., 110.
19. Ibid., 123.
20. Isayev, 128.
21. Arkhipenko, 24.
22. Ibid., 24.
23. Isayev, 127.
24. Arkhipenko, 26.
25. Isayev, 128.
26. Skripko, 115.
27. Ibid., 113.
28. Ibid., 117.
29. Ibid., 122.
30. Bagramyan, 81.
31. Ibid., 83.
32. Ibid., 85.
33. Ibid., 86.
34. Ibid., 89.
35. Ibid., 102.
36. Ibid., 105.
37. Zhukov, vol. 2, 14.
38. *Collection*, vol. 36.

39. Bagramyan, 105.
40. Ibid., 107.
41. Ibid., 110.
42. *Collection*, vol. 36.
43. Zhukov, vol. 2, 10.
44. Ibid., vol. 2, 11.
45. Halder, 412.

CHAPTER 7

1. Bagramyan, 77.
2. Sbornik, vol. 33.
3. Popel, 21.
4. Ibid., 21.
5. Ryabyshev, 6.
6. Popel, 22.
7. Ibid., 23.
8. Ryabyshev, 8.
9. Ibid., 10.
10. Popel, 29.
11. Rokossovskiy, 11.
12. Ibid., 12.
13. Bagramyan, 125.
14. Kalinin, 7.
15. Rokossovskiy, 13.
16. Ibid., 13.
17. Rokossovskiy, 14.
18. Sbornik, vol. 33.
19. Ibid., vol. 33.
20. Moskalenko, 21.
21. Ibid., 22.
22. Halder, 413.

CHAPTER 8

1. Bagramyan, 114.
2. Ibid., 114.
3. Ibid., 115.
4. Ibid., 117.
5. Ibid., 120.
6. Malygin, 12.
7. Rokossovski, 14.

8. Kalinin, 8.
9. *VIZh* (April 1989): 55.
10. Ibid., 55
11. Ibid., 55
12. Popel, 38.
13. Ibid., 39.
14. Ryabyshev, 12.
15. Sbornik, vol. 33.
16. Schrodek, 124.
17. Ibid., 125.
18. Ibid., 127–128.
19. Sbornik, vol. 33.
20. Ibid., vol. 33.
21. Isayev, 142.
22. Schrodek, 129.
23. Isayev, 146.
24. Moskalenko, 24–26.
25. Ibid., 26.
26. Fedyuninskiy, 20.
27. Malygin, 13.
28. Sbornik, vol. 33.
29. Fedyuninskiy, 14.
30. Arkhipenko, 26.
31. Kalinin, 9.
32. No relation to commander of the Sixth Army.
33. *Moskovskiy Zhournal 3* (2003).
34. Ibid.
35. Isayev.
36. Schrodek, 129.
37. Popel, 56.
38. Gross, 181.
39. Popel, 61.
40. Ibid., 61.
41. Ibid., 62.
42. Ryabyshev, 15.
43. Zhukov, vol. 2, 21.
44. Bagramyan, 124.
45. Sbornik, vol. 33.

CHAPTER 9

1. Bagramyan, 132.
2. Ibid., 133.
3. Ibid., 133.
4. Sbornik, vol. 25.
5. Lyudnikov, 3.
6. Isayev, 158.
7. Moskalenko, 33.
8. Ibid., 33.
9. Ibid., 34.
10. Malygin, 14.
11. Schrodek, 131.
12. Kalinin, 9.
13. Rokossovskiy, 17.
14. Ibid., 29.
15. Popel, 66.
16. Ibid., 71.
17. Ryabyshev, 16.
18. Ibid., 16.
19. Popel, 69.
20. Ibid., 76.
21. Ryabyshev, 17.
22. Ibid., 17.
23. Sbornik, vol. 36.
24. Vladimirski, 60.
25. Ibid., 60.
26. Vladimirskiy, 62.
27. Isayev, 159.
28. Ibid., 160.

CHAPTER 10

1. Mlodowa is now an eastern suburb of Dubno, Molodava.
2. Schrodek, 131.
3. Ibid.
4. Isayev, 168.
5. Rokossovskiy, 16.
6. Ibid., 19.
7. Ibid., 19.
8. Isayev, 169.

9. Popel, 78.
10. Ibid., 80.
11. Ibid., 80.
12. Ibid., 81.
13. Ibid., 83.
14. Ibid., 86.
15. Ibid., 87.
16. Ibid., 88.
17. Ibid., 89.
18. Ibid., 94.
19. Ibid., 94.
20. Ibid., 96–97.
21. Ibid., 99.
22. Ryabyshev, 22.
23. Popel, 101.
24. Ibid., 103.
25. Bagramyan, 129.
26. Sbornik, vol. 33.
27. Ibid., vol. 33.
28. Bagramyan, 131.
29. Halder, 424.
30. Malygin, 15.
31. Schrodek, 132.
32. Ibid., 133.
33. Popel, 124.
34. Ibid., 126.
35. Ibid., 128.
36. Ibid., 129.
37. Ibid., 129.
38. Ibid., 130.
39. Ibid., 130.
40. Ryabyshev, 25.
41. Ibid., 26.
42. Ibid., 27.
43. Ibid., 27.
44. Popel, 137.
45. Ibid., 140.
46. Ibid., 140.
47. Ibid., 140.
48. Ibid., 140.

49. Ibid., 140.
50. Ryabyshev, 29.
51. Popel, 147.
52. Bagramyan, 133.
53. Ibid., 134.
54. Ibid., 134.
55. Ibid., 135.
56. Sbornik, vol. 36.

CHAPTER 11

1. Bagramyan, 146.
2. Ibid., 149.
3. Fedyuninskiy, 19.
4. Ibid., 20.
5. Bagramyan, 151.
6. Sbornik, vol. 36.
7. Ibid., vol. 36.
8. Ibid., vol. 36.
9. Bagramyan, 151–152.
10. Ibid., 152.
11. Sbornik, vol. 36.
12. Ibid., vol. 36.
13. Bagramyan, 152.
14. Ibid., 150.
15. Ibid., 150.
16. Rokossovskiy, 18.
17. Malygin, 16.
18. Ibid., 17.
19. Ibid., 18.
20. Vladimirskiy, 66.
21. Schrodek, 133.
22. Sbornik, vol. 36.
23. Ibid., vol. 36.
24. Ibid., vol. 36.
25. Schrodek, 134.
26. Isayev, 196.
27. Ryabyshev, 31.
28. Ibid., 31.
29. Schrodek, 133.
30. Ibid., 133.

CHAPTER 12

1. Sbornik, vol. 36.
2. Ryabyshev, 34.
3. Ibid., 34.
4. Ibid., 34.
5. Halder, 438.
6. Ibid., 430.
7. Bagramyan, 163.
8. Ibid., 165.
9. Ibid., 166.
10. Ibid., 169.
11. This formation was shifted from the southern front.
12. Sbornik, vol. 36.
13. Bagramyan, 169–170.
14. Popel, 168.
15. Ibid., 169.
16. Ibid., 170.
17. Halder, 437.
18. Ryabyshev, 37.

CHAPTER 13

1. Isayev, 218.
2. Halder, 444.

3. Popel, 185.
4. Ibid., 187.
5. Ryabyshev, 38.
6. Bagramyan, 156.
7. Sbornik, vol. 36.
8. Ibid., vol. 36.
9. Bagramyan, 161.
10. Ibid., 162.
11. Schrodek, 134.
12. Ibid., 171.
13. Ryabyshev, 38.
14. Ibid., 42.
15. Popel, 252.

CONCLUSION

1. I am stretching quite a bit to include the 109th Motorized Rifle Division (MRD) from Task Force Lukin into this number. The 109th MRD was part of 5th Mechanized Corps, already departed for Byelorussia.

Bibliography

ENGLISH LANGUAGE SOURCES

Burdick, Charles, and Hans-Adolf Jacobsen, ed. Abridged. *The Halder War Diary*, 1939–1942. Novato, CA: Presidio Press, 1988.

Center of Military History. *The German Campaign in Russia, Planning and Operations, 1940–1942*. Washington, D.C.

Churchill, Winston. *The Grand Alliance*. Kingsport, TN: Kingsport Press, 1950.

Clark, Alan. Barbarossa: *The Russian-German Conflict, 1941–1945*. New York: Quill, 1985.

Cooper, Matthew. *The German Army, 1933–1945*. Chelsea, MI: Scarborough House, 1978.

Dupuy, Trevor. *A Genius for War: The German Army and General Staff, 1807–1945*. Englewood Cliffs, NJ: Prentice-Hall, Inc., 1977.

Feist, Uwe, and Heinz Novarra. *The German Panzers from Mark I to Mark IV* "Panther." Fallbrook, CA: Aero Publishers, 1966

Fugate, Bryan. *Operation Barbarossa: Strategy and Tactics on the Eastern Front, 1941*. Novato, CA: Presidio Press, 1984.

Glantz, David. *Stumbling Colossus: The Red Army on the Eve of World War*. Lawrence, KS: University Press of Kansas, 1998.

Glantz, David, and Jonathan House. *When Titans Clashed: How the Red Army Stopped Hitler*. Lawrence, KS: University Press of Kansas, 1995.

Gross, Jan. *Revolution from Abroad*. Princeton, NJ: Princeton University Press, 2002.

Guderian, Heinz. *Panzer Leader*. Cambridge: Da Capo Press, 1996.

Habeck, Mary. *Storm of Steel: The Development of Armor Doctrine in Germany and the Soviet Union, 1919–1939*. Ithaca, NY: Cornell University Press, 2003.

Haupt, Werner. *Army Group South: The Wehrmacht in Russia, 1941–1945*. Atglen, PA: Shiffer Military History, 1998.

Jentz, Thomas. Panzertruppen, *The Complete Guide to the Completion and Combat Employment of Germany's Tank Force 1933–1942*. Atglen, PA: Shiffer Military History, 1996.

Kahn, David, *Hitler's Spies: German Military Intelligence in World War II*. New York: Macmillan Publishing, 1978.

Kosyk, Volodymyr. *The Third Reich and Ukraine*. Translated by Irene Rudnytzky. New York: Peter Lang Publishing, Inc., 1993.

Lefevre, Eric. Brandenburg Division: *Commandos of the Reich*. Translated by Julia Finel. Paris: Histoire & Collections, 2000.

Montefiore, Simon Sebag. Stalin: *The Court of the Red Tsar*. New York: Alfred A. Knopf, 2004.

Perrault, Gilles. *The Red Orchestra*. Translated by Peter Willes. New York: Simon and Schuster, 1967.

Reed, Anthony, and David Fisher. *The Deadly Embrace:* Hitler, Stalin, and the Nazi-Soviet Pact, 1939–1941. NY: Norton, 1988.

Stolfi, R. H. S. *Hitler's Panzers East. World War II Reinterpreted*. Norman, OK: University of Oklahoma Press, 1991.

Trevor-Roper, Hugh, ed. *Blitzkrieg to Defeat. Hitler's War Directives 1935–1945*. NY: Holt, Rinehart & Winston, 1965.

Warlimont, Walter. *Inside Hitler's Headquarters, 1939–1945*. Translated by R. H. Barry. New York: Praeger, 1964.

Weitz, John. Hitler's Diplomat: *The Life and Times of Joachim von Ribbentrop*. New York: Ticknor & Fields, 1992.

RUSSIAN LANGUAGE SOURCES

Bagramyan, Ivan. *How the War Was Starting Out*. Moscow: Military Publishing, 1977.

Baryatinskiy, Mikhail. *Soviet Tanks in Battle*. Moscow: Yauza, 2006.

De Lanney, Francois. Translated by Olga Wainer. *German Panzers in Ukraine, 1941*. Moscow: Eksmo Publishing, 2001.

Drogovoz, Igor et al. *The Iron Fist of RKKA, 1932–1941*. Moscow: Tekhnika-Molodezhi, 1999.

Irinarkhov, Ruslan. *At Dnieper's Banks*. Moscow: AST Publishing, 2006.

Irinarkhov, Ruslan. *Kiev Special*. Moscow: AST Publishing, 2006.

Isayev, A. V. *From Dubno to Rostov*. Moscow: Transitkniga, 2005.

Kholyavskiy, Gennadiy, ed. *Complete Encyclopedia of World's Tanks, 1915–2000*, Moscow: Harvest Publishing, 2000.

Makarov, Mikhail, and Andrei Pronin. *Red Army's Anti-Tank Artillery*. Moscow: Strategiya KM, 2003.

Moschanskiy, Ilya, ed. *Operation Barbarossa: Tank Battle in Western Ukraine, 22nd June–7th July, 1941*. Moscow: BTV-MN Publishing, 2002.

Moskalenko, Kiril. *On the South-Western Direction, 1941–1943*. Moscow: Nauka Publishing, 1975.

Popel, Nikolai. *During Difficult Times*. Moscow: AST Publishing, 2001.

Rokossovskiy, Konstantin. *Soldier's Duty*. Moscow: Military Publishing, 1988.

Shtemenko, Sergei. *General Staff During the Years of War: From Stalingrad to Berlin*. Moscow: Transitkniga Publishing, 2005.

Vasilevskiy, Aleksandr. *Endeavor of My Whole Life*. Moscow: Politizdat Publishing, 1988.

Zhukov, Georgiy. *Reminiscences and Thoughts*. Moscow: Novosti Publishing, 1990.

GERMAN LANGUAGE SOURCES

Grams, Rolf. *Die 14. Panzer-Division, 1940–1945*. Eggolsheim, Germany: Doerfler Verlag, 2004.

Schrodek, Gustav. *Die 11. Panzer-Division "Gespensterdivision": Bilddokumente, 1940–1945*. Eggolsheim, Germany: Doerfler Verlag, 2004.

Schrodek, Gustav. *Ihr Galube galt dem Vaterland: Geschichte des Panzer-Regiments 15*. Woelfersheim: Podzun-Pallas-Verlag, 1976.

von Mackensen, Eberhard. *Vom Bug zum Kaukasus*. Nekargemund: Kurt Vowinckel Verlag, 1967.

Werthen, Wolfgang. *Geschichte der 16. Panzer-Division, 1939–1945*. Woelfersheim: Podzun-Pallas-Verlag, 1958.

MAGAZINE ARTICLES

Parrish, Michael. "Formation and Leadership of the Soviet Mechanized Corps in 1941." Military Affairs 47, 2 (April 1983): 63–66.

Ratley, Lonnie O., III, "A Lesson of History: The Luftwaffe and Barbarossa." Air University Review (March–April 1983); English.

Richardson, Charles O. "French Plans for Allied Attacks on the Caucasus Oil Fields January–April 1940." French Historical Studies 8, 1 (Spring 1973).

Rokossovskiy, Konstantin. "Previously Unpublished Excerpts from Rokossovskiy Memoirs." Military History Journal (Voenno-Istoricheskiy Zhurnal) (April 1989).

Sella, Amnon. " 'Barbarossa': Surprise Attack and Communication." Journal of Contemporary History 13, 3 (July 1978): 555–583.

Yakovlev, Ivan. "Baptism by Fire." Moscow Journal 5 (May 2003).

E-BOOKS from http://www.militera.lib.ru/

Arkhipenko, Fyodor. *Memoirs of Fighter Pilot*. Moscow: Delta, 1999.

Collection of Combat Documents of Great Patriotic War, Volume 33. Moscow: Military Publishing, 1947–1960.

Collection of Combat Documents of Great Patriotic War, Volume 36.
Moscow: Military Publishing, 1947–1960.

Fedyuninskiy, Ivan. *Awakened by Combat Alarm.* Moscow:
Military Publishing, 1961.

Grigorenko, Petro. *Only Rats are Encountered in Underground.*
New York: Detinets, 1981.

Kalinin, Nikolay. *This is in My Heart Forever.* Moscow:
Military Publishing, 1967.

Lyudnikov, Ivan. *The Road Whole Life Long.* Moscow:
Military Publishing, 1969.

Malygin, Konstantin. *In the Center of Combat Deployment.* Moscow:
Military Publishing, 1986.

Ryabyshev, Dmitriy. *The First Year of War.* Moscow:
Military Publishing, 1990.

Skripko, Nikolay. *To Objectives Near and Far.* Moscow:
Military Publishing, 1981.

Vladimirskiy, Aleksey. *In the Kiev Direction. Experiences of
Combat Operations of 5th Army of South-Western Front in
June–September 1941.* Moscow: Military Publishing.

WEBSITES

www.militera.lib.ru

www.rkka.ru

www.mechcorps.rkka.ru

Index

People's Commissariat for Defense
(Narodniy Kommissariat
Oborony, or NKO), 16, 31, 71
People's Commissariat of Internal
Affairs (NKVD), 12, 43, 54, 55, 64,
66, 68, 75, 103, 116, 128, 135, 154,
155, 270
Pershakov, Mikhail A., 250
Petrov, V. F., 247
Pisarevskiy, D. S., 88, 104, 267
Pleshakov, Ivan N., 190, 191, 225, 241,
254
Plyashevka River, 168, 184, 225
Podoprigora, A. I., 197, 236
Poland, 1–4, 6, 20, 29, 30, 47, 52, 53,
56, 59, 60
Laszczow, 3
Stalowa Wola, 1
Wlodawa, 4
Politburo, 62, 71, 105
Ponedelin, P. G., 70, 193, 268
Popel, Nikolai, 20, 69, 112–116,
136–138, 154–156, 169, 170,
184–191, 199–203, 205–210,
214, 218, 224, 225, 227, 228,
232, 233–235, 240–242, 247–249,
254, 271
Popov, N. A., 184, 201, 202, 215, 268
Poretsky, Ignac, 55
Potapov, Mikhail I., 63, 83, 88, 103,
104, 110, 121–123, 133, 148, 157,
159–163, 172, 180, 194, 213, 216,
218, 219, 229–232, 245, 247, 250,
267
Pripyat Marshes, 29, 149
Pripyat River, 148
Prussia, 3
Ptukhin, E. S., 67, 90, 91, 95–97, 192,
265
Purkayev, Antonia, 62
Purkayev, Maxim A., 62, 63, 67, 68,
71, 89, 97, 98, 100–104, 126, 127,

135, 157, 193, 211, 213, 217, 230,
238, 254, 261, 265
Pz 38(t) tank, 22
Pz I tank, 7, 19
Pz II tank, 7, 22
Pz III tank, 7, 22, 186
Pz IV tank, 7, 58, 186

Red Army, the, 3, 13–18, 20, 21,
24–26, 28, 30–33, 43, 47, 48, 57,
58, 61, 62, 77, 79–82, 85, 89, 90,
102, 105–108, 116, 121, 124, 130,
134, 135, 150, 151, 165, 178, 199,
242, 254, 255, 258, 261
Reed, Anthony, 52, 53
Reichenau, Walther von, 3, 263
Renesse, Lieutenant von, 140, 141,
153
Rezun, Vladimir (pen name Viktor
Suvorov), 30
Riebel, Lieutenant Colonel, 142
Rokossovskiy, Konstantin K., 12, 43,
44, 100, 116–120, 133–135, 149,
152, 162, 166, 167, 179, 180, 181,
195, 196, 207, 211, 220, 221, 231,
240, 242, 245, 272
Romania, 2, 4
Rommel, Erwin, 2
Rowehl, Theodor, 60
Royal Air Force, 52
Rumania, 3, 4, 29, 30, 99, 101, 106,
107
Ploesti, 3
Rundstedt, Gerd von, 3, 5, 263
Russia, 2, 4–6, 12–18, 21, 23, 37, 42,
51–54, 57–60, 75, 76, 82, 84, 86,
93, 107, 135, 140–142, 150, 152,
153, 165, 179, 182, 225, 226, 228,
230, 234, 235, 242, 252, 258, 261
Kazan, 17–19
Kremlin, 71, 105
Kursk, 118, 262